CONNECTED COMMUNITY

SUBTLE FORCE IN A SYSTEMIC WEB

CONNECTED COMMUNITY

SUBTLE FORCE IN A SYSTEMIC WEB

Leonard Caum Moffitt

Nova Science Publishers, Inc.
New York

Art Director: Maria Ester Hawrys

Assistant Director: Elenor Kallberg

Graphics: Eddie Fung, Barbara Minerd, and Kerri Pfister

Cover Designed: Gavin Aghamore

Manuscript Coordinator: Gloria H. Piza

Book Production: Gavin Aghamore, Joanne Bennette,
Christine Mathosian and Tammy Sauter

Circulation: Irene Kwartiroff and Annette Hellinger

Library of Congress Cataloging-in-Publication Data

Moffitt, Leonard C.
Connected community: subtle force in a systemic web / Leonard Caum Moffitt.
p. cm.
Includes bibliographical references.
ISBN 1-56072-324-6
1. Community. 2. Community organization. I. Title.

HM131.M5675   1996
307—dc20   96-26533
                                                                                    CIP

© 1996 by Nova Science Publishers, Inc.
6080 Jericho Turnpike, Suite 207
Commack, New York 11725
Tele. 516-499-3103   Fax 516-499-3146
E Mail Novascil@aol.com

Printed in the United States of America

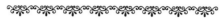

CONTENT

PROLOGUE

The April 1995 car-bombing of a federal building in Oklahoma City did more than shock Americans for its brutal carnage, especially its killing 19 little children. Discovery that its perpetrators had not come from some "blood-thirsty" terrorist-supporting country abroad—that the bombers were actually home-grown white American males—deprived us of that initially seized presumption of an "us versus them." Instead, we came face to face with an "us against us" dilemma. Reality made this deed even less comprehensible. What's more, it threatens to expose some dark aspects of our American experience potentially too troubling for many Americans to cope with.

We as a nation and a society might at last have to come to grips with an uncomfortable degree of strained divisiveness within our own national community. For many decades we had readily credited internal strife to "unAmerican" elements—be they labor union organizers in the 1930s, racial minorities (the very victims of race riots) in the 1940s and 1950s, "agitators" (the nonviolent civil rights marchers attacked by police dogs) in the 1960s, the "unpatriotic" anti-Vietnam protesters (shot at Kent State University) in the 1970s—even to a point of forgetting about our assortment of such true extremist groups as the Weathermen, Black Panthers, and Aryan Nations.

Just as we found it somehow comforting initially to credit such violence as the Oklahoma City bombing to foreigners, we seem quick to adopt again the presumption that surely any home-grown senseless violence could only spring from a few twisted minds. Emotionally we reject it as somehow incongruent with our vaunted life style. Yes, we might acknowledge that a rather wide undercurrent of bitterness, suspicion, cynicism, even fear of governmental conspiracies (after learning how often government officials have deceived the American public, witness Robert McNamara's belated confessions about the Vietnam War) has stressed cracks into our sense of nationhood. But re-examining what really generates a sense of national community in the first place —and hence what can erode it—falls by the wayside. More urgent seems a need to quick-fix the latest pothole in the road (this one dug by the Oklahoma City tragedy) so that we can speed on by as we had before it momentarily slowed and shook us up.

This latest wave of paranoia and alienation among self-touted rock-solid, God-fearing, patriotic, Middle Americans appears fed by repeated tensions between the social justice and sensitivity we expect from our government as against what government seems to represent—much the way such tension sparked the populisms of the Know Nothings in the 1850s, the American Protective Association (after the late 1800s' fiscal crash), the post-WWI's neo-KKK, the Depression era'a outburst of socialism, and the McCarthy and John Birch Society movements after WWII, among others.

Our American application of John Locke's version of social contract never thinks in terms of an integrated political system. Rather, with our Jeffersonian roots, we tolerate government only as the people's servant. We expect our national government (state and local governments, too) to serve individuals' needs expertly, fairly, and for our benefit, not for its own aggrandizement or any one segment's. Problems begin to creep in however when we try to draw a clear line between our national society and its government so that we can evaluate government's performance for our individual interests. But where does government end and society begin in a democratic system?

When we pledge allegiance to the flag of the United States of America and to the republic for which it stands, do we refer to a country of mountains and rivers, of farms and cities, of people with diverse ethnic, religious, political, cultural, and artistic orientations? Do we think of a complex web of interactive transactions, symbols, and linkages that function for our biological, intellectual, economic, social survival and exuberance? Or, isn't it easier for our minds simply to conjure up an image of a distant national government headed by a President and represented by a Congress: strong in war and supposedly expedient with those essential services we need and pay for? But can we readily delineate between a nation of diverse albeit interdependent people and a unifying governmental apparatus for serving those people?

Consider this question: Had our founding fathers not managed to establish a unification of separate states and had the 1860s' war between those states not ended with victory for reunification, would we today enjoy the same sense of national community? Wouldn't we more likely sense several distinct national communities each drifting apart? Yet it was our national community which gave birth to this thing we call the United States of America made tangible by its nationwide political institutions. Our polity and its instrument for governance exist by interacting to the point of blending. For, we are more than a collection of people contracting for services, public or private. We are a web of mutual dependence within a society and a culture. More specifically it appears, we are a web of nested, multi-scaled, participatory communities.

How then did our American society create this culture and how did this culture create this society? Indeed, how does any society create its culture and any culture create its society? And what role does community play in such an interactive process? Tackling this basic enigma might open up some valuable views of what makes us (and other nations) tick. *Therein lies the impetus for this book.*

A multitude of professions and interests deal with something they label "community." City managers, elected officials, educators, welfare directors, police chiefs, League of Women Voters, environmentalists, civil rights advocates, and religious leaders, to name a mere few, journey its political processes, keenly aware of this "something" and its centrality yet vague about what it really is and how it functions.

This is not surprising. We all use this term "community" in an array of ways. We refer to our neighborhood or town as a community. (Brooklyn once sensed itself a community by identifying with "them Bums," the

Dodgers, until that baseball team moved to another region, Los Angeles, equally in need of an identifying symbol to ritually rally around.) We talk of the business community, the scientific community, and even the community of nations. Can any word used so broadly to encompass so many different situations have any true meaning? And yet, a "thing" so frequently referred to must have some kind of importance in our culture and probably in our lives, whether or not we can concretely define it.

Chances are you use the term community without giving it much thought. Chances run equally high that your university education and subsequent reading, like that for others concerned about civic affairs, provided you little more depth than segmented pickings on this subject. If you studied political science or economics, for instance, you focused on one or another limited set of indicators: certain interactions and institutions. Your anthropology and geography courses might (if you were lucky) have encompassed a wider range of indictors but, alas, either for small-scale, relatively simple societies or with reference mostly to the spacial distribution of those indicators. Had sociology been your major, you might have encountered a reluctance even to acknowledge the existence of community as more than either a simple place or a network—judging at least by how introductory college textbooks handle it.

Those few whose studies made them aware of a systemic dimension to community most likely never had that dimension related to its interface with biological systems. Little wonder then that the politics of welfare, crime/punishment, violence, environmental protection, and similar high-profile modernday issues boil and churn yet escape the remedies constantly sought and repeatedly touted. As each academic discipline and professional field zeros in on its special area (or as in sociology, largely gives up and avoids contemplating it), few if any of us have much of an incentive to examine the totality of community as a living system in its full web of complexity.

For the most part, proposed solutions for contemporary issues arise like skyrockets on the Fourth of July—a big loud burst, a fall, and quick oblivion. We tend to consider today's problems as if they had no past and no context and no ramifications. Take violence, for example. Is it so unique to modern society or is it a natural facet of human behavior with a long history? And is it an individual or a societal phenomenon? (We'll come back to these questions late in this book when we have a firmer basis for addressing them.)

A working premise here holds that today's issues are seldom unique. They have a past with precedents which can throw useful light on shadowed aspects too readily overlooked in today's fast drive for quick-fixes. By probing for how the cultural context of community evolved and by drawing on historical case studies, our odyssey of discovery should find useful insights for making decisions in the here and now.

Be assured: "Community" used in this book is no vague catch-all. It is a specific entity: a highly interlinked system. And as we shall discover, this *connected community* is a real, functioning, meaningful, dynamic part of our lives, though for the most part vaguely defined and complex beyond imagination.

To understand the nature and hence the importance of community, it turns out, we do best to see it as part of a trinity rather than as something standing alone. It is a mutually interdependent—three in one—trinity composed of society, culture, and community. The larger and more complex the case, the more important the integrated functioning of this trinity. What's more, community (because it is so amorphous and easily neglected) takes on the role more of a hidden force than of a mere place or "thing." Community may provide the stage, so to speak, for society to act out its culture. But it also becomes an active participant in the play. Indeed, one key to comprehending community, which I found from my research and participant-observer work, lies in focusing on interactions—both functional and symbolic.

We will delve into the interaction of this trinity and its seemingly hidden force of community. Toward that end, this book unfolds in four parts, each with its own introduction, chapters, sources, and a different angle of attack. Part One explores the beginnings of simple community. It examines what we know (and what still lies in the realm of academic controversy) about how our biological evolution facilitated the emergence of extensive, syntactically symbolic thought and hence the evolution of human culture from a primitive level of complexity to the present proliferation of highly complicated societies. Here we find the foundation for subsequently discerning the intricate context and ingredients of community systems.

Part Two zeros in on the processes of change considered in the previous section by narrowing the time and place contexts. It briefly compares two somewhat parallel cultures—those of Japan and Hawaii—for how they coped (or failed to cope) with the pressures of change. In their contrasting records of resilience and collapse we can sense the presence (or absence) of some less than obvious force.

Ferreting out the ingredients and workings of this force must await Part Three where we unravel, in still more detail, Orange County California's fascinatingly rapid community evolution as it dramatically demonstrates in capsule form an America metamorphosing from broadly rural to highly urban, from a nation energized by a work ethic to one devoted to entertainment as exemplified by the world's first theme park at Disneyland in Orange County, from a nation split between rural villages and teeming cities to the pioneering of a new political environment composed of small municipalities and school districts clustered into larger-scaled cooperating amalgams and now (of necessity after its recent fiscal debacle) perhaps on toward the privatization of public functions.

Having thereby exposed what this "something" of a connected community really is, we can turn to Part Four where we apply what we have learned toward evolving strategies for the challenges of survival as we enter the twenty-first century. (We also pull together some broad findings that provide a workable set of premises for further research by scholars on how the resulting systems theory might bridge those academic chasms which now impede application of much current science.) Most important, we pull this analysis back to Part One in seeing how a society creates its culture and a culture creates its society, all within the process that is a connected community.

One bright note for the non-mathematicians debating whether to continue reading this book: Although it delves into systemic complexity, it nowhere resorts to mathematics to communicate observations. It simply explores real cases in real time and place contexts. At this stage in our understanding of human behavior, we would do better, I suspect, to clarify concepts and processes in such contexts before we can safely launch abstract theories in mathematical formats.

If reading this book happens to whet your appetite for taking the serious plunge into chaos and complexity analyses with their esoteric mathematics, so much the better. But that can come later and need not trouble you here.

L. C. M.
Corvallis Oregon
December 1995

PART ONE

THE COMING OF CULTURAL COMPLEXITY

INTRODUCTION

Humans today do not live as our ancestors did a hundred thousand years ago. Nor as they did fifty or twenty or just ten thousand years ago. Even those few scattered societies who still practice a hunter-gatherer lifestyle differ from our common ancestors in those earlier times. Moreover, people ten thousand years ago departed in their cultures from their ancestors fifteen thousand years before them—who likewise differed in behavior and social/economic organization from their progenitors of thirty thousand years still earlier. No single stereotype can realistically conjure up a singular, cliché "primitive man."

Cultural evolution goes back a long way. By culture I include the utensils people use, their forms of communication, their social structure and kinship relationships, their mores and spirit worlds. Paleoarcheological evidence and other analytical bases point to continual change and at an accelerating rate over the last fifty-thousand years.

What we think today, how we behave today, how we communicate today, all that is human today evolved. What we, the species *Homo sapiens*, are today reflects what we were all along myriad branching continua of change and the prolific set of factors which contributed to that change. Knowing our past could conceivably help us understand something about our present and about the processes of change propelling us today.

This first section of THE CONNECTED COMMUNITY addresses the questions: How did human cultures evolve (from a relatively simple system only slightly more complex than other animal species) into the vast array of massive societies with highly complex cultures? And what set of factors/forces participated in this evolution?

This task involves questions about how our early ancestors migrated across the world, how they gained the capacity for syntactical thought, how most societies underwent the transition from matrifocal to patriarchal, from hunter-gatherer to sedentary agricultural or organized pastoral economies. In the course of this exploration we discover the central role women likely played in cultural development and how (not all that long ago) previously peripheral males took over. Male-female relations today look quite different if viewed in the perspective of the last thirty thousand years of cultural evolution.

Part One sets the stage for addressing that fundamental chicken-and-egg enigma (in Part Four) of how a culture creates a society and a society creates a culture, from which there emerges the trinity of society, culture, and community.

CHAPTER ONE

ORIGINS

On the basis of language alone there exist hundreds of distinct cultures around the world; some scholars say possibly eight thousand. Add religion, marriage customs, family and community structures as indicators; the number of cultures grows even more prolific. Yet for all of this diversity, certain features do appear in all of those that maintain their viability.

All on-going cultures provide for kinship arrangements, for directions in food preparation, hygiene and health care, for processes to reach communal decisions and accommodate external and internal challenges. While specifics vary widely between cultures for each such basic function, cultural directives of some sort do exist for each of them in some way. Human cultures have grown complicated enough to necessitate such provisions as essential for survival.

Similarly, virtually all societies (all large societies at least) subscribe to male-dominant cultures to some degree, most of them quite extensively. Their male members offer a variety of explanations: such as that dimorphism and strength make men responsible for women's safety (and hence for their behavior), that men are "naturally superior," or that Divine Providence as a male put men in charge.

Like other myths, these allow people to rationalize their relative social-political-economic-legal positions with little further thought or conscience. Such myths can soothe the oppressed as well as the oppressors in providing little or no room for other cultural options; they provide built-in excuses.

Knowing no other way, people live with what is for them preordained and inevitable; they simply make the best of it. At least they do until they face a severe challenge, as we shall see happen to ancient Hawaiian culture (in Part Two). Then any sort of cultural rebellion can erupt—even a king destroying the foundation of his own authority.

TRACING HUMAN ANCESTRY

All humans have something else in common: their biological ancestry. Since all humans today can interbreed fertile off-spring, we are all members of the same species and therefore of necessity had to have had at least one ancestor in common somewhere in our past. Though seldom acknowledged, it is theoretically possible that a common ancestor might have occurred more than once in our species' long, meandering evolution.[1] In contrast, our cultural heritage had countless sources and routes of development. While linguistic and genetic lines do correspond in many regions, elsewhere they confuse ancestry tracking.

A systematic exploration of our biological and cultural evolutions has emerged only since the late nineteenth century. Until quite recently, that exploration depended on the diligent (and lucky) digging for fossilized skeletal fragments and artifacts by a rare breed of scholar, the paleoanthropologist, and his/her perceptive interpretation of such finds. Unfortunately, the wide degree of uncertainty inherent in this methodology too often produced more controversy than consensus.

By the 1960s a few scientists sought firmer ways of dating evolution (for other species as well as for humans). They turned to laboratory research by drawing on recent advances in genetics. The Watson-Crick breakthrough on double helix DNA had opened new horizons. Unfortunately, nuclear DNA (the chromosomes) were still far too complicated for the new science of reading the billions of rungs. Mitochondrial DNA, with only 37 genes as against some 80,000 or more chromosomal genes, offered a potentially more workable tool for analysis.

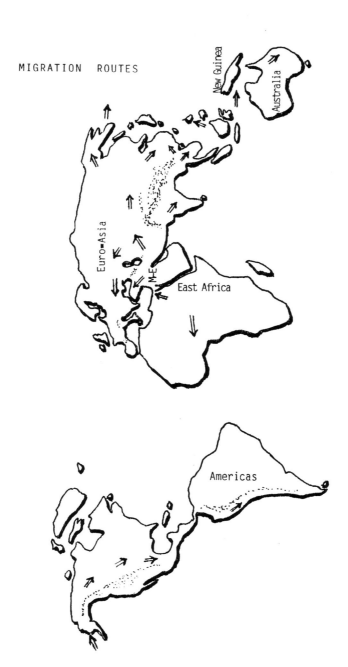

MIGRATION ROUTES

New Guinea

Australia

Euro-Asia

M-E

East Africa

Americas

Mitochondrial DNA (abbreviated to mtDNA) has two particular features. First, it is sex specific. Unlike chromosomal DNA in the nucleus (abbreviated nDNA) which is derived equally from the haploid genomes of the biological father and mother (equally, at least, in a normal nucleus), mtDNA lies outside the nucleus. Consequently, it does not follow the procreative process of meiosis. Instead, it passes without alteration from generation to generation through mothers—unaltered except for periodic mutations. Therein lies its second significant property: mtDNA has a reputedly constant rate of mutation, so constant that it should allow a far more reliable way to date when races and species branched than any other method could do today.

Paleoanthropologists had unearthed a collection of hominid skeletal fossils in East Africa ranging from nearly ape-like in morphology to proto-modern human. Although some scientists championed other locales for the origin of the human line (such as Asia, even Australia and Europe), more favored east Africa for that distinction. An analysis of mtDNA mutational distances between contemporary "races" also pointed to an East African genesis. Instead of settling the controversy however, the Berkeley group which reported this mtDNA finding turned up the heat by dating our common ancestor (unfortunately dubbed "Eve") far more recently than most paleoanthropologists could accept.

The mtDNA date for a common female ancestor of 200,000 years ago (plus or minus some 50,000 years) presented paleoanthropologists with a dilemma. For them, a common ancestor meant the subsequent presence of no prior racial diversity. Yet this flew in the face of observed markers for racial distinctions which seem not only present in much older skeletal remains but which they believe have remained consistent in those sectors of the world through to today. Teeth and bones found in China and dated back many hundreds of thousands of years, for instance, do resemble those of contemporary Chinese (such as the shovel-shaped incisors), just as fossils in Java and Europe show some similarities to peoples living in those regions now.

Science suffered in that several factors got lost in the scuffle. First, the reliability of mtDNA analysis had yet to be thoroughly established. Allan

Wilson had previously shown with another form of biological test that the temporal distance back to when the hominid and pongid lines had separated was five (at most seven) million years ago instead of the previously held ten to fifteen million years. His earlier success in upsetting paleoanthropological orthodoxy gave him undue confidence in his latest foray into recalibrating the evolutionary record.

Second, the prospect of a common female ancestor a mere 200,000 years ago does not mandate (contrary to contentions by Wilson's detractors) that all other proto-human races scattered across the Africa/Asia/Europe land mass had to die out and be replaced by the particular race represented by that common female ancestor. Actually, the phenotype of that common mtDNA ancestor may bear no resemblance to the nDNA-produced phenotypes of any of her descendants or to our common nDNA ancestors. Mitochondrial DNA and nuclear DNA serve quite different functions and hence operate quite differently.

Mitochondrial DNA handles the cells' need for energy so that (among other things) nDNA in the nucleus can perform its function of providing the blueprint for messenger RNA (mRNA) to implement the miracle of cytodifferentiation and morphogenesis. Our species' phenotype, which paleoanthropologists examine, express the information contained in our nDNA and (except for one disease) has nothing to do with the mtDNA used by Wilson's Berkeley group to date and locate common ancestry. Tracing a common female ancestor need not carry the same implications as pinpointing our common nDNA "grandparents," if the latter actually does become scientifically possible someday.

Leaving aside the debated date of 200,000 years ago for the moment, we can note several routes by which all contemporary humans could have at least one common ancestor somewhere in our past. One group could have conquered and concertedly vanquished all other hominid species, races, and groups, thereby eliminating all other genetic lines. In historic times we know of such genocide happening deliberating only once: for the Tasmanians. It may well have been more difficult under prehistoric conditions when technological advantages were not so unequal between racial groupings.

(The Israelite tribes believed Yahweh had directed them to slaughter the entire indigenous population when they invaded Canaan, though later Biblical stories suggest that they may have failed to do so completely. In 1258 Hulego's Mongols, hating the Muslims, massacred a million residents of the world's most cosmopolitan metropolis, Bagdad, but failed to eradicate it; within a generation his followers, impressed with its sophisticated culture, had intermarried with those not killed and converted to Islam. Even Hitler, for all his Nazi ruthlessness, failed to exterminate his ethnic targets, also.)

Replacement however need not involve genocide. A group or race might die out when exposed to disease by invaders for which it has no natural immunity. But seldom does an entire race disappear. Usually some percentage manages to survive some how and develop immunity. This pattern occurred repeatedly as Europeans intruded into Asia, Africa, Polynesia, and the Americas within recent centuries.

If an invading group has more efficient organization and/or better tools, it might out-compete the indigenous population for limited resources and thereby reduce them numerically until eventually they cease being a recognizable group or race. It may do so without resort to war. In the process, the intruders simply reduce their competitors to political impotence or discredit and thereby topple the indigenous culture. We see this happen dramatically in Part Two for Hawaii. In the Incas' case, the leadership strata just quit reproducing.

Then of course there is interbreeding; the larger, faster breeding group swallows the other—provided that both parties of protohumans consisted of the same species. Since all *Homo sapiens* can interbreed fertile off-spring, there most likely has occurred genetic sharing globally from time to time over the past several hundred thousand years to prevent speciation which total isolation would have induced. If instances within historic times provide any clues for prehistoric cases of migratory encounters, chances run high that various combinations of these several processes would have occurred.

Actually, common mtDNA ancestry (unlike nDNA) could have happened also by each local race absorbing small bands of intruders, provided they included females, a prospect discussed more fully later. Given the scarcity of human population back then and likely lack of social organization larger than small bands, this last alternative (though neglected in the debate) may well have typified what happened until rather recently.

But just how frequently over the millennia and how extensively did proto-humans migrate about the Asia/Europe/Africa land mass, including into Australia and New Guinea? Fossils found in Java and China, as well as throughout the entire expanse of East Africa, suggest that hominids classified as *Homo erectus* spread out as long ago as ten- to nineteen-hundred millennia. If other species can do it, surely primitive hominid groups could have migrated, adapted, and survived great changes.

Archeological and historic evidence makes it abundantly clear that humans, even with limited technological sophistication, have constantly migrated—sometimes displacing others which in turn had to migrate thereby pushing still another population, or on occasion combining into new ethnics. Ancients Greeks, Sythians, Huns, Turks, and Mongols have swept out of Asia and into Europe. Roving Phonecians, Macedonians, Persians, Romans, Vandals, Goths, Vikings, Arabs, and Crusaders spread their genes, as have Burmese moving down from Tibet, Thais and Vietnamese out of China, Indians eastward, as well as Malays in several directions. Polynesian sailors regularly navigated thousands of miles of open ocean at a time when Europeans could not venture beyond sight of land.

We have no basis for not granting the possibility that, given the time available, protohumans and early humans could have repeatedly crisscrossed Asia, Africa, and Europe. This likelihood of frequent, if not almost constant, movement holds relevance to the primary focus of this section, that of cultural evolution—once we can surmount these ancestral enigmas with their genetic underpinnings. Certainly evidence of climatic fluctuations (with resultant Ice Ages) must have necessitated repeated migrations no matter how reluctantly undertaken.

The significance here lies in the distinct possibilities: (a) that many more than one "wave" of proto-humans and humans emerged out of East Africa to populate Europe, Asia, Australia, New Guinea, and later the Pacific Islands and the Americas as well as the rest of Africa; (b) that some if not most of these so-called waves may have tended toward the almost imperceptible such as averaging a mile a decade; and (c) that they eventually, albeit per-

haps fitfully, would have eliminated all remnant pockets of any other hominid species except that which happened to lead genetically to a single *Homo
sapiens* species.

Returning to the issue of the 200,000 year age for our common female
ancestor: While subsequent mtDNA and other genetic analyses continued to
point to an East African genesis, the fudge factor widened for when that
elusive ancestor lived. Consequently, the controversy may boil down to
these options.

#1. Was she a member of an early *Homo erectus* group which spread
from Africa to Asia something like a million years ago? Those paleoanthropologists who prefer a multi-regional development of races lean toward this
option. For reckoning nDNA grandparenthood, they are probably correct.
But are they for mtDNA?

#2. Was she our ancestor purely by the chance of being the first to have
had daughters in every succeeding generation of proto-humans who migrated out a quarter to a third of a million years ago, interbreeding around
the world as they traveled? Some adherents to mtDNA dating feel more
comfortable with an older time than 200,000 years ago for this occurrence.
Indeed, there is nothing to suggest that the generation of our common ancestry moved anywhere. For all we can tell now, several generations might
have elapsed before a migration took place—and without their having to be
a wild horde of rapacious cutthroats.

There remains still another option, one which complicates the issue for
everyone yet will not go away. #3. Did her common ancestry coincidentally
result from some particular nDNA genetic development within her
deme/race, such as the fundamental changes that became evident between
120,000 to 40,000 years ago and accorded some definite advantages in reproductive dominance ("fitness" in sociobiological terms) over all other extant demes and races? Quite possibly also; which means that all three options contain plausibility in their own, nonexclusive ways.

Short of finding many widely dispersed, quick-frozen hominid remains
dating back hundreds of thousands of years with DNA available for analysis, ancestry issues which plague paleoanthropology will likely remain un-
decided. Without such a tremendous stroke of unlikely luck, we face a pros-

pect long resisted but mathematically possible: that *Homo sapiens* may have experienced common ancestry several times in its mobile evolution.

Whether or not our common female ancestor identified by mtDNA analysis partook of these late genetic changes, these changes did eventually spread everywhere. They constitute the core phenotype of today's single species. In any event, it would appear that our genetic history is far more complicated than any of the combatants in this controversy acknowledged. Not surprisingly then, the cultural dynamics of that genetic process is likely to prove no less complex. Here we come to the core concern for analysis in this section of the book.

Launching Pad of Cultural Evolution

Early in that crucial span of 100,000 to 50,000 BP (Before Present) there emerged a population in East Africa with a sufficiently gracile face as well as gracile body to earn the sobriquet of anatomically modern: a biologically and morphologically true *Homo sapiens*. Looking modern and acting such are two quite different matters, however. But by the end of this era these *Homo sapiens* could also fully warrant the designation of *Homo sapiens sapiens*; their mental capacity was fully modern as well.

It was not just a matter of communicating verbally; hominids up to then most probably had learned to do that. Since other species can communicate and many apes have a mental capacity to understand perhaps a hundred symbols, we may safely surmise that the hominid line was at least that neurologically complex. By the time the human larynx had dropped in the throat sufficiently (perhaps as far back as 100,000 BP) to allow far greater articulation, our ancestors could at least speak ad hoc pidgin—that is, individual words albeit with exceedingly limited, if any, grammatical structure.

The crucial advance stems not from talking more but in the underlying thought process. This change involved structuring symbols—any kind of symbols—systemically in what we may term syntactical thought. Perhaps the phrase "synergistic process" comes closer to reality than "syntax:" Far more is involved than just words where single sounds directly equal meaning. In this view, words (and other symbol systems as well) have meaning mostly in a virtually interactive fashion within themselves.

Learning a vocabulary accomplishes little unless one can grasp the inter-relating process of that language. Denzel Carr, a wonderful professor during my student days at UC Berkeley, aptly personified the basic idea here. In mastering more than fifty languages during his life, he treated each language as a distinct mathematical formula. It should not come as a surprise, either, that so many mathematicians love to play music, for it is also inherently another form of syntactical formulation.

Whether a Stravinsky or Mozart, a Mondrian or El Greco, a Henry Ford or Leonardo da Vinci, Copernicus or Einstein, Lao-Tzu or Aristotle—or you and me—we all think in intricate systems. A capacity for syntactical thought allows us to envision the distant past and future and then to modify current thinking and behavior (to plan and implement) accordingly so as to seek remote or imaginary, even mythical objectives.

The greater a capacity for syntactical thinking—beyond merely using symbols—the greater the capacity to gain nuance and comprehend abstractions in both thought and communication. Since nuance and abstractions underlie a capacity for more complex social organization, religion, and art, they are prerequisites for sophisticated cultures to emerge. This capacity for systemic thought seems also to underlie advances in fabricating complex tools. While many animals (crows, dogs, porpoises, elephants) can occasionally experience insights into problem solving, achieving insights (or at least conjuring explanations) daily comes rather natural to most of us with our capacity for interrelating diverse phenomena and their potential inferences.

Let me reiterate: Use of symbols alone does not distinguish *Homo sapiens sapiens* from earlier humans and protohumans even though our vocabularies no doubt expanded dramatically. Our vocabularies could expand because we now could effectively use more words with more meanings to express far more subtle complexities of thought. The crucial factor not evident among our cousin apes and probably not evident until quite recently in the human line is this capacity for syntactical (synergistic and systemic, though not always systematic) thought. With syntactical consciousness, words become interactive and sentences become processes, just as temporal, spatial, and aesthetic contemplations take on systemic dimensions.

Please note: as used here, "syntax" goes far beyond merely the structure of grammar. It encompasses a systemic process of viewing and hence comprehending (or comprehending hence viewing) the world we live in, in such a way as to replicate it via one medium or another of interactive symbols, be they words, music, math, or pictures. Humans do not then need a set of language genes per se to have a "universal language" sense. But we do need a brain wired for syntactical perception that we can translate into coherent sets of mutually understood symbols.

This syntactical consciousness allows us, for instance, to hear music instead of a series of sounds the way birds hear. It allows us to sense deep emotions from looking at a painting, sculpture, or film and relating them to personal experiences and to the emotions those experiences generated. It prompts us to emphasize aesthetic as well as functional construction of our tools, be they houses, clothing, or autos. It allows us, perhaps it makes us structure meaning to life and death, to create heavens, hells, and gods. It allows the human community to adhere effectively through rituals of identity rather than merely through and for functional operations—and at scales far larger than the family, band, or clan within immediate eyesight. It enhances and can enlarge our awareness of others, of our interactions, and hence our identity beyond what other species experience with pheromones or plumage.

Quite possibly, this evolutionary achievement more than any other allowed humans to cease being a part of nature and to begin to see themselves above nature —and giving rise to the Adam and Eve legend. Until then, the environment involved interaction between the physical and ecological worlds. Afterward, this interaction turned into a three-way dance with humans becoming an equally influential partner. For above all, this new mental capacity allowed far larger and far more effective social organization. And how did we get to this point in our evolution? Why might we surmise that a capacity for true syntactical thinking might have occurred only as recently as fifty or sixty millennia ago? Many factors count.

Over the course of the last five million years, the hominid line experienced: (1) modification of knee, foot, tibia and pelvic bones that made upright bipedal locomotion not only possible but the preferred, more comfortable form; (2) modification of hand bones to allow a truly opposable thumb; (3) loss of estrus and "gain" of menstruation among females; (4) enlarged cranial capacity; (5) loss of body hair; (6) diminution of canine and molar teeth; (7) overall skeletal modification gracilely and a subsequent similar modification of the facial structure, such as lss of brow ridges and prognathism; and (8) a lowering of the larynx in the throat until, among mammals, only humans above the age of three months cannot breath and swallow simultaneously; but we can talk a lot. Our chromosomes also differ: 46 for us, 48 for the great apes.

Except for the number of chromosomes, most of these modifications had profound impact upon human cultural evolution. The first two directly facilitated our eventual tool-making/using proclivities. The third affected male/female interaction. The fifth (possibly in conjunction with the first, third, and seventh) may have prompted a need for clothing and hence for tool-making with our freed hands. The eighth, already noted, allowed us to articulate the expanded vocabularies made possible by number four. Additional impacts from number four hold particular significance for matters better discussed later.

In the course of these genetically provided alterations, numerous hominid species participated, then died out. As far as the paleoanthropological record indicates, apparently each succeeding species was more gracile, more dexterous and/or more brainy than those species/races which died out. From surface appearances, the process of adaptation seems simply to have prevailed, each new genetically provided advantage possibly facilitating the next biological or cultural phenotype, albeit without any basis for attributing orthogensis to the result.

CULTURAL EVOLUTION TAKES OFF

Contemporary with this newly "anatomically modern" race of *H.sapiens* in East Africa and Middle East, whom we might call proto-CroMagnon, there lived a relatively much more robust race (or species). Encased in a thick-set skeletal frame with quite pronounced brow ridges, limited vocal tract, and a large head, they spread across Europe into central Asia and the Levant. Not without reason are Neanderthal (named for the site of initial discovery) sometimes looked upon as either a throwback to *Homo erectus* or an actual remnant of that earlier form of hominid. (Other anthropologists see them as equal to the East African race of proto-CroMagnon albeit adapted to a colder climate.)

From findings in what are now Israel, Syria, and Iraq, apparently Neanderthal and the much more gracile people from Africa lived for some forty to fifty thousand years in proximity to each other, between variously estimated 90/95,000 and 45/50,000 BP. Yet they seem to have remained distinct: some cultural borrowing perhaps but doubtfully inconclusive evidence for fertile interbreeding. Neither seems to have had any distinct technological or organizational advantage over the other. Neither conquered or displaced the other—until the end of that era.

By the mid-40,000s BP, something occurred to change the world's population picture profoundly. By that date, those now fully modern proto-CroMagnon were on the move from northeast Africa in a big way. As already noted, extended migration was nothing new to the hominid line. *Homo erectus* had reached Java and China. Then the increasingly "anatomically modern" protohumans and humans during the hundred to two hundred thousand years prior to this point slowly migrated out and likely mixed their genes with indigenous groups/races across Asia and Africa. Now with a booming population, CroMagnon is on the move.

Although the earlier movements of humans may have proceeded leisurely, what happened no later than 43,000 BP differed. It seems to have progressed swiftly enough and strongly enough to set off a bow-wave of migrations ahead of it. Christy Turner's dental evidence has major population movements underway by 40,000 BP in Southeast Asia and into Australia, fully moderns arriving Down Under not later than 32,000 BP.

While evidence remains less than certain for China and on to the Americas, a new wave of migration did head there via Central Asia at almost the same time, reaching China no later than 22,000 BP. All the islands of even Indonesia and Philippines held fully modern humans by 17,000 BP and Japan no later than 12,000 BP. Whether or not earlier peoples may have reached South America, *H.sapiens sapiens* surely had by 11,000 BP.

This out migration from northeast Africa or the Middle East turned also toward Europe. Sometime before 35,000 BP, CroMagnon had invaded that continent. By 32,000 BP, Neanderthal as a distinct race (or species) and culture had effectively disappeared. Only CroMagnon remained as a people and culture. (Migrations in sub-Sahara Africa, probably even earlier, remain as yet far less clear.)

Something must have happened to at least some of those CroMagnon progenitors in east Africa or in the Middle East (most likely between 65,000 and 45,000 BP, possibly earlier in southern Africa) to so drastically upset stability. Until then neither CroMagnon nor Neanderthal had a decided advantage over the other in terms of sophistication in organization and implements, if archeological finds are extensive enough to be indicative. After all of those millennia of proximity and likely contact, neither side could annihilate the other—until after 45,000 years ago when it occurred with suddenness and on Neanderthal's home turf. Something drastic changed to favor CroMagnon over Neanderthal, and over all other hominids and other human races encountered anywhere thereafter.

By 30,000 BP, marked improvements in tools are unmistakable. Some of the world's most striking art work, those famous cave paintings by ancient humans, begin to occur prolifically. This geometric acceleration in technological innovation and artistic expression becomes undeniable by 20,000 BP and has yet to subside. Not left in tangible form for our present day analysis are likely accompanying advances in linguistics, social organization, and the imagining of a spirit world.

What changed to favor that gracile East African race of now anatomically and mentally modern humans (the proto-CroMagnon) in leapfrogging all other humans if it was not the last bit of neurological rewiring to facilitate extensive syntactical formulation of symbolic thought and the advantages it accords in social organization and tool fabrication?

With the organic/morphological evolution to anatomically moderns, there had already come an expeditious combination of human tongue, lips, and larynx. With the right wiring (to the neo-cortex, cerebrum, left hippocampus, Wernicke's or Broca's areas?) came greatly expanded thinking power that would grow into syntactical insight. Or might this advance in mental power have possibly come not just from rewiring in those parts of the brain used for speech but in conjunction with an expansion of the brain function which processes what many animals and quite likely proto-humans had well developed: a capacity for complex spatial comprehension—mental mapping? (A large portion of today's humans still think *initially* in spatial or tactile syntax, something our word-thinking school teachers and professors could neither envision nor tolerate.)

By 1.7 million years ago, hominid cranial capacity had begun to expand. Having more brains may facilitate more complex processing of neurological stimuli, but it does not necessarily equate with sophistication in thought. After all, we only ever use a portion of our total brain capabilities anyway; and some geniuses have small brains while morons may have large ones. That Neanderthal had a larger cranial capacity for brains did not apparently equate with more sophisticated thinking, judging by their production of unsophisticated implements and their clumsy efforts to copy CroMagnon tools. The real difference must lie not in size of brain but in how it is neurologically "wired" for total, integrated functioning.

Much has been made of supposed burials by Neanderthal to indicate a capacity for complex symbolic thought by imagining a hereafter and spiritual links to the dead. Perhaps. But this kind of emotional demonstration—if those actually were real burials —need go no further than expressing a deep personal loss, which proves little about thinking powers. Even dogs can display that kind of feeling upon the death of a kind master or longtime canine playmate. Elephants show great reverence when coming upon the skeletons of other elephants. Whales have been known to stick with sick family members in tidal waters even at an obvious risk to their own lives. Mother chimps and baboons sometimes even carry around a dead infant for days while denying its death. Young chimps go into utter trauma at the death of a close relative.

Since we can point to no *conclusive* evidence for sophisticated thinking among any hominids before 45,000 years ago but do see it unmistakably no later than 35,000 BP, the right combination of requisite neurological rewiring must have occurred (or at least spread) in this general era. It is not hard to imagine that such a marked increase in thinking might have soon evoked (or provoked) restlessness as well as competitive advantages for the group so benefited. Little wonder then that a real wave of outward migration would follow (in the mid-40,000s BP) and continue until all major inhabitable lands were populated by a single, mentally quite sophisticated, human species.

Hypothesis Testing

Is it possible to prove this hypothesis? No, not really; not any more than for any other scenario on the anthropological table. While we can date bone fossils with some reasonable degree of reliability, neural systems simply do not fossilize for later-day paleoanthropologists to examine. Even evidence in the form of artifacts is quite limited — to non-disintegrative tools (such as those made of stone and bone) and whatever wall paintings survived, all traditionally presumed to have been created by men. Biodegradable artifacts—those made of leather, reeds, and bark (such as in clothing, baskets, and housing) all traditionally presumed the realm of female work—have long since disappeared.

Not only are we denied a major portion of early human artifacts to analyze; traditional interpretations about what existing ones might tell us appear to carry heavy loads of bias. For example, we actually have no proof that only males produced stone tools. It is simply an assumption made by male anthropologists and hence one we must question later in this section.

If available artifacts offer us only limited evidence, we might check for clues against how apes and contemporary hunter-gatherers behave. Again we face severe limitations. In the five million years since the hominid and pongid lines split, great apes have undergone their own evolutions and have had their natural habitats continually altered and intruded into by humans. How they look and behave today do not provide a sure baseline for hominids when the split came five million years ago.

Contemporary hunter-gatherers also may offer behavioral possibilities for consideration but must be handled cautiously too. We cannot take their cultures as models of a by-gone era ten or twenty millennia ago. All practicing hunter-gatherers today have had contact (often close symbiotic association) with sedentary societies. Moreover, some of them may have once practiced a sedentary culture themselves and chose (or were forced) to convert to hunting-gathering subsequently.

Checking against these sources, however, may at least help us to eliminate the less than plausible explanations. We might recognize probable parameters for human culture back to thirty thousand years ago. Human culture then would most likely fall between cultures of inarticulate apes on the one hand, and the fully articulate, mentally sophisticated, yet technologically and organizationally limited, modern day hunter-gatherers on the other. A broad span, admittedly; but a start.

This acknowledged, we must note, too, that no amount of desire to be as "scientific" as possible will eliminate an unavoidable need for some speculation about possible scenarios. Available evidence simply is too limited, too uneven, and already too tainted by earlier interpretations. All we can do is take every precaution possible and avoid sounding as if we know more than we really do. We are simply left with using what evidence does exist to formulate hypotheses for further testing.

One question underlying the scenario sketched here immediately arises. It asks how realistic is it to see the emergence of syntactical thought as coming rather abruptly after millions of years of glacially slow biological and cultural evolution. Most of us have had our educational experience oriented to traditional Darwinianism that allows evolution to proceed only at an excruciatingly slow pace. So is it possible for genetic changes to occur abruptly enough to make this scenario plausible? Yes, apparently—at least some cases suggest so.

Studies by University of Hawaii's Shiela Conant on finches introduced not long ago into the Laysan Islands northwest of Hawaii found dramatic physiological changes favoring adaptation to food sources in only a few dozen generations. Observations by others of rock wallabies released into Oahu's Kalihi Valley two-thirds of a century earlier indicated changes great enough already to portend a new speciation. In both cases the initial gene pool was extremely small: a matter of a few individuals.

Actually Darwin allowed for various courses of evolution. It is the Darwinianism of his followers (especially T.H. Huxley) that narrowed in on only one form, that of gradual adaptationism. Research on drosophila (fruit flies) in Hawaii and elsewhere has studied other modes and shown how important, for instance, female selection can be—even when the female's choice achieves no discernible evolutionary advantage.

In formulating his remarkable insights into evolution, Darwin (Wallace also) did not have the advantage of even our current, albeit admittedly limited, knowledge about genetics. Gregor Mendel's pioneering work in that field followed Darwin's publications and then lay unrecognized by the scientific community for some 35 years. Eventually by mid-twentieth century, a "new synthesis" integrated Mendelian genetics and Darwinian evolution. Since the Watson-Crick breakthrough on double helix DNA in 1953, genetics has become one of the most rapidly paced fields of scientific research, its core concepts and paradigm seemingly revised by the year.

Unfortunately a "virus" lurks in Darwinian evolution, that of confusion over acquired characteristics, known incorrectly as Lamarckism. Adaptationism sees chance mutations providing alternative genetic instructions within a species' gene pool. When the environment changes and a new phenotype becomes necessary, this genetic variation might contain a better phenotypic fit. Applying this seemingly clear-cut idea to specific cases, however, is where "Lamarckian" distortion can arise. We see it in the debate over whether biology adapts to environment which changes behavior, or biology adapts to behavioral changes which create a new environment, or whether behavior changes to fit biology.

For example, in his pioneering book on sociobiology, E.O. Wilson explains stereoptical vision in primates as acquired in arboreal living. He does not, however, consider the alternative that primates moved into trees because their genetic system had already somehow evolved a stereoptical capability. Indeed, would enough primates have survived their falling out of trees over enough millennia to have had their eyes switch from side to front? Wouldn't it have been better for them to have had the requisite vision before they left the ground and ventured up into the precarious perches of an arboreal life? Might they not have gone into the trees because they had gained this chance added capacity?

Or take human teeth. Did our molars steadily diminish in size over several million years because we could create tools and so no longer needed large teeth, as adaptationism might contend? Or might our ancestors have fabricated tools because they no longer had built-in tools in the form of large canines? So can anyone prove any of these alternative scenarios? Which explanation leans more toward acquired characteristics—the traditional evolutionists' one or the suggested alternative?

Since hominid teeth began to diminish in size a million years before hominids became effective tool makers, it would appear that hominid culture did the adapting rather than their genomes providing characteristics to fit hominid life styles. Moreover, once started, the genetic diminution of teeth size continued without regard to adaptive needs generated by human behavior. The point here is our very limited understanding of the horrendously complicated genetic system; the latter's possibilities far exceed what scientists had for long credited it.

Geneticists know that genes function in a highly complex system where some genes control other genes which interact with still other genes. The challenge looming before them now concerns whether some genes (or viruses) somehow also influence the evolutionary process itself. How otherwise to explain such cases of rapid genetic adaptation as those Laysan finches and displaced wallabies in Hawaii, given the extremely small size of the gene pool available? These alternatives need not and should not be unfairly linked to Lamarckianism simply because adaptationism does not provide for such possibilities. Too much scientific work remains to be done first before any judgment is either warranted or convincing.

S.J.Gould and N.Eldredge's research into "punctuated equilibrium," though still denied by some biologists, rests on evidence that genetic change can come quicker than traditional views allow. Gould contends that entire new species can emerge quickly and then remain rather stable for millions of years before suddenly dying out. This view seems somewhat more plausible than steady gradualism for adaptive purposes, as distinct from gradualism (such as for teeth diminution) without speculating adaptive value.

While gradualism can readily rationalize "final" phenotype, its credibility can suffer when trying to explain how a species could be adaptive at every point along a drawn out evolution—unless its environment changed at the same glacial rate, a far from believable prospect. For, we know that environments—especially the climatic factor—can and do change quite abruptly in the temporal scale of evolution. More likely, evolution proceeds in stages, like steps, when it either fits into new niches or adjusts to abrupt environmental change.

Determining whether evolution goes slowly or fast still leaves unexplained the particular process involved in adaptation. Is it entirely a matter of chance mutations? Or might nature have evolved—along with all of its vast cornucopia of amazing biological innovations—a feedback process to enhance its own rate of adaptability? Given all of its multitudinous accomplishments in genetic "engineering," we might think it quite likely that nature would early on have reduced its losses by helping to ensure faster and surer ways to achieve a phenotypic fit than depending solely on mere random chance.

Yet as late as 1982, highly respected Ernst Mayr of Harvard stated emphatically that genetic information can flow only one way: from gene to soma. Within a few years, John Campbell would argue that the genetic system probably has built-in feedback processes to favor more advantageous mutations and genetic drift. Subsequent experiments with *E.coli* found mutations favoring available nutrition well beyond what chance alone would render. If the genetic system could develop feedback in simple organisms, the argument asks why it would abandon that strategy in more complex organisms where it is needed more. In his book, Christopher Wills lucidly sketches the complexities involved.

Some kind of genetic feedback or "self-organizing" system would certainly help explain so much remarkable and otherwise lucky complementarity among adaptive evolutionary changes in apparently disparate parts of an organism. This expects less from chance. On the other hand, expecting every genetic change to have adaptational value may prove too limiting a concept. If nothing else, some changes may simply have piggybacked (as via sexual selection) on other changes which had adaptive value.

How many generations it took to rewire the last part of the human brain necessary to transform *Homo sapiens* into *Homo sapiens sapiens* remains unresolved. Genetic evidence now might not preclude it taking only a dozen or so generations within one deme. Certainly the ten to fifteen thousand years (500 to 750 generations) suggested here should have proven ample for the altered phenotype to prevail genetically throughout a sufficiently large population to launch a massive outmigration and a revolution in communications, social organization, and technology. Especially so, given its advantages. Those advantages in turn would have facilitated its genetic inbreeding as Cro-Magnon overran a world population estimated at only one million or so *Homo sapiens* at the beginning and perhaps ten million when completed by 12,000 BP, some thirty-thousand years later.

Unfortunately in the final analysis, we remain dependent on circumstantial evidence for this or any other scenario offered for consideration. Since we have no way of knowing today what language consisted of thirty or forty thousand years ago (linguistic science has at most gone back 14,000 years), we must judge the emergence of a capacity for syntactical thought by when some human culture made a relatively abrupt change in both the rate and quality of change from what typified human existence during the prior hundreds of thousands of years.

Significance

Two aspects of this discussion call for particular attention relative to their implications for our concern with community. The first involves evolutionary processes; the second, the centrality of females in that evolution.

Geological, biological, paleoarcheological evidence overwhelmingly points to evolution of living systems on Earth. Far less clear is the process involved. And therein may lie a major problem: looking for a single process when many processual routes may have occurred. Indeed, change and the processes of change may have come about more by chance than for readily attributed "causes" and rationalizations. Quite likely, too, they were interactive. This prospect becomes increasingly evident as cultural diversification picks up speed. (More on this in Part Four.)

Once adaptationists locked in onto gradualistic natural selection, their sensitivity to alternatives became boxed in. They had to ascribe causality where causality may not have happened so cleanly, as in saying toolmaking contributed to, rather than followed, diminished canine teeth. Adaptationists had to see human efforts in toolmaking as encouraging the evolution of a truly opposable thumb/fingers by crediting a large degree of determinism to human activity. They had, also, to credit a dropped larynx to increased talking. But what if humans simply expanded speech willy-nilly as they learned to use a fortuitously dropped larynx? Adaptationists saw our current extensive capacity for full syntactical thought taking hundreds of thousands of years of natural selection, whereas this capacity may have emerged rather suddenly and spread throughout the population by sexual selection as its tangible benefits happened to materialize and become quickly utilized.

Linking cultural change and biological change unavoidably faces problems with Larmarckism because acquired characteristics definitely do typify processes of cultural evolution.

Either we premise explanations of causality on exceedingly gradual change or we acknowledge the possibility of built-in feedback processes of some sort which bring genetic change to fit life-style. The tremendous amount of change for our human line within so short a timespan of only five million years—in the feet, pelvis, back/neck, hands, cranial capacity, estrus, and neural system, among others—however, strains credulity for gradualism alone. Unless! unless we either allow change to occur with a more accidental, chaotic, self-organizing cast to it than the causality of natural selection by itself provides, *or* we fall into a creationist trap of omniscient orthogenesis?

While we have no basis for inevitability in the emergence of *Homo sapiens*, possibilities do exist for a complex of diverse routes interactively producing the multitude of changes. As in military strategy, so in scientific strategy: advantages tend to gravitate to viewpoints which keep their options open.

More ironies lie in the second item, that of the female role in human cultural evolution. Its most significant facet seldom draws the attention it deserves. This concerns mtDNA and the interaction of migrating humans with indigenous people.

From historical cases of one society overrunning another, we can readily conjure up scenes of forced interbreeding via male domination and rape. In those cases, males would have distributed their genes into new breeding demes. But the mtDNA question involves a continuous *female* line worldwide. Obviously it took more than just males to move and interbreed.

Short of wholesale slaughter of all races around the world which definitely does not seem to have happened, women had to have played at least as important a role as men. Males could have spread genes for a gracile body and face and syntactical thought. But racial features could not have persisted on different continents **and also** have all humans today share evidence in their mtDNA of a common female ancestor without sexually independent women in (if not dominating) the outmigrating bands of CroMagnon and proto-CroMagnon. Having the indigenous people also matricentral would have facilitated mate selection by intruding females who exploited local males for stud as needed. In short, mtDNA evidence indicates that females back then had to have had the social/political power to call the shots as they migrated around the world.

This possibility opens quite a different window through which to view the next (and more significant question) of how to account for the pervasity of male dominance in human cultures. It suggests that females of yore might well have behaved far more assertively than the wretch cowering behind a club-wielding caveman so widely pictured traditionally by male writers and anthropologists for our supposed ancestors. Early females held a social position which must have accorded them more choice than evident in most societies today. It certainly suggests a recent retrogression in female power, rather than a progression—at least for European and Semitic societies.

My questioning of traditional male bias on the issue of how human culture evolved began with the deeply favorable impressions I gained for the resilience and strength, the determination and subtle command displayed by women in Korea, Vietnam, and China as I observed them under the severe strains of wartime. Fortunately, a reevaluation of the role of females in human cultural evolution has emerged in recent years, thanks largely to a new generation of female anthropologist. Their work has begun to alter how we view female/male relations in today's world as well.

CHAPTER TWO

SEX AND
SOCIAL STRUCTURE

Other than a male bias among earlier anthropologists, no real evidence exists to preclude hominids (in the five million years between the hominid/pongid split and the relatively recent emergence of a syntactically thinking humanity) from living in female-centered societies not unlike some of their primate counterparts. From what evidence does exist, it would appear that technology had not developed so far that women could not have just as expertly made and used the full range of implements then available for survival. Sex-specific specialization of labor lay largely in the future.

Indeed, until at least 35,000 years ago, women could, just as readily as men, have fully fed their children by gathering nuts, fruits, grains, etc. and caught small game and fish with traps. The crudeness of weapons back then indicates that males did not bring in protein as great hunters. The best they could do was scavenge for dead or dying animals, or trap small ones. Quite possibly their most effective weapon was fire: to stampede animals into bogs or over cliffs to their slaughter.

No evidence exists to preclude women from being equally effective as men with such inefficient methods. Even today among hunter-gatherers, female efforts still account for from sixty to seventy percent of a group's food and as much as all of the clothing and shelter. Throughout history, the vast majority of women around the world worked harder than their male folks; women are seldom the weaker sex in the way Western men might portray them recently as an excuse for dominating them.[2]

Additionally, females may have a better record at innovating. As Nancy Tanner points out, females among our nearest primate relatives tend to demonstrate greater dexterity in fabricating tools than males. Japanese anthropologists observed major cultural shifts among macaques (snow monkeys): that of throwing handfuls of sand/grain onto a pond to let the sand sink so that they could easily skim off the floating grain; and that of washing sweet potatoes before eating. Both sprang from female insights and were quickly picked up by young females. Last to catch on: the old males.

In gathering food, females among early humans would have had a chance to gain familiarity with plants and to have recognized advantages in manufacturing food-carrying baskets, clay food-storage pots, and baked pottery. They would have had a greater opportunity to discover a correlation between sticking seeds or plant parts (depending on locale and type of vegetation present) into the ground and the reliable availability of food later. They were, then, more likely than men to have recognized the possibilities of agriculture.

Habitually the ones closer to the children on a daily basis, women would more likely have heard and given in to entreaties from their daughters to keep an orphaned wild puppy or orphaned wild lamb. They would have, however inadvertently, thereby taken humans' first steps toward animal domestication. As Chester Gorman points out, it would have required a major reordering of the male perspective for hunters to perceive what had always been prey as now a friendly servant and handy source of fiber and protein immediately available without the macho rewards of hunting for it. Unburdened by a male outlook, women could more readily have become nascent pastoralists.

Arguably the emergence of syntactical thinking (even prior to female innovation in domesticating plants and animals) must have sparked major sociocultural change. Again, women most probably played the leading role. Throughout the world today, little girls tend to master language quicker than do boys. Raising children and having to cooperate with other women for survival functions would have afforded females more opportunity to develop complex speech into language and practice using it.

Besides, males had less need for language. Children can learn hunting by imitation without verbal instructions; the last thing a hunter needs on the hunt is talk. (Male chimps can conduct complicated raids with minimal signals and grunts; groups of lions hunt with even more complex tactics/strategies albeit with no observable communications among them. Why not male hominids?) Articulate speech may well have had more adaptive survival value for women than for men—initially at least.

If contemporary hunter-gatherers offer any clues to our past, women likely also had responsibility for maintaining a group's fire. We should not be surprised, then, if women became the first storytellers around a nightly campfire. From creative storytelling they would take a relatively short step to weaving tales about spirits, itself a first step toward becoming shamans who called on supernatural forces: for assistance and protection, for a supply of food, and for success in childbirth. In gathering, women could have observed the recuperative powers of certain herbs. Their nascent shaman activity could then have widened to encompass healing, a common practice among folk and tribal societies around the globe and one most often conducted by those shamans who also show effective understanding of psychosomatic illness. These advanced societal activities would have further established their magical powers and hence strengthened their matriarchal influence.

Associating the female menstrual cycle with an awe inspiring monthly lunar cycle could have added an aura of mystery to women already deemed mysterious in their power to give birth. A basis exists for so much importance attributed to goddesses among early religions: Isis and Hathor in ancient Egypt; Hara, Aphrodite, Artemis, Gaia, Rhea and Cybele in ancient Greece; Magna Mater in Rome; Ishtar and Inanna in Mesopotamia; Kali, Sri Lakshmi, and Radha in India; Kuanyin in China; Amaterasu the Sun Goddess in Japan; Pele (in the mold of Kali) in Hawaii; Mother Earth among Amerindians; residually to some extent in the cult of the Virgin mostly among Mediterranean Catholics.

(One major thread in the Old Testament concerns repeated conflict between the male-supremacy orientation of the twelve Israelitic hunter-herder tribes as against surrounding agriculturalists who honored goddesses. Goddesses continued to exert an enticing appeal, much to the utter horror of Moses and later prophets.)

SOCIAL BONDING

Over the last 1.7 million years, one evolutionary factor in particular must have brought marked change in hominid society from that evident among our closest primate species. The continually expanded large hominid head forced two significant adjustments, one biological and the other sociological.

First, to exit the pelvic cavity, babies had to be born more "premature" in the sense of being helpless and hence demanding far longer care. A longer time of parental involvement would facilitated the inculcation of more cultural information, particularly verbal symbols for communication. Second, as childbirth became increasingly difficult, it would have had to evolve from an individual matter (as it is for other primates) into a social affair. Other members in the group would have had to assist in an increasing number of births.

Since men are seldom of much use here, most likely the woman's mother and sisters would have been expected to take part. Herein lay a major impetus for a more structured social bonding; and its impetus was female, not male. Moreover, the increased need for sociability and social reliability among women could well have contributed to a hominid propensity for sharing food, quite unlike our primate relatives. (The much touted theory of "old boy" male bonding for warfare having brought on food sharing must raise grave doubts, principally because it took far too long—into historic times—before warfare became a disciplined endeavor of individual submission and group bonding instead of a competitive exercise in individual heroics.)

Given the probable levels of verbal communication, social organization, and technology prior to 45,000 years ago, a distinct possibility exists that males held a rather peripheral place (socially and physically) in hominid

society. Like female apes, hominid females could have performed all functions—including defense—necessary for group and species survival on their
own without the burden of having also to feed, clothe, shelter, and serve
men. Women had no need to tie themselves down to one man. As in chimp
societies, males might have operated largely on their own or in their own
group, their usefulness limited to insemination at the female's choice. Indeed, female promiscuity may have accorded a strategic advantage, that of
gaining greater protection for offspring, as it does among chimpanzees, in
decreasing infanticide or at least infant abuse by males.

In some societies, males might have served a protective role—as even
orangutans do where tigers and siamangs live but don't do in the absence of
such a threat to their offspring. Or as occurs in some tribal societies today,
a woman's brother (rather than the biological father) might have taken responsibility for his sister's child. This arrangement avoids inbreeding yet
holds the matricentral family in tact. Whatever arrangement existed, we can
only guess from the scant evidence available. A wide range of possibilities
may exist for males; but in all likelihood, species survival rested squarely on
female effectiveness.

THE SHIFT TO MALE DOMINANCE

With the markedly heightened mental powers gained by neural rewiring,
men (as well as women) could have gained a heightened capacity for more
effective tool making. This shows up unmistakably in paleoarcheological
evidence by twenty to thirty thousand years ago. With accelerating technological advances, humans could for the first time become effective hunters.
Being unburdened with the care of children (and the infirmed) and the collection of daily food, males could for the first time become big-game hunters
on extended excursions. Moreover, they could at last make a significant
food contribution to their group.

The era of "man the hunter" (so prevalent in anthropological as well as
popular concepts for our "primitive" ancestors and so ballooned by such
writers as Robert Ardrey) probably only emerged some 20/30,000 years
ago. And it began to pass as early as ten thousand years ago in various lo-

cales around the world. Yet that rather brief era of change may well have been crucial in providing a base for the profound revolution in human culture which we have experienced in historic times.

Certainly by twenty thousand years ago, the enhanced technological capabilities (evident in paleoarcheological finds) would have facilitated more productive hunting, especially for big game and hence the supply of protein. However, that success would have come sporadically. Since people must eat daily, human bands would have had to continue to rely on the daily gathering and small-scale hunting and fishing traditionally accomplished for survival by women.

But when men did bag a large animal, it would have to be eaten quickly before spoiling. This meant that the entire band, not just the hunter's immediate family, would all share the bounty. What better time than a moment of surplus protein for community festivities with fun and games to go along with the feast. About this time, men might have celebrated their victories with artistic creations, either as sculptures or paintings on cave walls; perhaps by dancing, too.

We have then a situation where it would remain women's responsibility to sustain the family on a daily basis while men contributed what amounted to surplus production. What food, clothing, shelter a woman provided would be shared with her family members routinely and as a matter of course. What food a man might occasionally bring in to camp would contribute to communal well-being and hence to a grateful community feasting.

Consequently, even though men still contributed a minority of the food, what they did provide would more likely be associated with celebration; whereas women, in keeping the family alive, would be seen simply as doing what was expected of them routinely and without festivity. Male activity/production became a societal affair; women's work remained a family matter. Cultural evolution was passing women by and converting them into domestic servants for males to play the role of "big man."

Furthermore, with art, men could glorify their own contributions. Artwork would also provide a means for communal identity, aggrandizement, and enjoyment as well as possibly facilitating interaction with the spirit world. It would become lasting, tangible evidence of productivity, unlike consumed food provided routinely by women. Male presence, by asserting itself initially in communal affairs rather than in the family, would have inadvertently promoted an expanding community.

This new male importance socially, in boiling down to a matter of surplus production, was probably not enough in and of itself to revolutionize society. It depended on how each group dealt with the social spinoffs. The most stubbornly persistent of today's hunter-gatherer cultures do not countenance ownership nor grant honor to hunters for what they bag; it is deemed unmanly to hog the spotlight, to be acquisitive, or to presume to create art for gain. In those societies (such as among Eskimo) the wives rather than the men distribute the meat from a kill, and little had changed in their cultural systems—until the recent deluge of Western utensils and consumerism.

In other groups, however, male prowess at hunting and artistry could have grown into prestige and communal leadership. These would likely have translated into enhanced reproductive advantages in terms of attracting the most desirable females for mating. It also would have involved a nascent concern for ownership—ownership both of the surplus production generated and of the instruments used, be they especially effective talismans, especially good spears, and larger huts (from the larger animal skins). Perhaps secrets in artwork and accumulated wives eventually assumed exclusive ownership characteristics, too.

Once the idea of ownership begins to take hold, concepts of property are not far behind. Then comes concern about how to pass it on, even to controlling it after death. Questions about what may be owned and who constitutes an heir would soon follow. Inheritance always poses a significant problem in societies which recognize property and ownership. (Some Amerindian tribes avoided the inevitable communal conflict by outright forbidding any inheritance.) Where recognized, ownership necessitates institutionalized ways of reckoning, protecting, and trading it. Thus a once relatively simple society/culture grows complicated as its community system evolves this way.

Inheritance poses a more difficult problem for men than for women. A woman knows she gave birth to a child; a man can never be certain that he is the true father of the child he claims is his and then expends energy and prestige in rearing. In virtually all societies, nothing humiliates a man like being cuckolded, especially if he identifies with the resulting child and must deny to the public what really happened.

Settling Into a Regimented Life Style

What incentive could have induced men to forsake their recently emerged, relatively easy, macho life of male hunting and female gathering for the always more demanding, more precarious, more regimented life of farming or herding? Might not this new combination of status and ownership, a thirsting for power with its sexual advantages, and anxiety over paternity have done the trick? These certainly have made men do all manner of crazy things in historic times!

So long as women took responsibility for the children during the previous millions of years, women most probably were independent enough to select their own mates when they chose to do so, much as other independent female primates have always done. (Recall that with the loss of estrus, hominid females had gained a far greater say in when and if, hence with whom, they might choose copulation and pregnancy.) Males could only strut and bear gifts, but short of rape could not dictate selection. And with nothing to inherit, there existed little if any reason to bond the parents together for child-rearing.

Now introduce ownership, inheritance, male pride (and fear of cuckoldry); the social equation changes. How could a man honored by his community risk not only humiliation but uncertainty over his genetic reproductivity if women could continue selecting their own mate at their own chosing? With increased self-awareness and community involvement, this prospect might have generated real anxiety; and anxiety has frequently been the irritant for cultural change, the most often recognized example being the contribution of Calvinist anxiety to capitalism

One obvious solution to this dilemma would involve drastically curtailing women's opportunities for selecting mates. But so long as men specialized in hunting which took them away from the band for days at a time, they would have lacked a way to control women. So, either men had to stop traveling around or they had to take their women with them. Abandoning their new skills of hunting to stay home was no solution; they would have lost their new status and selectivity advantage. Ironically, it was women who provided men with the means for curtailing female mating caprice by being able to keep their wives near them.

As noted already, women more likely than men initiated animal and plant domestication. But true agriculture and true animal husbandry could not succeed within the limits of time and resources available to women alone. Either option required the input of many people—an entire family, preferably as part of a group of families to maximize mutual support, labor sharing, and increased needs for defense. By switching to either sedentary agriculture or regularized nomadism for herding, a man could ensure the paternity of his children by keeping his wife always within eyesight

As men became more proficient in organizing production, they rose in wealth and power while women remained limited to their traditional responsibility for family sustenance. And as men gained wealth and power hence communal honor and status, they could focus on public affairs, be it trade, government, religion, and war. This move enjoyed a quantum leap from enhanced mobility when men domesticated horses (then camels and elephants)—in contrast to the so-called barnyard animals domesticated by women much earlier.

It should not surprise us that the major era of cultural change in economic activity and social organization (from hunter-gatherer to organized agriculture or herding) of between ten and six thousand years ago happens to correspond with the emergence of larger social/political community systems, long-distance trade, organized warfare, and eventually forms of governance that transcend tribal groupings.[3]

While this shift by males seems plausible, two questions arise: Why did it not come sooner? And why would women go along with it when they had previously exercised—and may have still retained in many societies—a preeminent position within family, clan, and community?

Horrendous climatic change may go far in accounting for the matter of timing. It took the rather abrupt end of the Ice Age to provide the requisite conditions for this momentous switch, even in lands quite distant from the nearest ice sheet. Although small initial permanent settlements may have appeared as early as 15,000 years ago (possibly as trading posts), intentional agriculture begins to appear by 12,000 BP, either by part-time farmers or simply by hunter-gatherers who planted crops to harvest during their next swing through the area.

By 10,000 BP, climate favored farming; true agriculture could proceed in several parts of the world, most notably the Middle East for grain production and Southeast Asia for certain tropical fruits and possibly primitive rice; soon in Africa, New Guinea, and Americas.[4] Regularized nomadic herding began in various sectors of the world (depending on the kinds of animals and geographical conditions) at roughly the same time period.

The second question presents a more difficult enigma to unravel, mainly because the evidence is so skimpy. We cannot safely project contemporary female attitudes toward marriage and family back to an age when those social institutions were still in their nascent state. The extent to which a desire for certainty or for competitive reproductive advantage may have played a role is anyone's guess; it appears plausible though.

The drive for reproductive success of one's genetic material imposes a tremendous force within all species, the quintessential basis for species survival without which you and I would not exist. In watching the behavior of teenagers and young adults, it takes an exceedingly strong bias to not see the same drive in humans as well. It appears more prudent to accept than to deny that the reproductive drive exerts a major influence on human behavior for both sexes. Coping with reproductive pressures constitutes a central aspect of all cultures and community systems. Male/female interaction still permeates virtually all sociocultural phenomena no matter how much we encrust daily life with other busy activity, consumerism, and moralisms. (Appendix D Provides a further consideration of politics in mating).

The centrality of a species' drive for reproductive perpetuation seems especially relevant here when we acknowledge how surplus production among our ancestors could garner communal power and hence increase possibilities for still greater assured reproductive success ("fitness" in sociobiological lingo) for men recognized as successful. Women's individual natural desire to do whatever it takes to enhance their children's survival prospects could, conceivably, have rather early seen the value of monopolizing successful men toward this fundamental objective. In this situation, women would have acted without ever recognizing that it could lead to their own enslavement.[5]

If this scenario occurred, then we have an irony. Men (not women) may have taken the lead in committing themselves to pair-bonding—to avoid being cuckolded. Having seen the advantage for their own reproductive success, women would have given up their previous freedom to gain optimal benefit from a communally recognized bonding with a male. This gradual change, apparently, stems from expectations of advantage by both sexes.

But until this latter shift (which may have begun imperceptibly some 30,000 years ago and accelerated after 10,000 BP) the likelihood exists that migrations were as much or more a decision by women to make and push than a male prerogative. Until the latter era, small bands probably had no need for leaders as such; consensus, so essential for survival, would have determined issues. Until Middle Eastern and European cultures intruded, women in such diverse societies as Indonesian, West African, and Iroquois had considerable (if not a majority) say in community affairs.

With this scenario in mind, the debate over a common mtDNA ancestor need not have grown so acrimonious. An mtDNA ancestor could have been a member of any "wave" of outmigration; no need to conjure up mass slaughter. With the prevalence of matrifocal groups, migrating females could simply have chosen local males for stud service wherever they moved or settled.

Common ancestry then would have taken entirely different routes for nDNA and for mtDNA. The breakthrough here comes in not imposing any current cultural system on our ancestors of many millennia ago and thus not presupposing a set of male-biased restrictions on females back then which are neither proven nor necessarily the most plausible.

CHAPTER THREE

CULTURAL DIVERSIFICATION

Late nineteenth century theories that saw an almost total determination of culture resting on geographic environments have long since experienced appropriate repudiation. However, we cannot completely eliminate geographic location and historical processes over time as important considerations. They do constitute factors among a gigantic web of factors which did exert all manner of influences (in a diversity of possibly conflicting directions) on how each human culture might have evolved, eventually split, collided, merged, and changed.

Latitude, altitude, and wind patterns associated with a locale would certainly affect how people lived—in terms of clothing worn and shelters built, if for no other reason. Geography, climate, and availability of herdible animals, for instance, would certainly have gone far in favoring whether any particular group of humans shifted from hunting-gathering into farming or into herding. If they went into farming, whether the domesticated plants propagated through planting seeds or inserting parts of the plants (vegetative reproduction) and whether the seeds could be planted by broadcast or required insertion, even transplantation—these variables would have significantly affected the amount, kind, and timing of work as well as the availability of manpower.

Manpower considerations would call for organizing an optimal division of labor. Whether they needed to remove trees and whether they had to provide irrigation and flood control would have affected how farmers would organize their individual and collective lives and hence their culture. Then would come problems of defense against wild animals and raiding parties. Out of these efforts would emerge the beginnings of government—while the raiders converted themselves into ruling conquerors.

A need for exchanging vegetables for wild meats, fish, and fruits would become necessary since farmers seldom enjoy total self-sufficiency. For effective trade, mature, sedentary societies would need to develop diplomacy, rituals of mutual trust, additional forms of leadership and arrangements for further divisions of labor, all major cultural accomplishments.

Just these few variables alone (and many others would have applied) would allow a vast diversity of cultures to emerge. In each case they would have required a believable rationale for decisions made and the translation of those rationalizations into alleged divine guidance and political organization. Strong personalities by individual leaders of either sex at crucial junctures along the way could have pulled small societies toward one collective choice or another without their being aware that choice had occurred. Climatic shifts would have forced societies to migrate; mountains and rivers would have channeled the directions those migrations took and hence have affected which societies and cultures would collide.

The original shift from hunter-gatherer to some more regimented form of community probably happened in several places individually and without contact between them. But subsequent transformations in those regions could have followed contact with the originators. When a group of people undertook their conversion would have posed different kinds of sociocultural models to observe, different levels of technological sophistication, and different religious/economic/political rationalizations as well as different social structures to adopt from. (Part Two provides a rather well-documented case in point.)

Developments in technology and mobility surely affected how cultures around the world evolved. While the genetically provided superior mental capacity had recently facilitated the formation of larger and more complex communities, their actual realization had to wait until sophistication in technology (in mining and smelting, for example) and mobility (for trade and transportation of goods) could make truly large-scale societies practical. This did not gel until some seven thousand years ago

With so vast a variety of variables involved, there should be no surprise that societies in similar geographical contexts might exhibit contrary sociocultural formats while other, quite unrelated societies in rather different geographical contexts might pursue somewhat parallel cultures. Consequently, some societies reckon matrilineal descent whereas others reckon it patrilineally. Some make males into tyrannical gods whereas others accord them only titular authority. Some allow women relatively greater participation in communal affairs and economic transactions whereas others circumscribe their realms to near slavery or dependence within the home. Some still allow women a major voice in mate selection whereas others have her parents make the arrangements to favor family interests.

That no truly female-centered society exists today does not prove that some form of matrifocal organization of society could not have existed many places, perhaps everywhere (as is common for apes), at least until twenty/thirty thousand years ago. Vestiges of it still persist in some cultures in the form of matrilineal descent and matrilocality of residence, such as in parts of northern Thailand and traditional Java.

For lack of written records to trace how each culture on the "tree" of cultures has evolved along its entire course over the last ten thousand years, there now exists virtually no way to reconstruct realistic explanations for specific cultural practices in any particular society much less globally. While it may be impossible to trace the evolutionary routes of individual cultures, one overall irony has begun to emerge.

A Modern Ironic Twist

We noted that women appear to have taken the foremost initial strides in the evolution of human culture as we know it today: Women were most likely the first tool fabricators (for baskets, clothing), the originators of language and religion, and took the lead in domesticating plants and animals. Unburdened by pregnancy, lactation, and child-rearing, men could eventually build complex cultures/communities on women's technological advances.

Eventually men went on to usurp control of religion and civic affairs, particularly so with the advent of writing and its monopolization by men. A monopoly on writing meant they could justify as sacred any cultural provision beneficial to elite males. From there they could establish and run government, thence to take charge of defense and engage in warfare. Meanwhile they dominated tool fabrication to build industries and exploit natural resources, including the enslavement of captives and the exploitation of women and children.

Each "advance" was made possible by further advances in technology and knowledge. Holding monopolies on these forms of power made males increasingly unchallengeable by women. Instead women might likely have found it advantageous to try to solidify the institutions of family and marriage (even concubinage) for their individual protection and as socially ordained ways to ensure that as many males as possible would accept responsibility for the offspring they sire. Females (or at least their families) would seek to achieve an optimal pairing as security for themselves and their children.

This situation has long prevailed in many cultures. But a problem has arisen and herein lies the irony. At an accelerating rate over recent decades running back into the last century, the technological monopolization which originally allowed men to dominate has now grown increasingly sophisticated. It is now so demanding and extensive in modern societies until there are no longer enough talented men in the upper strata to handle all the tasks required to keep a highly complex technological culture functioning. Men had no choice (even if they refused to admit it as such) other than to allow universal education: for commoners, then for ethnically suppressed men, and finally for women—to become productive workers, willing soldiers, skilled technicians, and even effective managers/professionals.

Not surprisingly, decision-makers tried (successfully at first) to limit what educational opportunities they opened to women. They sought to limit openings to what they could readily rationalize as akin to women's supposed "proper place," namely mothering and child rearing—tasks not leading to communal power and competition with men. Thus women were, at least in the West, allowed to enter teaching and the arts, then nursing, then secretarial, and (during wartime) routine assembly line jobs, all previously thought to be exclusive areas of "male work."

Since WWII, the rampant, insatiable demands of modern technology no longer allow men to bar women from such recent male monopolies as law, medicine, government, science, management, even the military, and finally religion. The "iron curtain walls" protecting WASP male bastions are coming down for women, as they are for men from other ethnic backgrounds. And women have demonstrated that they can just as readily master the intricate rituals and games of science and management—even when they get less pay for the same performance.

In short, the technological innovations (which females inaugurated thirty or forty thousand years ago and which ten thousand years ago began to enslave them) have at last accelerated to a point where they have begun to offer choices about how women might want to organize their own individual lives and careers. Moreover, technology makes it possible for women not only to live longer but to face pregnancy and lactation for a far shorter portion of their lives now. They have an opportunity (for a change) to make the most of the options opened by advanced educations, whether it be in a career, traditional "homemaking", some combination of both, or single parenthood.

Of course, just as the shift from hunter-gatherer to farming or herding did not happen everywhere simultaneously but took a multiplicity of routes and transition times among different societies, so too this process of female emancipation is not taking, and will not pursue the same identical route everywhere. But just as Euro-American industrialization, capitalism, and democracy have infected virtually all other societies to some extent; so too the impact of female emancipation due to the demands of technological change will eventually disrupt male monopolies of power in all societies. Social ferment, once started, seems most difficult to dam off or turn off—especially in this age of global communications and travel.

The process of change will not, of course, be universal and certainly not simultaneous. Men will fight any threat to a supposedly God-given right of dominance; no bloc surrenders power and privilege meekly. Communist countries promised equality for women but continued to relegate most to the least technologically demanding tasks. Wealth from natural resources may allow some societies (Arabic Middle East countries with oil for instance) to postpone instituting universal education and opening employment doors to women; they can for awhile still buy their technological sophistication from others who have released women from the home. The fascinating Japanese case, examined in Part Two, reveals a somewhat different dilemma.

A SECOND IRONY

In this section's scenario for the evolution of human cultures, women probably had to defend their families virtually throughout the hominid evolution. But as males came to dominate human society during the last ten to twenty thousand years, they have assumed increasing roles in defense. A sociobiological perspective would contend that males simply sought to protect their genetic investment in progeny.

This sounds plausible until (a) we ask why males have only recently developed a concern for genetic investment, and until (b) we look at how "defense" has evolved into warfare with varying degrees of masculinization. Have males in some cultures expressed their genetic concern through an increasing fixation on material goods—as a way to attract the most desirable females and subsequently as a way to ensure the survival of their children? Have they then engaged in ever larger scaled warfare both to protect that material wealth and to accumulate more—perhaps spreading their genes along the way in the process?

Or perchance have the games of acquiring power and wealth come to dominate for their own societal and psychological rewards regardless of any possible genetic incentive? The glory of war can come to dominate, and men can—perhaps as they did during the five million years of human evolution until a dozen or so millennia ago—find more empathy with other men (even with their enemies) than with women and children. When a society thereby develops a deep divide between the sexes over the assignment of labor, status and power, it is not uncommon for any of several results to emerge, none of which sociobiology would predict.

Either women become mere chattels to be exploited, ignored, and abused; or men turn to other men for social and eventually sexual gratification; sometimes both. You can find these developments in characteristically warrior cultures—in earlier Samoa, earlier Amerindian tribes, Turkish conquerors, China and feudal Europe, to name but a few of the better known cases. We see this clearly in Part Two for Japan's thirteenth to nineteenth centuries.

All of which leaves us wondering whether the current controversy over allowing women and homosexuals to serve combat roles in America, Britain, and other "modern" societies might stem not only from a resistance to admit that women and gays can perform just as well as macho men, thereby demeaning male claims to dominance. Might it not stem a bit also from a preference for male company but a fear of acknowledging this as yet nonsexual homophilial orientation? Hence the resort to a rather common "Tailhook syndrome" to prove masculinity among modern day "warriors" who face an increasingly feminized world (or at least a non-macho, bureaucratized, domesticated world) and who instinctively know no other response except to abuse.

It is at this level of question, if at no other, that answers may depend on a far more historic and cross-cultural analysis than generally pursued. Indeed, looking only at contemporary cultures may likely miss much of what is involved by concentrating on superficial indicators. Here is where we may well need a far fuller appreciation of living systems in their utter complexity.

In Conclusion

A few final points: First, for hundreds of thousands of years—since they started using fire purposefully—hominids exerted sufficient impact on the ecological system of their habitat to have affected it. Since 10,000 BP, human capacity for markedly altering nature has become increasingly evident. We humans may now impact the environment sufficiently to affect even our own genotype as well as phenotype (examined in Part Four).

As important as the new capability for markedly enhanced thought and communication by individuals was for human communities, people individually could not have so profoundly altered the ecological context in which we live and on which we depend for survival. The real power here lies in the new capacity for highly organized, highly structured, and highly disciplined behavior. This greatly expanded competence in social process over the last ten thousand years or so made our cultural complexity and creativity possible. It also made our destructiveness all the more devastating as well as profitable, especially as it facilitated greatly accelerated population growth.

Second, all of this compounding of culture seems to have required an instrument with enough built-in flexibility to accommodate both the accelerating rate of change and its breadth. This instrument had to have provided a process for meeting members' functional needs, for coping with external threats, for adapting to challenges, and for stirring emotional loyalty and a sense of mutual responsibility. Quite likely, this instrument had to have had a familiar arena in which societies could act out their cultures in such a way as to both maintain and modify them in the face of recurring challenges.

From the observations in this book, the most natural candidate to serve this need was community. At the outset it might have involved no more than a band of related women, their children, perhaps some peripheral juvenile brothers, all bonded together under a matriarch. From there, community could expand to accommodate bands of subbands, then tribes and clans, eventually villages and towns, until now we have an overwhelming combination of multi-scaled and variously oriented community systems at megatropolis and national levels. Instead of just coming naturally, community is so complex now that it requires its participants to work at their own integration into it.

END NOTES

1. Although reality is far, far more complicated, consider this simplified, imaginary scenario for illustrative purposes only. Suppose that at some point in the past, the human line consisted of a group of people with black eyes and black hair. Eventually they separate into two geographically separated demes. After a while, there occurs a mutation in one group for blue eyes which proves dominant. The other group experiences a mutation for blond hair which also proves dominant. After centuries or millennia apart, the two demes meet up with each other and begin to interbreed, the blue-eyed/black-hair people with the blond-hair/black-eyed people. That would result in most people having blue eyes and blond hair. Consequently, all of those so endowed would share the same "original" black-hair/black-eyed common ancestral pair and also both the common black-hair/blue-eyed and blond-hair/black-eyed ancestral pairs in the temporarily separated demes. They would, then, share at least three sets of common ancestors. And this involves only two of thousands of features.

2. Please note that barring women from combat has little to do with their effectiveness as warriors. Joan d'Arc in France and several empresses in Japan (among other examples around the world) quite effectively led armies and personally engaged in combat. Nearly two-thousand years ago, the Trung sisters led one of Vietnam's mightiest armies which happened to consist entirely of women. As late as the fourteenth century, some female Japanese warriors could outperform their male counterparts. A most perceptive analysis of the masculinization of war appears in Cynthia Enloe's *The Morning After: Sexual Politics at the End of the Cold War* (1993).

3. Not only did community systems increase in size and complexity, availability of more food energy might likely have facilitated shorter intervals between pregnancies. Shorter intervals could give rise to population increase, as would mothers giving birth to fewer stillborns and being able to care for more children during their early, fully dependent years. And apparently the beginnings of population increase do occur some twenty to forty thousand years ago, accelerating during the last ten thousand as various cultures have increasingly emphasized reproductive success for family continuity.

4. Boserup and others have argued that increased population provided the critical factor for the shift to agriculture. A global population of only ten million at the time hardly makes that theory compelling. No doubt local increases in population may have facilitated a sedentary culture, whether for trade or farming. But that possibility does not establish its causality any more than the timely change in climate globally could have "caused" the cultural metamorphosis. Both climate and population (along with other factors) were only contributory.

In complex systems where all variables are essentially dependent in their linkage webs, we may not attribute causality. We may only explore and describe processes of change in which various factors facilitate or contribute to the outcome.

5. After completing this analysis I was astonished to discover that Friedrich Engels a century ago had come to a parallel hypothesis. My astonishment springs from my normally not seeing the world the way he did. Unlike his ideological commitment, I had the advantage of a century of more extensive ethnological and genetic findings by scientists to draw upon.

BIBLIOGRAPHY

In addition to interviews with Professors Derek Bickerton, Rebecca Cann, Hampton Carson, Sheila Conant, Kenneth Kaneshiro, and feedback from Professors Bryce Decker and Mary MacDonald, all at the University of Hawaii, the following provide an indication of sources drawn on, checked against, and questioned:

Aiello, Leslie C. "The Fossil Evidence for Modern Human Origins in Africa: A Revised View." *American Anthropology*. Vol.95 #1. 1993.

Alexander, Richard D. *Darwinism and Human Affairs*. 1979.

Alexander, Richard D. & D. W. Tinkle. *Natural Selection and Social Behavior*. 1981.

Ardrey, Robert. *The Hunting Hypothesis*. 1976.

Barash, David P. *Sociobiology and Behavior*. 1977.

Bar-Yosef, Ofer & B. Vandermeersch. "Modern Humans in the Levant," *Scientific American*, Apr. 1993.

Barkow, Jerome H. et al. The Adopted Mind: Evolutionary Psychology and the Generation of Culture. 1992.

Bateman, Richard. et al. "The Feasibility of Reconciling Human Phylogeny and the History of Language." *Current Anthropology*. Vol.31, No.1. Jan. 1990.

Bateson, Patrick. [ed.]. *Mate Choice*. 1983.

Berghe, Pierre L. van den. *Human Family Systems*. 1979.

Bickerton, Derek. *Language and Species*. 1990.

Blumer, Herbert. *Symbolic Interactionism: Perspective and Method*. 1969.

Bock, Kenneth. *Human Nature and History: A Response to Sociobiology*. 1980.

Bonner, John T. *Evolution of Culture in Animals*. 1980.

Boserup, Esther. *The Condition of Agricultural Growth*. 1965.

Boulding, Kenneth E. *The World as a Total System*. 1985.

Bower, Bruce. "A World that Never Existed," and "The Strange Case of the Tasaday," *Science News*, Vol.135, Nos. 17 and 18, Apr. & May 1989.

Boyd, Robert & Peter J. Richerson. *Culture and the Evolutionary Process*. 1985.

Brandon, Robert N. & Richard M. Burian [eds.]. *Genes, Organisms, Population: Controversies Over the Units of Selection.*1984

Brown, Michael H. *The Search for Eve*. 1990.

Calvin, William H. "The Emergence of Intelligence." *Scientific American*. Oct. 1994.

Campbell, Bernard G. *Human Evolution: An Introduction to Man's Adaptations.* 1985.

Campbell, John. "Autonomy in Evolution," in *R. Milkman* 1982; also in Depew & Weber. 1985.

Cann, Rebecca. "DNA and Human Origins," *American Review of Anthropology,* Vol.17. 1988.

Carson, Hampton. "Genetic Imbalance, Realigned Selection, and the Origin of Species," in *L.V. Giddings,* 1989.

Ciohon, Russell L. & John G. Fleagle [eds.]. *Primate Evolution and Human Origins.* 1987.

Cohen, Mark Nathan. *The Food Crisis in Prehistory.* 1977.

Commoner, Barry. *The Closing Circle: Nature, Man, and Technology.* 1971.

Conant, Shiela. "Geographic Variation in the Laysan Finch," *Evolutionary Ecology,* Vol.2, 1988.

Conant, Shiela. "Saving Endangered Species by Translocation," *BioScience,* Vol.38, No.4, 1988.

Daly, Martin & Margo Wilson. *Sex, Evolution and Behavior.* 1978.

Dawkins, Richard. *The Selfish Gene.* 1976.

Dawkins, Richard. *The Extended Phenotype.* 1982.

Depew, David J. & B.H. Weber. *Evolution at a Crossroads.* 1985.

Degler, Carl N. *In Search of Human Nature.* 1991.

Diamond, Jared. *The Third Chimpanzee.* 1992.

Diamond, Jared. "The Golden Age that Never Was," *Discover.* Dec. 1988.

Diamond, Jared. "Sexual Deception," *Discover.* Aug. 1989.

Diamond, Jared. "The Accidental Conqueror," *Discover.* Dec.1989.

Diamond, Jared. "Ten Thousand Years of Solitude." *Discover.* March 1993.

Diamond, Jared. "Sex and the Female Agenda." *Discover.* Sept. 1993.

DISCOVER. "What is Consciousness?" Nov. 1992.

Dobzhansky, Theodosius & Earnest Boesiger. *Human Culture: A Moment in Evolution.* 1983; Bruce Wallace editor.

Ebil-Eibesfeldt, I. *The Biology of War and Peace.* 1979.

Ehrhardt, Anke A. "The Psychobiology of Gender," in Alice Rossi, *Gender and the Life Course.* 1985.

Eldredge, Niles. *Unfinished Synthesis: Biological Hierarchies and Modern Evolutionary Thought.* 1985.

Eldredge, Niles. *The Miner's Canary.* 1991.

Ellen, Roy. *Environment, Subsistence and System.* 1982.

Filsinger, Erik E. *Biosocial Perspectives on the Family.* 1988.

Flohn, H. & R. Fantechi. *The Climate of Europe.* 1984.

Fox, Robin. *The Search for Society.* 1989.

Freedman, D. G. *Human Sociobiology: A Holistic Approach.* 1979.

Futuyma, Douglas J. *Evolutionary Biology.* 1986.

Galdikas, Birute M.F. "Waiting for Orangutans." *Discover*. Dec. 1994.

Gargett, Robert H. "Grave Shortcomings: the Evidence for Neanderthal Burial," *Current Anthropology*, Vol.30, Apr. 1989.

Geertz, Hildred. *The Javanese Family: A Study in Kinship and Socialization*. 1961.

Gibson, Kathleen R. & Tim Ingold. *Tools, Language, and Cognition in Human Evolution*. 1993.

Giddings, L.V., K.Y. Kaneshiro, W.W. Anderson [eds.]. *Genetics, Speciation and the Founding Principle*. 1989.

Goodall, Jane. *In the Shadow of Man*. 1971.

Gould, James L. & Carol Grant Gould. *The Animal Mind*. 1994.

Gould, Stephen J. "Is a New General Theory of Evolution Emerging?" *Paleobiology*, Vol.6, No.1, 1980.

Gould, Stephen J. "The Meaning of Punctuated Equilibrium," in *R. Milkman*, 1982.

Gould, Stephen J. "An Asteroid to Die For," *Discover*, Oct.1989

Gould, Stephen J. "The Evolution of Life on the Earth." *Scientific American*. Oct. 1994.

Gove, W.R. & G.R. Carpenter. *The Fundamental Connection Between Nature and Nurture*. 1982.

Gray, Patrick J. *Primate Sociobiology*. 1985.

Greene, Majorie [ed.]. *Dimensions of Darwinism*. 1983

Griffin, Donald R. *Animal Minds*. 1992.

Halverson, John. "Art for Art's Sake in Paleolithic," *Current Anthropology*, Vol.28, No.1, Feb. 1987.

Hapgood, Fred. *Why Males Exist: An Inquiry into the Evolution of Sex*. 1979.

Harding, Robert S.O. & Geza Teleki [eds.]. *Omnivorous Primates and Hunting in Human Evolution*. 1981.

Harpending, Henry C. et al. "The Genetic Structure of Ancient Human Populations." *Current Anthropology*. Vol.34, No.4, 1993.

Headland, Thomas N. & Lawrence A. Reid, "Hunter-Gatherers and Their Neighbors from Prehistory to Present," *Current Anthropology*, Feb. 1989.

Hebb, Donald O. *Essay on Mind*. 1980.

Heiser, Charles B. *Of Plants and People*. 1985.

Hill, James N. [ed.] *Explanation of Prehistorical Change*. 1977

Hrdy, Sarah Blaffer. *The Woman That Never Evolved*. 1981.

Isaacs, Harold R. *Idols of the Tribe*. 1975.

James, Steven R. "Hominid Use of Fire in the Lower and Middle Pleistocene," *Current Anthropology*. Vol.30, No.1, Feb.1989

Jaroff, Leon. "The Gene Hunt," *Time*, 20 Mar. 1989.

Johanson, Donald C. *Ancestors: In Search of Human Origins*. 1994

Johnson, Allen W. & Timothy Earle. *The Evolution of Human Societies*. 1987.

Johnson, L. Lewis. "The Neanderthals and Population as Prime Movers," *Current Anthropology*, Vol.30, No.4, 1989.

Jonas, Hans. *The Phenomenon of Life.* 1966.

Kaneshiro, Kenneth Y. "The Dynamics of Sexual Selection and Founder Effects in Species Formation," in *L.V. Giddings,* 1989

Keller, Evelyn Fox. *A Feeling of the Organism: the Life and Work of Barbara McClintock.* 1983.

Kevles, Daniel J. *In the Name of Eugenics.* 1985.

Kimura, Motoo. "The Neutral Theory of Molecular Evolution," *Scientific American,* Vol.241, No.5, 1979.

Knecht, Heidi. "Late Ice Age Hunting Technology." *Scientific American.* July 1994.

Kuhn, Thomas S. *The Structure of Scientific Revolutions.* 1962.

Laitman, J.T. "Evolution of the Upper Respiratory Tract." in P.V. Tobias [ed.]. *Hominid Evolution: Past, Present, and Future.* 1985.

Lancaster, Jan Beckman. *Primate Behavior and the Emergence of Human Culture.* 1975.

Lancaster, Jan Beckman. "Evolutionary Perspectives on Sex Differences in the Higher Primates," in *Gender and the Life Course,* Alice S. Rossi editor, 1985.

Lazell, J.D. Jr, R.W. Sutterfield, W.D. Giezentanner, "The Population of Rock Wallabies on Oahu," *Biological Conservation.* #30, 1982

Leacock, Eleanor. "Women's Status: in Egalitarian Society," *Current Anthropology,* Vol.19, No.2, 1978.

Leakey, Richard E. *The Making of Mankind.* 1981.

Lederman, Leon. *The God Particle.* 1993.

Lee, Richard B. *The !Kung San.* 1979.

Lee, Thomas F. *The Human Genome Project.* 1991.

Lewis, G.J. *Human Migration.* 1982.

Lieberman, Philip. *The Biology and Evolution of Language.* 1984.

Lieberman, Philip. *Uniquely Human.* 1991.

Lieberman, Philip. "On Neanderthal Speech and Neanderthal Extinction," *Current Anthropology,* Vol.33, No.4. 1992.

Lindly, J.M. & G.A. Clark. "Symbolism and Modern Human Origins," *Current Anthropology,* Vol.3, No.3, 1990.

Lovejoy, C. Owen. "Evolution of Human Walking," *Scientific American.* Nov. 1988.

Lumsden, Charles J. & Edward O. Wilson. *Genes, Mind, and Culture: the Coevolutionary Process.* 1981.

Mackenzie, W.J.M. *Biological Ideas in Politics.* 1979.

MacKinnon, John. "The Behavior and Ecology of Wild Orangutans," *Animal Behavior,* Vol.22. 1974.

Martin, Glen. "Killer Culture." *Discover.* Dec. 1993.

Mayr, Ernst. *The Growth of Biological Thought: Diversity, Evolution, and Inheritance.* 1982.

McCarty, Maclyn. *The Transforming Principle: Discovering That Genes Are Made of DNA.* 1985.

Mellars, Paul. "Major Issues in the Emergence of Modern Humans," *Current Anthropology,* Vol.30, No.3, Jun. 1989.

Meltzer, David J. "Coming to America." *Discover.* Oct. 1993.

Milkman, Roger [ed.]. *Perspectives on Evolution.* 1982.

Montagu, Ashley [ed.]. *Sociobiology Examined.* 1980.

Montgomery, Geoffrey. "Molecules of Memory," *Discover,* Dec.1989.

Mysior, Arnold. *Society—A Very Large System.* 1977.

Newman, L.F. [ed.]. *Hunger in History.* 1990.

Nisbet, Robert A. *The Social Bond.* 1970.

Olsen, Carl [ed.]. *The Book of the Goddess: Past and Present.* 1985.

Perper, Timothy. *Sex Signals: the Biology of Love.* 1985.

Persinger, M. *Neuropsychological Bases of God Beliefs.* 1987.

Pfeiffer, John E. *The Emergence of Man.* 1978.

Pinker, Steven. *The Language Instinct: How the Mind Creates Language.* 1994.

Pfennig, D. W. & P.W. Sherman. "Kin Recognition." *Scientific American.* Vol.272, No.6. June 1995.

Potter, Jack M. *Thai Peasant Social Structure.* 1976.

Pullman, H. Ronald & Christopher Dunford. *Programmed to Learn: An Essay on the Evolution of Culture.* 1980.

Radetsky, Peter. "Silence, Signs, and Wonder." *Discover.* Aug. 1994.

Radetsky, Peter. "Speeding Through Evolution." *Discover.* May 1994.

Raup, David M. *Extinction: Bad Genes or Bad Luck.* 1991.

Reed, Charles A. [ed.]. *Origins of Agriculture.* 1977.

Renfrew, Colin [ed.]. *The Explanation of Culture Change: Models in Prehistory.* 1973.

Renfrew, Colin. "The Origin of Indo-European Languages," *Scientific American.* Oct. 1989.

Reynolds, Vernon. *The Biology of Human Action.* 1976.

Rhoades, R.E. "World Food Supply at Risk," *National Geographics.* April 1991.

Rosenberg, Karen R. "The Functional Significance of Neanderthal Pubic Length," *Current Anthropology.* Vol.29, No.4, 1988.

Ross, Philip E. "Eloquent Remains," *Scientific American,* Dec. 1990.

Ruffie, Jacques. *The Population Alternative: A New Look at Competition and the Species.* 1986.

Sauer, Carl O. *Life and Land.* 1963.

Sauer, Carl O. *Agricultural Origins and Dispersals: The Domestication of Animals and Foodstuffs.* 1969.

Savage-Rumbaugh, Sue & R. Lewin. "Ape at the Brink." *Discover,* Sept. 1994.

Schneider, Stephen H. "The Changing Climate," *Scientific American.* 1989.

Schrodinger, E. *What is Life.* 1944.

SCIENTIFIC AMERICAN. Human Ancestors. 1979

_____. Prehistoric Times. 1983.

_____. The Molecule of Life. 1985.

_____. "Masters of Mutation." Nov. 1988.

_____. "Developmental Dialects. Nov. 1988.

_____. "Grave Doubts." June 1989.

_____. "Molecular Archeology." July 1989.

_____. "Trans-kingdom Sex." Oct. 1989.

_____. "First Impressions." Oct. 1989.

_____. "Hungry to Evolve." Nov. 1989.

Shaw, Evelyn & Joan Darling. *Female Strategies.* 1985.

Shepher, Joseph. *Incest: A Biosocial View.* 1983.

Shreeve, James. "The Dating Game." *Discover*, Sept.1992.

Shreeve, James. "*Erectus* Rising." *Discover*. Sept. 1994.

Silverberg, Robert. *The Challenge of Climate.* 1969.

Smith, Curtis G. *Ancestral Voices: Language and the Evolution of Human Consciousness.* 1985.

Smith, Fred H. & Frank Spencer. *The Origins of Modern Humans: A World Survey of Fossil Evidence.* 1984.

Stanley, Steven M. *Macroevolution: Pattern and Process.* 1979.

Stanley, Steven M. *The New Evolutionary Timetable: Fossils, Genes, and the Origin of Species.* 1981.

Stent, G.S. [ed.]. *Morality as a Biological Phenomenon.* 1980.

Symons, Donald. *The Evolution of Human Sexuality.* 1981.

Tainter, Joseph A. *The Collapse of Complex Societies.* 1988.

Tanner, Nancy M. *On Becoming Human.* 1981.

Thorne, Alan G. & M.H. Wolpoff. "The Multiregional Evolution of Humans," *Scientific American*, Apr. 1992.

Thomas, William L. Jr. [ed.]. *Man's Role in Changing the Face of the Earth.* 1956.

Thompson, John N. *Interaction and Coevolution.* 1982.

Thornhill, Randy & John Alcook. *The Evolution of Insect Mating Systems.* 1983.

Tobias, P.V. [ed.]. *Hominid Evolution: Past, Present, and Future.* 1985.

Tomlinson, Ian. "How Females Choose a Mate," *Nature*, Vol.335, No.6185, Sep. 1988.

Torrey, E. Fuller. *Witchdoctors and Psychiatrists.* 1986.

Totman, Richard. *Social Causes of Illness.* 1979.

Trigg, Roger. *The Shaping of Man: Philosophical Aspects of Sociobiology.* 1983.

Turnbull, Colin. *The Forest People.* 1961.

Turnbull, Colin. *The Mountain People.* 1972.

Turner, Christy G. II. "Teeth and Prehistory in Asia," *Scientific American*. Feb. 1989.

Tuttle, Russel H. *Apes of the World: Their Social Behavior, Communication, Mentality and Ecology.* 1986.

Waal, F.B.M.de. *Chimpanzee Politics: Power and Sex Among Apes*, 1982.

Wall, F.B.M.de. "Bonobo Sex and Society." *Scientific American*. March 1995.

Wald, William H. [ed.] *Sociophysiology*. 1984.

Walker, Stephen. *Animal Thought*. 1983.

Wallace, Robert A. *The Genesis Factor*. 1979.

Wallace, Ron. "Cognitive Mapping and the Origins of Language and Mind," *Current Anthropology*. Vol.30, No.4, 1989.

Wasser, Samuel K. [ed.]. *Social Behavior of Female Vertebrates*, 1983.

Watson, James D. *The Double Helix*. 1968.

Wenegrat, Bryant. *Sociobiology and Mental Disorder*. 1984.

White, Douglas R. "Rethinking Polygyny," *Current Anthropology*, Vol.29, No.4, Aug. 1988.

White, Leslie A. *The Concept of Cultural Systems: A Key to Understanding Tribes and Nations*. 1970.

White, Randall. "Visual Thinking in the Ice Age," *Scientific American*. July 1989.

White, Raymond L. "Human Genetics," *The Lancet*, Dec. 1984.

Wiegle, Thomas C. [ed.]. *Biology and the Social Sciences: An Emerging Revolution*. 1982.

Wills, Christopher. *The Wisdom of the Genes*. 1989.

Wilson, Allan. "The Molecular Basis of Evolution," in SCIENTIFIC AMERICAN's *The Molecules of Life*. 1985.

Wilson, Allan & Rebbeca L .Cann. "The Recent African Genesis of Humans," *Scientific American*, Apr. 1992.

Wilson, Edward O. *Sociobiology: the New Synthesis* (condensed version). 1980.

Wilson, Edward O. *On Human Nature*. 1978.

Wolpert, Lewis. "DNA and Its Message," *The Lancet*, Oct. 1984.

Wrangham, Richard W. et al [eds.]. *Chimpanzee Cultures*. 1994.

PART TWO

CONTINUITY AND COLLAPSE: TWO CULTURES IN CONTRAST

INTRODUCTION

The evolution of human culture sketched in the previous section of this book obviously rests on evidence from numerous branches of science, none of which stands above challenge. How much more reassuring it would be to have a rather well documented case history that demonstrates the reasonableness of this suggested scenario. Fortunately, we have one.

Japan's cultural evolution telescopes into two thousand years the last ten to twelve thousand years of transition examined in Part One. What's more important, archeological and written records for this time span are not only continuous for a specific society and place but are relatively extensive and authentic. We can see Japan going from matrifocal tribal to patriarchal tribal to feudal to centralized and on to modern—and with an exuberant gusto at every stage.

Although forms of social organization and cultural expression changed, a central core of consistency remained strong throughout. Indeed, this core of consistency facilitated the frequent bouts of rapid, always traumatic change. This core "something" must impress the observer for its great resilience.

The last chapter in this section of the book looks at a society with many parallels to that evident in Japan. Yet when tested, its core collapsed. When challenged, community in Hawaii became unstrung—with dire consequences for its members. Both societies were island kingdoms (the "emperor" of Japan is really a king) with limited outside contacts for several centuries prior to recent European contact. Both were managed by a warrior class. But where one's community system could bend and snap back, the other proved brittle and broke.

The significance of insights gained from looking (in this part) at the processes of change in Japan and Hawaii will become more evident when we closely examine (in the next part) the processes of rapid urbanization recently in America.

CHAPTER FOUR

THE JAPANESE CASE IN CONTEXT

No larger than the state of California in square miles, Japan now has four times California's population yet must do with far less arable land for producing food and fiber for its people. Like California, Japan contains great mountain ranges and volcanoes. Unlike California, Japan's valleys are small, three-quarters of Japan's area having slopes of 15 degrees or steeper; only 14 percent is suitable for farming.

Warmed by the southern Kuroshio (the Black Current similar to the Gulf stream along the eastern US seaboard), Japan's southwestern half enjoys a semi-tropical climate. It differs from the northeastern half which is cooled by the Okhotsk current flowing from the north. During summers, warm tropical winds from the south bring heavy rains and frequent killer typhoons, especially in September. In winter, the winds reverse direction. Blowing dry and cold out of Siberia, they pick up moisture as they cross the Sea of Japan and dump heavy snows, sometimes in blizzards that leave three or more feet of snow in a single day where they hit north-facing mountains.

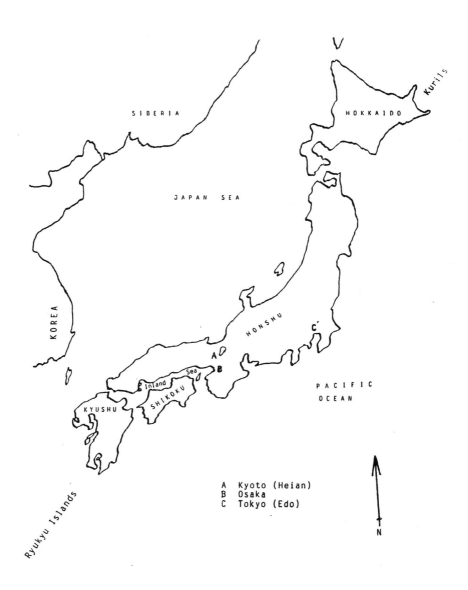

A Kyoto (Heian)
B Osaka
C Tokyo (Edo)

The rugged terrain, great forests, and tumbling rivers readily lent themselves to veneration. Markedly separated valleys facilitated tribal delineations and later feudal organization. The land itself underscores the impermanence of existence. Sitting at the edge of the Pacific Plate, Japan constantly experiences destructive earthquakes, tsunamis, and volcanoes. School children must hold earthquake drills the way American schools practice fire drills.

With 127 million people, seventh largest in the world, Japan must export to finance its essential imports for survival. Even with the world's lowest birth rate currently, Japan's population continues to increase because it also has the lowest death rate of any country; people average a life expectancy of nearly 80 years. With limited space, property values have soared. The estimated total land value of Japan in 1990 reached four times the total value of all land in the United States. The Tokyo-Yokohama metropolitan region, presently the largest conurbation anywhere, contains some 26 million people.

At 99 percent racially Japanese, this country ranks well above any other large nation for its ethnic homogeneity. But it was not always this way. Ancestors of those considered Japanese today derived from a diversity of racial origins.

The first hominids may have reached Japan as long ago as 50,000 years, during one of those times when the islands were connected to the mainland, when large animals could have come. *Homo sapiens sapiens*, however, did not arrive until 12,000 or at most 15,000 years ago. Paleoanthropological evidence from teeth suggests a non-sinitic derivation, possibly a Malaysian strain from southeast Asia and/or a Chukchi connection from Siberia. However, nine thousand years of isolation (along with possible inbreeding with the earlier paleolithic inhabitants?) could have produced a genotype that only coincidentally resembles either a north or south Asian ancestry—or both.

Archeological evidence reveals two distinct pottery styles both of which were artistically quite advanced. The Jomon culture of these early people existed for several thousand years and is deemed to have had the world's finest neolithic pottery, found mostly in northeast Japan. Then in the third century BC a new culture, called Yayoi, begins to displace Jomon in western Japan, most likely coming with waves of sinitic migrants via Korea or perhaps even Yueh from what is now Fukien and Taiwan.

This would correspond with the great upheaval of the Ch'in and Han dynasties which ended China's feudal era and began its centralized imperial/mandarin system of governance, an upheaval that not only resulted from movements of people but likely set off an even greater exodus. Chinese records do speak of settlers being sent out to the land of the rising sun.

It appears, too, that this era corresponds with the introduction of rice agriculture. Only with the beginning of what we now globally call the Christian era does rice become a principal food among inhabitants of southwest Japan known to the Chinese as the Wa. They were, according to Chinese accounts, at least semi-hunter-gatherer and matrifocal with female leaders as high priestesses or priestess chiefs, some of whom had sent trading missions to China.

Linguistic evidence is even less definitive about the origins of the Japanese. *Nihongo* (the language of Japan) is polysyllabic stemming from Tungus-Altaic, the root language of Mongolian and Turkish from which Korean is also derived. As late as thirteen hundred years ago, at least some residents of what are now Japan and Korea spoke a mutually understandable language, although only a specialist can detect similarities now. And like some features of Japanese culture (such as a residential architecture more suited for southern climes), there may remain traces of Malayan and Ainu in Nihongo. For at least fourteen hundred years, Japanese have so readily adopted foreign words and forms of writing (first from China and recently from the West) until their language amounts to a unique eclectic creation.

THE SWEEP OF HISTORY

By the first century AD, rice cultivation had gained prominence in southwest Japan—among peoples recently arrived from the mainland and possibly among former semi-hunter-gatherer tribes as well. (Centuries would pass before a fully sedentary way of life would characterize Japan south of Hokkaido.) By the first century, too, Chinese goods had become rather prevalent, at least among tribal leaders, if archeological finds are indicative. Mostly home and personal utensils show up, such as pots, coins, bronze mirrors, and combs.

By the fourth century AD, the kind of foreign artifact had changed. Now they took a characteristically more military hue: weapons, saddles, and symbols of authority. Archeologist found them most often at the sites of massive moat-and-rampart works unmistakably shaped like a modern keyhole. In scale, these structures match anything created in ancient Egypt, Babylon, or medieval Europe. So distinctive were these structures that the era acquired their Japanese name: *Kofun*. For, they mark a dramatic cultural shift, namely the introduction and adoption (by some tribes in Japan) of the mounted-warrior chieftain culture of nomadic Tungus origin then dominant in Korea.

Although the imperial Yamato clan dates itself back to a mythical time in the seventh century BC, it may well have crystallized among those tribes in the eastern Inland Sea (modern Osaka) area whose clan leaders had secured a dominant place through the success of their priestesses in superior ritualism and magic. The arrival of a horse-based warrior culture with its male dominance would have presented a formidable challenge to the previous matrifocal culture with its emphasis on ritual purity.

The eventual result was a de facto compromise. Faced with a threat of eradication, the emerging imperial Yamato clan made some adjustments— such as adopting Turkish/Mongol purification rites for brides which involved stepping over fire. In return, the horse-culture warrior clans granted the imperial line to the old Yamato clan to represent the people of Japan before the gods. However, this imperial line would never rule as such; some other tribal power (eventually centuries later, some feudal clan or other) would always exercise actual governance for, and in the name of, the imperial Yamato clan.

This titanic struggle between a traditionally matrifocal, shamanistic/animistic orientation in central Japan resisting the newly imported cultural system with its male-dominant power politics in Western Japan actually took more than several centuries to resolve. Indeed, it would take a second wave of cultural importation from China via Korea. Again some Japanese factions would embrace a foreign system of governance and religion for its political leverage within the domestic power game between tribal blocs.

This latest instrument of staging extensive cultural change was Buddhism. Some tribal groups in western Japan retained such a close tie with their counterparts on the mainland that they kept being drawn into the wars between the several Korean kingdoms during the fourth through seventh centuries AD. As part of this relationship, one king in Korea dispatched a Buddha statue complete with priests and nuns to his ally in Japan in 552. Although most Japanese groups resisted this new religion, their resolve weakened as they came to see advantages for themselves in the superior Chinese organization and technology which came as part of the package.

This "package" of Chinese culture included a script for recording language, an elaborate form of centralized government (and the power its dominant clique could wield), city planning and impressive architecture, as well as a formalized religion, itself quite useful for political control. In only one generation, there would arise Japanese scholars capable of reading Chinese and engaging in original exploration and commentary on the sacred writings. In 593, Shotoku Taishi, the brilliant prince who rose to power as regent for the empress, would champion Buddhism and institute law and rule based on the Chinese model of that day.

Within the coming century, people who had heretofore lived in scattered tribal villages would lay out entire cities for populations of several hundred thousand. These followed the gridiron pattern used in China albeit without comprehending the geomantic purposes of importance to Chinese. Despite such accomplishments, when their armies (sent to Korea to help an ally) lost, they withdrew from further large-scale official mainland contact for nine centuries.

By 645, clan leaders ostensibly prepared the Taika Reform to officially abolish the old ways of reckoning power on a tribal basis in preference for Chinese administration. While they adopted Chinese titles for public offices, they never instituted the core of Chinese public administration. This core involved a mandarin system of civil service examinations, known sociologically as meritocracy. In contrast, the essence of rule in Japan continued as before to be hereditary power exercised by tribal chieftain clans.

Within one generation, Chinese forms simply covered traditional tribal politics in Japan the way a table cloth covers a table without changing the table under it. But some things did change. Tribalism gave way to clans. Please note that "clan" in Japan differs markedly from its application in China where it encompassed only relatives with the same family name however remote. As J.W. Hall explains, the clan (known as *uji*) in Japan resembled its Tungus mainland antecedent as a "lineal group" composed of families related by either real or fictional blood lines, held together by patriarchal power and worship of the same *ujigami*. Comprising well under a tenth of the population, they constituted a tribe's upper-class.

From the fourth through eighth century, male-dominant tribal clans (most notably the Fujiwaras) clawed and manipulated their way to the top of political power, then held on into the twelfth century by tightly controlling emperors and empresses as their regents and determining who married whom. In particular, they used the sincere devotion of several empresses to Buddhism as an excuse for henceforth restricting the imperial throne to males. Until then, females had often been chosen to reign in preference over males if they demonstrated superior abilities. (Male primogenitor would not become fully fixed among Japanese until the feudal era several centuries later.)

Japan's first "permanent" national capital, constructed at Nara in 710, adhered to Chinese ideas of city design. Until then, a "capital" had to remain simple for ease in moving each time an emperor or empress died, so as to avoid the contamination of death so central to Shinto. Further political maneuverings among competing clans, however, led to a new imperial capital built at Heian (modern Kyoto) in 794. At last one could remain fixed—for nearly eleven hundred years.

For almost four hundred years, pre-eminent political power would stay in Kyoto under the tight fist of the Fujiwara clan. But what went on at the imperial court did not represent all that happened in Japan even if most histories draw upon the extensive writings of court ladies to depict Japanese culture of the Heian era.

While southwestern Japan became thoroughly remolded into a sedentary society centered on rice cultivation, northeast Japan remained a frontier land somewhat like that of the nineteenth century American frontier "out West." Sinitic Japanese continued to battle the nonsinitic aborigines, pushing them ever farther to the north. With rolling hills better suited for raising horses than rice, the earlier mounted-warrior culture introduced from Korea to western Japan finally caught on in the northeast. Life there bred fighters, individual heroism, and rugged machismo which would eventually become known loosely as *Bushido*, the way of the warrior.

Not surprisingly, these rough frontiersmen (many of them what would in America centuries later be called half-breeds) grew increasingly appalled at the sterile formalities, elaborate etiquette, and extensive female influence over the courtier administrators in the capital. Frontiersmen saw this cultural milieu inhibiting action when action was urgently needed to deal with state affairs, especially with enemy tribes. Moreover cronyism, clan ties, and bribery had allowed powerful clans to avoid paying taxes on their extensive land holdings while small holders without connections were either taxed to death or had to flee to the less regulated northeastern frontier.

Eventually the provincial ferment erupted into civil war during the second half of the twelfth century. First the Taira clan, a Fujiwara branch line from western Japan, seized power from the Fujiwaras. Then in 1185, the Minamoto (another Fujiwara branch line but centered to the northeast in the general area of what later became Tokyo) defeated the Taira.

To avoid becoming "feminized" by too close a contact with the imperial court in Kyoto, the Minamotos moved their de facto center of political power several hundred miles east to Kamakura while leaving the emperor to his ceremonial rituals in Kyoto. The year of 1185 conveniently marks the start of feudalism in Japan because the Minamoto had consolidated political power by buying allegiance with grants of land confiscated from defeated Taira clansmen, imperial courtiers, and Buddhist temple lands (the latter, a convenient subterfuge to avoid paying taxes).

As long as power remained in western hands, the traditional *uji* type of clan seemed to typify social organization outside the imperial capital. A different environment in eastern Japan, in contrast, gave rise to the more independent nuclear family and the family enterprise known as *ie*. An *ie* "family" might include numerous nonrelatives serving as maids and apprentices or even laborers but incorporated more fully into the family than blood relatives living some distance away. Whereas western Japan might have at times its pirate gangs, eastern Japan would develop the family managerial unit that would grow in entrepreneurial significance over the centuries until it provided a foundation for the late nineteenth century Meiji industrialization/ modernization drive. The Mitsubishi, Sumitomo, and Mitsui families exemplify this newer form of social unit.

Despite Minamoto's insightful innovations in governance at Kamakura, feudal stability would not last a century. In 1274 and 1281 the Mongols, then conquerors of China, sought to acquire Japan too and might have were it not for fortuitous typhoons ("divine winds," *kamikaze*) which sunk their invading armadas on Japanese shores. Although Japan escaped cheaply, Kamakura preparations for battle had produced considerable indebtedness—by the *Bakafu* (military government) to its loyal henchmen who in turn had their feudal subordinates to reward.

But how could anyone make rewards of land when no new lands became available in defeating the invading Mongols? No rewards, in turn, bred dissatisfaction, and dissatisfaction in a feudal system led to disloyalty and political breakdown. Warriors sold their services to the highest bidder, and treachery became rampant among warring factions with generals switching sides in the middle of battle.

In 1333, Ashikaga Takauji could seize power from Kamakura in the name of the emperor and establish a regime headquartered (and soon largely isolated) in the Muromachi sector of Kyoto. Unable to establish an effective, centralized regime, Ashikaga accelerated the centrifugal transfer of de facto administrative powers to outlying areas.

Some local warlords effectively developed mines and improved agricultural production through innovation and fair treatment of peasants. Others exploited and increased the general miseries of that era. Extravagance in castle-building and art typified the times, as did the fall of old elite clans and the rise of brigands to power and status. For the next century following commencement of the Onin War in 1467, civil warfare ravaged the country—like the Wars of the Roses in contemporary England.

Upon this scene there arrived the first Europeans in 1542. The Portuguese did far more than introduce Christianity to Japan; they introduced fire arms. Mastering the tactical use of these new weapons allowed Oda Nobunaga to begin a consolidation of power from 1568 until his death in 1582. Toyotomi Hideyoshi continued that consolidation, even diverting soldiers to invade Korea so as to minimize their potentially disruptive presence in Japan. Hideyoshi's death in 1598 left Tokugawa Ieyasu to finish the task of structuring all feudal power under a single regime centered at his castle in Edo (modern Tokyo), even farther eastward from the emperor in Kyoto than the earlier Kamakura regime had gone.

Although originally of commoner background himself, Hideyoshi disarmed all commoners thereby reestablishing a greater gulf between the classes. He also deprived the samurai class of a direct feudal base on the land by making them professional employees of town-based *daimyo* (lords) to be paid salaries in rice. And he froze everyone's place of residence, thereby prohibiting the movement of potential agitators and troublemakers; internal passports became mandatory.

Once the Tokugawa Bakafu (military authority) was ensconced, it would institute even more extensive restructuring of Japanese society in the interest of ending the recent centuries of almost continual feudal turmoil. Although they might likely seem harsh to modern American eyes, the draconian measures did accomplish their objective: Japan had two and a half centuries free from war and revolution. Those measures inadvertently gave Japan its closest thing to a centralized national government yet experienced and one not all that different from European kingdoms of that time despite its avowed feudal orientation.

One early step involved resurrecting and reinstituting the *goningumi* form of mutual responsibility. Whether taken from an indigenous form of five-family mutual self-help and social control of a much earlier era or adapted from the ten-family Chinese governance system, *goningumi* effectively made every person spy on everyone else to insure that he/she was not punished for a neighbor's wrongdoing.

Tokugawa also required everyone to register with the nearest Buddhist temple thereby co-opting all monks. Where armed monks had for five or six hundred years all too readily wielded swords in attacks against the ruling establishment, they were now disarmed and swallowed into that very establishment as part of its pervasive spy network. (George Orwell's *1984* had nothing over early Tokugawa—even with Big Brother's electronic surveillance going for it.)

Oda Nobunaga had used Catholic missionaries to check the power of various Buddhist sects. Toyotomi Hideyoshi began to have misgivings about the Catholics, using a few Protestants to check the Portuguese. The Tokugawas would eventually drive out all foreigners and brutally stamp out Christianity which had gained a threatening stronghold in westernmost Japan.

Even more ingenious than their means of controlling commoners was the Tokugawas' set of checks and balances among the ruling class. Those daimyo who had opposed Ieyasu at the crucial battle of Sekigahara in 1600 were considered "outside lords" and assigned provinces sandwiched between those who had been Ieyasu's allies; in this way they would find it impossible to form united blocs for revolt. Moreover, all daimyo had to live at least half of the year in Edo (Tokyo) and to leave families there as hostages when they visited their assigned domain.

In addition, all manner of expensive dress, formalities, large entourages when traveling, elaborate castles according to their status, and gift exchanges were imposed to keep daimyo from accumulating enough resources to stage a revolt. And if these did not suffice, a Tokugawa shogun need only announce his intention to visit a daimyo. The "honored" daimyo would have to spend lavishly to construct an entirely new castle for the occasion. This could bankrupt even the wealthiest feudal lord.

With warfare ended, samurai no longer had a real function; six percent of the population became effectively superfluous. Something had to be done to keep them productively engaged and out of trouble. To retain their privileged status—and thereby justify the entire Bakufu edifice—they needed a rationale and they found it in an exaggerated sense of discipline and loyalty (discussed in the next chapter).

Many lower-level samurai eventually did become competent public administrators. Others became scholars, replacing the monk scholars of previous centuries and marking this departure by leaving their heads unshaven in contradistinction from monkish practice. Samurai of all ranks were encouraged to practice the disciplined fine arts of calligraphy, poetry composition, and tea ceremony.

But most important for the future of Japan was the codification of Bushido as influenced by neo-Confucianism and Zen. Although intended to distinguish elite from commoner, Bushido would infect all strata of society and thereby unwittingly prepare Japanese for the heavy disciplined demands of industrialization centuries later at the end of shogunal rule.

Seventeenth century Japanese society had (at least in idealized theory) a four-tiered stratification. The ruling class, composed of numerous sublevels, was supported by hard-working peasants who in theory held tier number two. Below them supposedly came skilled craftsmen. True to a feudal structure elsewhere, merchants stood at the theoretical bottom.

Like feudal systems in Europe however, in actuality this bottom class (which became de facto bankers) soon accumulated much wealth and power. These came from grain speculation and supplying the elite in their enforced overspending. Not legally entitled to such wealth, the merchant class soon aspired to elite status through educations and sophisticated tastes and even more so via adoptions and marriage—just as European merchant/bankers similarly acquired "nobility" by saving impoverished noble families. They also came to wield (cautiously and subtlely of course) considerable influence over the financially weak ruling class. Not surprisingly, the peasant class, upon whose productive backs this entire precarious economic edifice rested, sank back into near slavery.

Paid in fixed amounts of rice, samurai suffered from merchant speculation, many of them mortgaging future income for several generations yet unborn, all to fulfill social expectations. Any economic/political system as unrealistic as this one was bound to generate internal conflict. By mid-eighteenth century, Japan had experienced the world's first true economic cycle of boom-and-bust.

As labor costs rose after 1720, farmers with large holdings found it more profitable to lease out their land than to farm personally. Soon, even this kind of rich landowner could afford to purchase swords from impoverished daimyo and educate their children as pseudo-samurai. As landlords moved up, their appetites for an elite lifestyle grew. This led to increased exploitation of poor peasants. With increased wealth also came opportunities for landlords to manipulate local officials, resulting in worsening administration, arbitrary injustices, and appointment of weak village headmen. Consequently, peasant revolts would steadily increase in frequency and scale until that chaotic end of the Tokugawa era.

Only the absence of a serious foreign threat allowed the Tokugawa regime to remain so long. It took a mere shove in the form of a US fleet under Commodore Matthew Perry in 1853-54 for it all to crumble. While regaining ascendancy for the imperial clan over the shogunate in 1868, Emperor Meiji had to move from Kyoto to Tokyo and occupy the shogun's palace to demonstrate that supremacy. Yet from out of that fallen so-called feudal regime there emerged with astonishing resilience a centralized government eagerly willing to learn from technologically advanced Europe and America—just as Japan would do eight decades later after its decisive defeat in WWII.

Although the Meiji era's unmatched transformation to a modern industrial culture cannot do other than impress, Meiji reforms did not go unchallenged. Once again—as in the adoption of a rice culture from China, the championing of a male-dominant mounted-warrior culture and *uji* clan structure from Korea, and the promotion of the new Buddhist religion (later Christianity also) for political objectives—challenge to central authority came from westernmost Japan. First, samurai there took the lead in restoring imperial dominance, then undertook a last-stand samurai revolt against the emperor's backers in Tokyo for opening Japan to Western cultural influence. Their utter defeat by a new conscript army of commoners signaled the actual, as well as symbolic, end of feudalism.

CHAPTER FIVE

ANXIETIES OF OBLIGATIONS

If we tried to rank all of the world's larger societies on a single scale to indicate their religiosity, those practicing Islam and Hinduism would likely appear at the more devotional end of the spectrum. China and Japan would tend more toward the other end. At least that is how a Westerner might scale them. From a European/American perspective, Japanese have never practiced religion with exclusivistic, black-or-white delineations so typical of the West. Until their recent adaptations of Western religious services, Japanese religions had no congregations and spanned the complete spectrum from polytheistic to atheistic, from pragmatic superstition to transcendental abstraction. But saying this does not imply that religious ritual was not a part of daily life or that religiously derived attitudes, values, and interhuman relationships did not occupy a major place in Japanese culture. Indeed, it is impossible to understand the Japanese experience (across society at any one time or Japan's cultural evolution over time) without digging into the many strands of religion that comprise the warf and woof of this culture.

With exceptions, Japanese religion has given little emphasis to the hereafter but placed tremendous emphasis on down to earth interrelationships either with the spirit world of Nature or with other people dead and living. Over the last four centuries this concern with relationships has taken the form of obligations, expressed by the neo-Confucianist terms: *on, gimu, giri, ko,* and *chu.* Benedict, Lebra, and Nakane dissect them in detail; I cover them here only in summary simply to convey the essence of the "spiritual" energy affecting Japanese behavior.

Bear ever in mind while considering these philosophical concepts that they are far from abstract ideas. They were and remain real enough to exert marked influence on people's daily lives, on their outlooks, and on their ways of dealing with challenges. Indeed, for all ordinary Japanese, there is nothing philosophical about them; they constitute "natural" (preordained) practices. They have been as real as any tangible mark of cultural distinction. They were and are inescapable and have had to be accepted by Japanese as such.

The earliest form of religious life here involved a version of animism not unlike that in many other simple societies, such as early Hawaiians and Amerindians north of Mexico. Everything had a spirit: trees, streams, fire, fish, birds, ocean, stars, mountains, and of course the sun and moon; even an oven or household utensils. A person would not cut down a tree without apologizing to its spirit (the *kami*).

Certain animals still command awe or fear, throwbacks perhaps to a still earlier totemism. Fertility held major importance; through to modern day, some Japanese villages retained their annual fertility festivals. Rocks exhibiting a natural phallic shape were set at road junctions where people could (and still do) place small offerings to achieve conception.

Until Buddhism arrived in the sixth century, indigenous animism had no name; people simply practiced it in their daily lives with no need for idols or theology. Spirits were real for them and that was all one need be concerned with philosophically, although chieftains of major tribes likely had more elaborate rituals to ensure the power of magic. Similar to practices found among Hawaiians and Amerindians, early Japanese had their shamans who practiced a carefully crafted communication with important spirits and undertook healing.

Chances are that those early shamans were female, the most successful of them being located among the tribal complex settled in Yamato (in the hills east of today's Osaka). Initially matrilineal, these shifting tribes would eventually consolidate into the Yamato clan which would provide Japan an unbroken imperial line for some sixteen or seventeen hundred years.

The advent of a much more complex religion, Buddhism, exerted a tremendous impact on this native spiritual experience. Everywhere highly organized religions with sophisticated theologies have altered, if not usurped and replaced, indigenous forms. That Japanese animism persisted so stoutly through the centuries in a popular form attests to its strength and resilience. (It probably attests as well to the Japanese propensity for preserving the past to the extent few if any other societies have.)

One of the first things Buddhist monks did was give the local religion a name. They called it Shinto, the Way of the Spirits. Then they began to organize it and give it statues, shrines, and rituals for commoners, beyond what had previously been the prerogative of tribal shamans and chieftains. Shinto, like Buddhism, had become a tool for political control.

By the time the Mahayana branch of Buddhism had diffused from India to Gandhara (today's Afghanistan, then under the influence of Alexander the Great's Greece) and across Central Asia to China, it had picked up a vast assortment of deities, myths, idols, and rituals that were totally alien to the basic teachings of Gautma Siddhartha. Yet to the less sophisticated rulers of Japan, it represented a superior form of magic as well as bringing with it the superior culture of China in the form of writing, administrative organization, and architecture.

Within the first century after its introduction, several Buddhist denominations had taken root among Japan's tribal chieftains and imperial court. These denominations included most notably Tendai and Shingon, formed earlier in China with varying mixtures of superstitious Taoism and paganism.

For people far distant from the Kansai Plain where the Yamato and other premier tribes lived, common Shinto persisted with minor competition from Buddhism for centuries. Buddhism did not really gain widespread acceptance until the tenth and eleventh centuries. Its success came largely from taking over the operation of Shinto shrines and rituals as it converted Shinto spirits into local manifestations of Buddhist deities.

The emergence of Amidaism in the eleventh century did the most to make Buddhism popular among commoners. Amidaism so closely parallels Christianity that early missionaries thought it a corrupted version of Christian salvation. (There exists the possibility that it actually was influenced a bit by Nestorian Christianity which had arrived and thrived in northern China about the same time as Amidaism evolved there.)

Original Buddhism sought Nirvana (enlightenment, not heaven) through one's own devotion. Amidaism, in contrast, proposed a heavenly eternity, not through one's own inadequate efforts, but by putting one's faith in the efficacy of Amida to expiate the "sin" of human frailty. All one need do is sincerely repeat the *Nembutsu* (the prayer "Namu Amida Butsu"). Although this religious format became popular, Shinto remained in everyday life.

Even today, most Japanese homes have a *kamidana* (a shelf for Shinto rituals) and a *butsudan* (an alcove for Buddhist rituals). Neither Shinto nor Buddhism demands a total rejection of other forms of worship the way Christianity, Judaism, and Islam do. Japanese say they marry Shintoist and die Buddhist. In the interim they now even celebrate Christmas.

The thirteenth century saw the rise of two new forms of Buddhism to prominence in Japan, and both became tied to the reemergence of the *bushi* (warrior) to dominance. One was a product of an indigenous prophet, Nichiren. The other, Zen, reached Japan from India via Southeast Asian and South China.

In the mold of an Old Testament prophet, Nichiren underscored his message of repentance and reform by accurately predicting severe earthquakes and the Mongol invasions. His denunciations of the corruptions, dissipation, and effeminization so evident in court circles in Kyoto made him most popular among the frontier warriors now self-conscious as a class having risen recently to power. His message of reform held particular cogency in a day when Shingon and Tendai monks ensconced on opposite mountain strongholds regularly engaged in pitched battles in Kyoto streets. (As a Buddhist denomination again preaching reform and a return to native purity, Nichiren enjoyed marked resurgence after WWII, even spreading abroad and winning converts among non-Japanese.)

Japan had long had Hachiman, the Shinto God of War. Nichiren went further in offering a positive approach to life for common soldiers. For better educated warriors, Zen would begin to make a strong appeal.

A Theraveda (Hinayana) form of Buddhism, Zen harkened back closely to Gautma's original teachings of ascetic self-discipline. But instead of seeking Nirvana, Japanese warriors practiced Zen for its mastery over human emotions and frailty—to make themselves better warriors, to allow them to gain life by learning to forsake it.

Some of these educated samurai joined Zen monks in studying neo-Confucian ethics recently introduced by scholars who had fled from Mongol-dominated China. Since it was largely in eclipse when Buddhism arrived in Japan, Confucianism had thus far exerted relatively little impact under its own name. One feature of Confucianism which Buddhist monks in the sixth century did introduce was ancestor worship, something alien to native Shintoism. As Benedict points out, Shintoism might recognize God as an ancestor but never turned ancestors into gods. After all, nothing was so defiling in Shinto as death and dead things.

Neo-Confucianism from the thirteenth century on would increasingly exert a major influence in shaping the ethics of human interactions and structured interrelationships for Japanese society. Two philosophical perspectives characterized the neo-Confucians which Japanese elite diligently studied during the Kamakura and Ashikaga eras.

Chu Shi emphasized reading the Sages and practicing prescribed rituals with an emphasis on loyalty and etiquette. Wang Yang-ming, in contrast, taught independent, intuitive perception; much like Zen. By the seventeenth century when the Tokugawa regime sought to end feudal warfare and establish stability and loyalty, the Bakufu naturally chose Chu Shi (Shushi in Japanese) over Wang Yang-ming (Oyomei).

Cut off from contact with China (and the outside world in general) during the Tokugawa era, Japanese warrior scholars undertook their own explorations into the writings of "Ancients" which sought to turn the clock back and learn from the past. The Mito School, founded in the 1660s with Tokugawa blessing, focused on Japanese history. Its studies, however, revealed that loyalty belonged to the emperor, not the Shogun. It thereby became a contributor to the growing dissatisfaction with shogunate rule that would eventually lead to the imperial (Meiji) restoration of 1867-68.

ETHICS, OBLIGATIONS, AND DISCIPLINE

We noticed briefly already the various measures taken by Hideyoshi and Ieyasu to institute an effective set of political /social/economic checks and balances—such as disarming commoners, fixing residency, separating samurai from the land, making samurai professional employees in towns, sandwiching of "inside/outside" daimyo, imposing *sankin-kotai* (alternative residency) on feudal lords while holding their families hostage, prohibiting foreign trade, expelling foreigners, suppressing Christianity, bureaucratizing monks, and officially encouraging (pressuring) warriors without a war to keep active through artistic and scholarly endeavors. These measures accomplished their objective; they brought stability.

No less important was the Tokugawa choice of Chu Shi as its official philosophy. It would at last codify Bushido, the Way of the Warrior. Bushido had long existed during the feudal era, primarily however as macho bravado. Its expectation of loyalty often stood out more in violation than in observance. Ironically, now that warfare had ceased, the ideal of loyalty gained supreme value. Bushido as a code became essential as justification for the continued existence of a privileged class of largely unneeded warriors.

What makes Bushido and neo-Confucianism important is what resulted in the long run. In the long run, the loyalty, ascetic self-discipline, and sense of obligation that supposedly marked a samurai would permeate the general public so thoroughly as to provide Meiji planners with a well-disciplined citizenry ready to make whatever sacrifices they deemed necessary to achieve national goals. So what were the particulars in this combination of Chu Shi ethics, Bushido loyalty, and Zen's ascetic self-discipline? And how did this "religious" amalgam infect the rest of society?

The central concept taken from Chinese philosophy and made an integral part of Japanese culture concerns *on*, a debt for blessings received. Christians have the concept of original sin; Japanese have *on*. In both, an individual is expected to do one's best to overcome this inherent human flaw even though total success is inherently impossible.

Christianity provides salvation; *on* provides no escape, only anxiety. A person owes his/her life to parents without whom that person would never have existed. For this reason, a person begins life eternally indebted to those parents. No amount of obedience, devotion, or loving care can erase that burden of debt; yet try they must.

When one person does a favor for another, the recipient acquires another burden of *on* for that favor which he/she must repay but never really can. Benedict suggests that a verbal "thank you" may not express appreciation for the favor as much as a protest that you have imposed a burden upon me. Consequently, Japanese erect cultural barriers so as to avoid acquiring *on*; and they must observe strict rules of limitations (*enryo*) to minimize it. Customarily refusing a gift three times ritualizes this resistance to assuming more burden.

The unredeemable debt one owes parents also applies to emperor as son of Heaven and symbol of the nation. The terms for these two forms of inherent debt (*on*) are *chu* and *ko*. *Ko* refers to the debt one owes parents; *chu*, the debt of *on* to the emperor—or during feudal days, debt to one's lord and shogun. While these concepts occurred in China as well as Japan, they received opposite priorities.

In China where clans have for at least two-thousand held the center of loyalty, *ko* has enjoyed supremacy over *chu*. In Japan, *chu* dominates— stemming from the rationale that, since parents and grandparents etc. owe *chu* to the emperor for *on* and since *on* can be inherited, obligations to ruler must exceed obligations to parents and all other *on*.

Debts owed to parents and ruler for blessings received differ from the burden of *on* to other people. The first kind (*ko* and *chu*) are known as *gimu*. People must show no resentment for this form of burden. Other debts for *on* are called *giri* which comes in various forms. An act of kindness by a stranger (whom one never thought of helping first) creates a situation of *giri* with more resentment than appreciation. The other person has, in effect, accomplished one-upmanship and placed the recipient in an undesired position of indebtedness.

Giri also relates to what one owes one's name as the current link in a long chain of generations. When Puccini has Cho-Cho-San commit suicide, he has her quite accurately evoke the crucial idea of death before dishonor. She had to clear her name as a matter of *giri* due to Lt. Pinkerton's inappropriate behavior.

Sensitivity to criticism among Japanese is more than simply ego pique; criticism attacks one's name and hence affects the *giri* of responsibility to that name. And a slur on one's performance amounts to a slur on one's name; in some way it must be cleansed. In times past, it meant either doing so by murder or by suicide for major offenses. Not surprisingly, Japanese find themselves ever having to carefully interpret everyone else's words and signals while judiciously weighing their own words and actions lest they affect *giri* in some way.

So long as each form of *gimu* and *giri* remains distinct from the other, life can proceed without undue anxiety. But life is never so simple; does anything so complex stay in neat compartments? Anxiety mounts when what Benedict calls the circles of *chu*, *ko*, and *giri* begin to overlap and conflict. Probably nothing so well illustrates both these concepts and their potential for complicating conflict than that most famous of Japanese stories, the *Forty-seven Ronin*. Indeed, it is beloved precisely because it so poignantly dramatizes the conflict which Japanese must cope with all of their lives.

In brief, not having received the customary bribe, Kira improperly instructs Lord Asano in etiquette. Asano's faux pas leads to a moment of extreme embarrassment in the presence of the shogun. Asano then does *giri* to his name by slashing Kira. No problem with that, except for the fact that Asano did so inside the shogun's palace, and drawing his sword there meant he violated *chu*. To demonstrate *chu* and correct his error, Asano had to die.

As a high samuai, he was permitted to die at his own hand by *seppuku*, that painful ritual of disembowlment. Were it a matter only of Asano and Kira, it could have ended there. But much more was involved. Kira's action amounted to a slur on all clan members, and Asano's suicide would terminate the entire clan. This would make Asano's samurai retainers became *ronin*; they were reduced to the status of masterless, hence useless.

The real story concerns how 47 of those faithful vassals demonstrated their absolute loyalty. To ensure success at inflicting revenge on Kira, they had to shame themselves through debauchery and even allow their swords to rust as evidence of faithlessness. Once Kira had relaxed his guard, the 47 struck knowing full well that by so doing they had decreed their own deaths. Not only did they endure the insults for appearing to fall from samurai standards; they neglected their families and had themselves disowned. But once they had killed Kira, they had fulfilled *giri*. Then they fulfilled *chu* by proudly committing suicide through ritualized disembowlment as their master had done. They thereby cleared their family names as well.

This seventeenth century true story provided the theme for many a kabuki play, popular novel, and painting. It so well dramatized neo-Confucian ideals and Bushido, commoners could readily comprehend them and come to identify with the characters as role models for everyone, not just samurai. Suicide became so widely accepted as a solution to conflict between love and duty that the Bakufu had repeatedly to issue prohibitions against it. In this, the Bakufu was caught in its own trap: permeation of samurai ideals throughout the populace made it easier for the regime to keep control, and keeping control constituted the Tokugawas' primary objective.

As the samurai ethic seeped through the general population, something quite unexpected and largely unobserved occurred. Not only did commoners come to accept Bushido and live by the ethics of loyalty and obligation; a new attitude toward an individual's place in life gained acceptance—an attitude strikingly like the concept of "calling" in Calvinist Christianity as it affected believers' self-image and world view.

Increasingly people recognized that, just as samurai had their roles to fulfill, so too did commoners. Services rendered the ruler and nation by farmers, craftsmen, and even by merchants were no less essential to the nation's well-being and survival than those functions performed by a largely superfluous (parasitic) ruling class.

As the era of peace continued, everyone could see that samurai had no more divinity about them than commoners. After all, Japan was not a caste society. Second and third sons of samurai did slip to merchant or village headman status while brilliant young men of humble background could and frequently did move up through adoption. Also, rich merchants married their sons or daughters into samurai families—or bought samurai rank from impoverished daimyo. Rank had become simply a matter of correct symbols and punctilious etiquette.

Given this well-instilled mix (this verve of Bushido, a deep concern for loyalty, and a very personal sense of utter responsibility for fulfilling one's duty/calling), the social stage was set for accomplishing the wholesale changes decided upon and planned by the elder statesmen (*genro*) behind the imperial restoration and modernization drive in the last third of the nineteenth century. Everyone's calling was important and so everyone was important in upholding *giri* to the name of Japan. Anyone's failure brought shame to the nation. Shame for the nation meant shame for each citizen; they must do their best. They all participated in the national community.

Herein lay great personal and collective anxiety—the anxiety about failing to fulfill one's duty of *chu*. In his famous study of the Protestant Ethic, Max Weber points out how forcefully a concerted search to conquer deep anxiety can drive people to accomplish formidable social/economic change. Anxiety, more than anything else then, spurred English merchants to bring about the West's industrial revolution.

As Calvinists, those merchants believed in predestination with absolute sincerity: that God in His infinite wisdom had preordained some people to Heaven and some to eternal damnation in Hell. Since Hell and Heaven formed such utter reality for them, the worry of their lives centered on whether they numbered among God's elect or not. The only way they found to assuage their anxiety lay in looking for how well a person succeeded in his calling. If a person succeeded, logic said he must be chosen of God.

Believing that people are assigned a calling by God, they reckoned that success in their calling (which happened to be commerce) would answer their worry. Success was not, however, simply a matter of making money; merchants had done that for thousands of years. No, they must rationally organize their work. This meant continually reinvesting profits, not in luxuries but in an ascetic expansion of business. This led them to rationally organize the entire economic stream from collection of raw materials, to designing tools and systems of production, to distribution, retail operations, and cost accounting, all for the irrational goal of convincing themselves that God had selected them for salvation. They became this-worldly ascetics.

The men who led Japan's industrialization process were not merchants. They came from the lower samurai ranks whose calling involved administering the realm. Their anxiety welled up from the horrendous burden of *on*, *gimu*, and *giri* as governmental functionaries responsible for Japan's status in the world. An inward compulsion drove them to ascetically devote their efforts at rational planning for the irrational objectives of imperial power and eliminating national shame.

But this burden was not their's alone. Meiji leaders drew upon everyone's sense of responsibility in their calling. Each person's contribution was essential. Workers were as important as military commanders. And Japan did finance its industrialization from the long, heavy toil of farmers and their wives who raised silk worms and of young women who painfully processed the silk for export. Note: Meiji leaders need not create this widespread attitude; they need only utilize it as a resource.

When the British and French fleets bombarded Shimonoseki in August 1864, they did more than demonstrate the weakness of Japan's defenses; they humiliated Japan. This intolerable shame cried out for expiation. Japan had to learn from the West so that it could arm itself as powerfully as Europeans had. All Japanese must devote themselves to carrying out their job and make whatever adjustments proved necessary—even if that included instituting Western-style education, adopting Western-style male clothing, constructing Western railroads, and building Western warships. In less than forty years they could decisively defeat China and then even Russia.

In the 1920s, Britain and the US pressured Japan into accepting the famous 5-5-3 naval treaty for major warships. Britain and America could each have five battleships for every three allowed Japan on the argument that American and Britain had several oceans to patrol whereas Japan had only one. Regardless of its logic, this treaty struck Japanese as an insulting slap to the face. It brought deep shame to Japan—rather akin to how insults between Westerner elite-class men once led to duels.

In Japanese eyes this incident meant a blatant racial affront to their *giri*. They must at any cost resolve it, quite likely with blood. It readily helped rationalize Japan's on-going drive for a colonial empire that would surely rank Japan among the world's premier nations. If colonialism made other nations great, then Japan must do so to achieve top status also. The end result, however, was Japan's utter defeat in WWII.

An interesting thing happened at that juncture. Once the military route to world-class status had proven errant, total defeat provided the means for satisfying *giri*. Japan had now cleansed itself with blood and sincerity. Japanese could start all over again, this time along a different strategic route, the route of economic excellence that has accomplished all Japan sought to do a century ago through military might.

While it does appear that contemporary Japanese outlook and behavior owe much to the inculcation of neo-Confucianism via Bushido well over three centuries ago, a question arises why Japanese would have responded as they did to it when it had no such impact in China, the land of its origination. Might not a much deeper and older strata of cultural influence predisposed them? Quite possibly.

This possibility finds support in earlier Japanese feats. For instance: Within one generation after clan leaders had adopted Chinese writing and Buddhism, Japanese scholars could hold their own on the finest points of philosophy with anyone. When Japanese began to build fifth century *kofun* burial mounds and seventh century Buddhist temples, they set out to construct the largest ones ever built in the world, and they succeeded in doing so.

This pattern—of having to master every adopted culture and then to outperform those from whom they had borrowed—is no new phenomenon. It runs through Japanese cultural history, even back to making the world's finest neolithic pottery in prehistoric times. Within one decade after receiving their first guns from the Portuguese in the mid-sixteenth century, Japanese artisans had mastered production of guns so well that they manufactured the world's best. They exported them to Europe instead of importing them. Their 17th century Christian martyrs match anything Europe can demonstrate for devotion. In WWII, they built the largest battleship ever attempted. And we know quite well their success in recent decades with Western technology.

Japanese have a phrase for it, a phrase every child hears sternly enunciated each day from parents: "*Issho kemmei!* (Do your best!)"—implying that the entire world is watching you; you must not bring shame. The burdens of *on* thereby became far greater among Japanese than anything Chinese philosophy intended. For, that philosophy had found ideal soil to flourish in, the soil of a Japanese communal spirit preconditioned for it. Japan had to become more Confucist than Confucist China.

Proper Place

Ruth Benedict made the argument that no one can comprehend Japanese culture and hence Japanese community without mastering its meaning of "proper place." While the European concern with class does not afflict Japanese, rank and order do exert powerful influences on social processes and communal bonding.

To stabilize a volatile war-ravaged nation, the Tokugawas, for instance, imposed rigid codes for comportment, fashions, and occupation. Built on traditions of relative status, Tokugawa rules of behavior, dress, and assigned work wove social place into their elaborate political structure. To this day, Japanese take great care in ranking everything, be it schools, corporations, public agencies, whiskey, sports, golf clubs, opera singers, families, you name it, to an extent not matched in Europe and America. And then they act toward all such items according to those rankings. Observing Japanese life in the nineteenth century, Lafcadio Hearn described how girls at age 14 had distinctly different hairdos from girls 16 whose hair style differed form girls 18; similarly married women in their early twenties from single women of the same age.

This sensitivity to fashion did not provide a means for personal expression. Quite the contrary. It sought to establish a comforting sense of belonging and acceptance. Fallows notes that "fitting in" reaches down even to pressures on mothers to prepare exactly the same standard *obento* (lunch) for their children to take to kindergarten. Embree observed in the mid-1930s what remains true for Japanese schools today: a brilliant student who does not conform receives less esteem than a mediocre student who never questions. To quote a much used old adage in Japan: a nail that sticks out gets hammered down.

No matter how carefully a foreigner (even a Japanese of Korean ancestry) might comply with all expectations, Japanese look askance. Such a person is inherently an outsider and therefore cannot possibly understand the nuances of Japanese life sufficiently to fit in. Indeed, nothing can disconcert Japanese like encountering a Westerner who does thoroughly know Japanese culture and how to function in it. There simply is no "proper place" provided in the Japanese community for that kind of person. And with no niche provided, Japaneses have no recourse than to treat that person as a nonperson. Only with the rank of ambassador could Edwin Reischauer achieve acceptance—because his rank at last provided him a recognized niche.

Japanese language does not draw the English distinction between status and role. The Japanese word *bun* combines status and role into a single relationship. The commonly referred to *oyabun/kobun*, derived from a father/son set, extends the familial relationship to nonrelatives as patron/client or master/follower. Ambitious employees in government and business seek out someone senior to attach themselves rather feudally to and thereby to rise (or fall) with their patron. Then if they succeed, a successive generation will do the same with them. Similarly among cult members.

Ranking so pervades that persons at obviously different levels find it easier to interact socially than can professional colleagues where their rank distinctions are too trivial to make a senior/junior relationship unquestionably evident to all. Inherently, they are rivals in a highly competitive world. They must guard rigidly lest a lapse or weakness with a colleague of equal rank be turned against them. Far safer to participate in clearly structured interactions within an unmistakable *sempai/kohai* (senior/junior) framework, there awaiting for one's eventual seniority to gain the top.

Consequently, Japanese colleagues find it quite difficult to brainstorm ideas or to critique someone's proposals because it immediately takes on the shades of an attack on one's name and one's status, thereby provoking a *giri* incident. Rather, they must see how the person of highest rank leans and then follow suit. The person of highest rank, however, must protect his status and secure the loyalty of others by demonstrating sensitivity to the feelings of all involved. One simply does not speak without considering its strategic impacts on all the potential relationships affected.

Not uncommonly, Japanese associates may communicate more through body language than through spoken words. Western-style logic holds less importance than "shared understanding" referred to as *hara-gei* (literally translated: "belly art:" our "gut feeling"). Society expects everyone to correctly read all the ranks and all the interests present as well as all the subtle signals and feelings of everyone else. Those failing this test find themselves outsiders and hence ineffective in social intercourse.

American business reps in Japan get frustrated with the rituals of socializing that can drag on for days before their Japanese counterparts get down to serious negotiations. They don't understand how essential it is for Japanese to get a feeling for the other side so that they can size up others and adjust their interaction accordingly. Japanese call it *omoiyari*, a sense for others' *kokoro* (spirit of the heart) without being told. Lebra notes that the customary solicitation of guests' desires by an American hostess strikes Japanese as the epitome of impropriety. A hostess (like a governmental official) is supposed to sense what others want without having to be told. Failure in this by a hostess (or an official) provides grounds for social banishment.

The ubiquitous exchanging of name cards in Japan takes on the appearance of an obsessive ritual carried to the absurd. But for Japanese it serves a most useful purpose. A name card conveys all the information necessary for total strangers to quickly evaluate their relative ranks—by occupation, employer, education, age, and any note of fame. Immediately establishing this ranking avoids embarrassment later when one of them must enter a door first. It determines who bows deeper, who may speak bluntly and who deferentially, and where each should properly sit around a table.

In this context, role identity takes on a different emphasis from that in America. People will more likely refer to another person by the latter's career position than by name—such as Mr. Dentist, or Mr. Company President. An employee in a public agency or a corporation will likely identify himself less by his profession (such as engineer or accountant) than by the organization employing him on a lifetime basis. He thereby expresses his primary linkage as the object of his loyalty.

MARRIAGE AND FAMILY

Japanese literature, arts, and tradition do not lack romance and sexual excitement. Yet marriage has never depended on those odd factors of romantic love and sex appeal so emphasized during this century in America. As typical throughout the world most of the time, marriage does not just unite two people. It unites two families and consequently has far deeper significance socially, economically, and politically—for the community as well as for the families involved. Add the Japanese neo-Confucian concerns with *on, ko,* and *giri;* marriage requires considerable hedging and buffering to ensure its success as an institution even if the individuals have to carry heavy burdens of responsibility and sacrifice.

In most business and political dealings, Japanese must make certain that careful preliminaries occur to avoid embarrassment in the event the intended project eventually cannot proceed. They must take all possible precautions to ensure that no one suffers shame. (Even Japanese police do not make arrests until they know they have at least a 99 percent likelihood of a conviction.) What then could need more careful scripting than steps toward marriage? The *baishakunin* (intermediary) played an exceedingly—and ritually elaborate—role in all marriage arrangements. A prospective bride and groom only met at the formal *omiai* ceremony once the go-between and families had found their opposite numbers satisfactory and all recognizable obstacles resolved.

Even today when love matches do occur, go-betweens retain at least a ritualized role. In addition, brides paid a visit to their family in the first year of marriage. This allowed her to dissolve the union by not returning to the husband's family who could tell neighbors that the bride had "taken ill and died" while on that visit. Result: no one incurred shame. But before resorting to such an extreme measure, the go-between as well as other family members interceded to buffer and resolve the problems. A couple need not cope with troubles on their own the way so many American marriages must.

Traditionally women did not accompany their husbands on activities outside of the home. Their lives revolved around managing their family. A wife even bore the responsibility for family finances, including hiding some savings from her spendthrift husband. Japanese call these savings *heso kuri*—"belly button money." While a man might receive deference as family head, even he knew who really ran the household.

Village women also bore responsibility for ensuring that their families fulfilled all social obligations and carried out the annual cycle of nearly monthly religious celebrations or festivities associated with cooperative planting, harvesting, and irrigation repair. Women achieved recognition on their own by how well they accomplished the prescribed household decorations and food preparation. Their degree of compliance marked how fully each family "fit in" and how fully each sought to promote communal continuity and vitality. Modern big-city life loses much of this deep social flavor.

Americans experience increased freedom as they mature, then less as they age; Japanese go through a reverse cycle. Given much pampering (especially boys) in early childhood, they take on increasing burdens of responsibility and restrictions into early maturity but enjoy deference and even wide tolerance for bizarre behavior in old age.

Children in Japan usually enjoy far more close bodily contact with adults than tends to occur within American families. They breast feed far longer, even up to kindergarten age. They are fondled more and allowed to sleep with their parents (which produces all manner of popular jokes). They usually bathe with a parent and seldom find themselves alone. One commonly sees older children playing ball with a younger sibling strapped on their backs. Consequently, Japanese grow up continuously feeling themselves integrated members of close-knit groups steeped in mutual responsibility.

CHAPTER SIX

CONTINUITY IN CHANGE

The last chapter may have conveyed an impression that ascetic Zen and neo-Confucian ethics, as they gave specific criteria for Bushido, fully answer questions about what drives the Japanese. Such a conclusion seems akin to saying that the Protestant Ethic analyzed by Max Weber fully explains the emergence of industrial capitalism in Europe.

It is, of course, far from so simple. Weber acknowledged other contributing factors, such as the development of double-entry bookkeeping without which rational accounting would have been impossible and the emergence of rational science, an outgrowth of the Renaissance and a platform for advanced technology. So, too, in Japan. Numerous factors went into the Japanese experience, many of them quite possibly not yet adequately recognized and probed.

Certainly the *goningumi* system of imposed mutual spying must have added to the anxiety inherent with *on/giri* as well as making conformity a national habit. Removing samurai from rural life made villagers far more self-sufficient in organizing community functions, in policing themselves, in maintaining the infrastructure of local roads, bridges, and irrigation systems, and in resolving conflicts on their own (as Embree describes for Suye Mura in the mid-1930s) than might have occurred otherwise. With only a badge of authority but no samurai at hand, local headmen had to achieve compliance through diplomacy, encouragement, and sincerely representing peasant interests.

Certainly neo-Confucianism could not in and of itself explain Japanese culture; it produced results too dissimilar in China. More likely, Japanese took from neo-Confucianism what already fit Japanese culture, and Chinese took what fit their particular cultural orientation and traditions. Perhaps the concepts in neo-Confucianism go farther in providing a convenient handle, than providing substance, for analysis.

Still, something did happen to Japanese society during Tokugawa. Take for instance peasant complaints and protest demonstrations over unfair treatment. The Bakufu adjudicated approximately one thousand cases, about half of their judgments favoring the peasants against daimyo and landowners. Most certainly those were not the only cases; more likely they reflect only the ones that had grown unbearable. We may surmise this because the peasants who petitioned their grievances knew what the end result would inevitably entail.

No matter how right their cause and no matter how fully a Bakufu's judgment might side with them, they would have to die nonetheless. Their petition would have posed a threat to the established order; for that, death must follow. Still, they protested, and at an accelerated rate during the eighteenth and early nineteenth centuries as Bakafu rule came more to preserve form than substance—more the letter of the law than its purpose and spirit—and as it became counterproductive of its own best interests as well as the people's.

We may have here another instance of what Ivan Morris has called the "nobility of failure." We saw it in the 47 ronin who methodically carried out the vendetta expected of them and then went without hesitation to their final act of *seppuku* to fulfill *giri*. Protesting peasants knew they would die, yet they willingly sought to save the villages and families who looked to them for recourse. They chose death above dishonor. Morris demonstrates with examples from all eras of Japanese history that the 47 ronin and the popular basis for their special reverence among Japanese were not a fluke. Heroism comes not from achieving victory but from perseverance in the face of obvious, certain defeat.

Kamikaze pilots in the waning days of WWII fit this pattern quite well. Admiral Onishi knew the war was lost; he had resisted using kamikazes earlier. But when all was hopeless, they found hope in the fulfillment of total loyalty—of *chu*. Once Japan surrendered, Onishi then took his own life in respect for the subordinates he had sent to their deaths.

Yoshida's graphic *Requiem for Battleship Yamato* grippingly captures the fatalism of absolute loyalty, also. Or take the dozen or so Japanese soldiers who held out in the mountains of the Philippines for 10 or 20, even 30 years rather than surrender. They knew their situation was hopeless, yet they steadfastly upheld their sense of duty and loyalty. They achieved "salvation" from human frailty through sincerity—not just for themselves but for all Japanese.

Buddhism's principle contribution here may come from an underlying sense of *karma*, an acceptance of fate. Yet that acceptance has seldom if ever meant resignation for Japanese as it may mean at times to Buddhists in other parts of Asia. Japanese society and culture are above all else vibrant, dynamic, competitive, or what American business folk-culture calls "hard driven." This is true despite the formidable obstacles imposed on interpersonal relations by the burdens of *on* and *giri* and the resulting anxiety over potential shame from failure if one acts on one's own. This vitality runs through Japanese history, back to the feudal wars, to the mega-sized temples and exaggerated burial mounds of earlier times.

From Tribe to Clan to Family

Clan in China involved blood relatives with the same family name no matter how geographically dispersed, in Japan it eventually rested on geographically concentrated feudal self-identification. Members were not necessarily blood relatives. By the time Minamoto established the Kamakura shogunate in 1185, tribe had given way to alliances of power blocs which hardly bothered any more to claim blood relations--except where it brought politically advantage, such as nominal ties to the previously dominant Fujiwara clan.

Indeed, due to intermarriage among tribal elites, by then all elites could claim some distant relation to the Fujiwaras and hence to the imperial Yamato clan. This interlocking network warranted their claim to elite status. Lacking this pedigree prevented Hideyoshi from assuming the title of shogun in the 1590s after uniting all of Japan for the first time by becoming the de facto supreme power.

Several paradoxes arise here. First, *uji* clans replaced tribal loyalty among the elite. Then eastern feudal clans undercut the cohesion of *uji* clan by "buying" vassal loyalty via land grants. Meanwhile the managerial unit known as an *ie* family of eastern Japan became increasingly common until it could provide the base for entrepreneurial accomplishment when the modern era dawned, not just in such tycoon families as Mitsui, Mitsubishi, and Sumitomo, but in every town and village.

Everywhere the power of tribe and clan over families and individuals must be broken before a manageable industrialized workforce can emerge. Mao sought this in China by unleashing Red Guards in a Cultural Revolution; colonial governments made it central in ruling their subjects. In Japan, it developed well in advance of the day it would prove crucial, just as it did among independent Americans on their self-contained family homestead. As Smith points out, continued innovations among farmers and widespread industrial enterprise in self-operating villages not only increased production throughout the century before Meiji but created a large technologically prepared, literate workforce already accustomed to industrial discipline.

Second, we can easily see the fulfillment of feudal ideals in the Tokugawa system. Yes, the Tokugawa Bakufu did manage to achieve a rigid balancing of feudal forces so as to maintain stability for over two centuries. Yet in that well-balanced arrangement, Tokugawa effectively took the vitality out of feudalism and hence out of any vestigial tribal elements still struggling between elite clans for domination. Whether intentional or not, by perfecting it the Tokugawa Bakafu sent feudalism sliding into what would become state centralism under the Meiji government. Tribal identification could merge into national scale with simply regionalized subcultures left over.

Third, the Meiji Revolution sprang not from class tensions but from the ambition among frustrated samurai frozen at lower rank whose educations and talents exceeded those of their incompetent lords. Having no landed rights, these samurai felt no need to defend the system; they could overthrow it. And they could shift their keen sense of loyalty from feudal lords to nation, even if that meant such unheroic "middle class" activity as managing industry and foreign trade.

The Tokugawa Bakufu did more than accomplish what was, de facto, a remarkably effective centralized system, as good as any in Europe at that time and comparable to the transition China underwent in the first two centuries BC. It completed the process of secularizing feudal allegiances which had begun during the tumultuous sixteenth century era of warfare. In that era, commoners, such as Hideyoshi, could rise to high position while elite clans, long associated with a sanctified power surrounding the throne, fell to oblivion and even disappeared.

No longer would daimyo have a quasi-religious function of tribal high priest under the supreme imperial priest, all linked to ancient shamanistic practices. They lost their clan identity and became little more than provincial governors. Meiji made it official by changing their title as well. While this pattern of change leaned toward linearity, others followed seemingly repetitive, almost cyclical patterns.

REGULARITY IN TURBULENCE

A case of consistent reaction to challenge occurs in the Japanese practice of undergoing wholesale absorptions of things foreign, be it dress, governance, language, art, or technology. The emergence of a horse-oriented warrior culture in Korea of the late third century got picked up and adopted in Japan. Some three centuries later came the embrace of a Chinese governance format, with Buddhism and Chinese writing. Sung art and neo-Confucianism, arriving seven centuries later, achieved official backing at the start of the seventeenth century. Western concepts of government and technology evoked the most extensive self-planned and self-implemented cultural reformation the world has ever seen, starting in the late nineteenth century.

Japanese, however, did more than adopt. As noted earlier, they always set themselves to successfully outdo the societies from which they had borrowed the new culture. On each occasion one Japanese power bloc would embrace a supposedly superior alien system of technology and governance.

It did so for the status leverage such an "advanced" culture might accord the clique's own political agenda domestically.

While readily wearing the manifest trappings of the adopted culture, the clique tended inadvertently (or intentionally) to miss its essence. Then after a few generations, Japanese leaders would withdraw from foreign involvement, seemingly to digest those aspects of alien culture they had swallowed, thereby gaining time to make them an integral part of the indigenous tradition. That accomplished, the internalized foreign cultural elements would be preserved devotedly henceforth.

The first withdrawal may have come in the first century BC or AD, which would account for the apparent suddenness of the introduced mounted-warrior and *kofun* culture in the late third century. The first documented turning inward came after a 663 defeat of an ally in Korea drove Japanese armies from the mainland. The cultural impact of Europeans on a chaotic Japan in mid-sixteenth century sent Japan's power elite scrambling: an invasion of Korea and adoption of thirteenth century Sung neo-Confucianism, followed by expulsion of virtually all foreigners and termination of foreign contact for two centuries.

Japanese withdrawal from the world under the Tokugawa Bakafu went so far as to ban guns—once it had secured supremacy using firearms. It did so for a very logical reason: a gun had proven too powerful an instrument of social leveling. In the hands of the lowliest peasant it could kill the mightiest of samurai. Only by returning to the use of swords could samurai assure their own preeminence.

Each succeeding era of change had a shorter interval between the time an elite group introduced and adopted alien cultural elements until their acceptance by the general public. The Tungus practice of male dominance did not reach fulfillment for a thousand years. Buddhism took some five hundred years to become the religion of preference or predominance for commoners; it never did replace Shinto. Neo-Confucianism had to wait four hundred years to gain full acceptance among the elite, then only a century for its practices to remold the ways of commoners. Westernization reshaped much of Japanese culture from top to bottom in less than a century.

Confucianism's central concern for harmony might not have meant much to what was a warrior-dominated society, as compared to China's where mandarin scholars provided the role models of ideal behavior. However, Japanese have long had a deep sensitivity to the natural environment as evidence in, and reinforced by, native Shintoism. The reciprocal mutuality principle of Confucianism, as expressed in *yin* and *yang*, occurs in Japanese thought even to finding complementarity in good and evil.

Beside glorifying loyalty, neo-Confucianism firmly fixed the five basic Confucian relationships into daily life—those of subject to ruler, child to parent, wife to husband, younger sibling to older sibling, and friend to friend. It provided a clearly known and structured place for everyone. Now society could expect everyone to comply and fulfill his/her place.

When the samurai-dominated government of Meiji determined to modernize Japan to a par with Western nations, its planners felt quite uncertain what all that might entail. Wisely they set out to discover what in Western culture would benefit Japan most. They sent observers to examine farms, legal systems, parliaments, school curricula, railroads, methods of factory production, etc. They even drastically redid fashions by prescribing Western dress for men. And for the most part they judiciously chose an eclectic collection of social, political, and economic alterations from various countries which Japanese could rather quickly apply.

Not surprisingly, even the most judicious study and planning could not keep out every new idea and alternate way of perceiving the world and socially interrelating. Not surprisingly too, all this rapid change produced serious tensions within society. Some sectors grew rich and flouted venerable mores while other sectors made the necessary sacrifices. As should have been expected, the tensions and inequalities—but even more so, the violation of honored ways of life—generated reactions by the 1920s. Those reactions grew particularly intense among the military officer corps who now came from peasant stock where both the greatest sacrifices occurred and the resentments against urban modernists/opportunists festered deepest.

World War II became for them more than an explosion of reaction. WWII was a modern expression of a repeated search for spiritual cleansing through blood, an emotional inclination that began to emerge by the arrival of a warrior culture from Korea some sixteen centuries earlier. Nichiren clamored for it in the thirteenth century. Seventeenth century Bushido viewed the world in those terms. WWII provided the means of demonstrating both *gimu* and *giri*, either by glory or in death. What counted above all then and now were sincerity and loyalty. Male workers in modern Japanese offices still must demonstrate that same sense of loyalty and devotion—and sacrifice of self.

Prestowitz points out that "proper" arrangements between Japanese businesses today amount to what Americans call collusion. They occur not for enhancing profits but to ensure harmony, the minimalization of dreaded "confusion." And they involve coalescence of old-time feudal-like loyalty. Security and growth come first; consumers and individuals come last.

OTHER PERSISTENCIES

The Japanese penchant for honoring by preserving the past has remained consistent. Today's scholar of ancient Persia, for instance, will find a unique source of artifacts in the eighth century Shosoin repository at Nara. In spite of heavy-handed efforts to use Shinto by Buddhist monks to dominate Japanese culture and by Meiji backers in the nineteenth century to create a cult of the emperor (after centuries of his utter eclipse in Japanese life, even to the point of poverty), traditional (not State) Shinto has persisted in people's lives. Japanese, better than Chinese, have even preserved the way Chinese pronounced words from fourteen hundred years ago.

Throughout Japanese history, the control of land has taken top priority among Japanese leaders in playing their political games. The Taika reformers sought to employ a Chinese system of surveying land ownership for the purposes of taxation—no doubt also to clip the power of rival tribes. Within a generation, Japanese clan leaders had found ways of subverting that reform and avoiding taxes through hereditary privileges, connections at court, and "donating" land to temples.

The feudal era was necessarily centered on land and the power its wealth created. Feudalism's loss of power stemmed from its inability to generate enough land grants. A center piece of the American Occupation after WWII was its land-reform program, quite possibly the most extensive ever conducted in the world. Now the tight squeeze on Japan's limited supply of land may spell future political changes in keeping with the social and economic impacts already evident from it.

Another rather constant pattern occurs: the turning over of operational power to someone else whose functions in turn similarly become so ritualized as to require yet another layer of substitutes to carry on the needed functions. Early emperors/empresses had regents to handle operational matters denied them due to the burden of fulfilling ritualized functions as the nation's chief intermediary with the gods. During Heian, an emperor was typically installed while still a small child so that his father could abdicate and then wield influence from behind the scenes.

At times, several ex-emperors maneuvered the fronting child emperor. This led to establishing councilors whose posts also soon become hereditary. Soon competing blocs within the Fujiwara family manipulated the abdicated emperors and their councilors. With the feudal eras of Kamakura and Muromachi, shoguns usurped real power but were soon manipulated by abdicated shoguns, councilors, and other tiers of hereditary functionaries for child shoguns.

Even the Meiji era saw actions of a supposedly reascendant emperor orchestrated and instituted by his advisors in his name. What differed this time, however, was that change now came too fast for the *genro* (a clique of "elder statesmen") to become hereditary as in previous eras. Soon the military dominated but fell with the defeat of WWII. Now politicians have their own day: they need no longer act in the emperor's name. People now see the emperor for what he has always been, a reigning monarch and high priest, a national symbol, but one who does not rule.

WOMEN IN A CHANGING JAPAN

Current idealizations of Japanese females include such qualities and roles as: long-suffering, obedient (to father, husband, and son), submissive, holding uppermost a desire to bear and raise children (especially sons) for her husband and the family line. Until the 1980s, popular movies and novels had unquestioningly employed this image, based on prevailing cultural practices—especially in movies and novels by men. More importantly though, even if somehow the overwhelming majority of Japanese women still act out this cultural mandate in all sincerity, these idealized feminine virtues have not always prevailed; they are relatively recent. Moreover, as occurs in other societies, a natural psychological variety in real life predisposes women to a wide variety of behavior—even in so rigidly regimented a society as Japan's.

The evidence for a female-led culture in Japan two thousand years ago rests on several factors: The highest divinity indigenous to Japan is Amaterasu, the Sun Goddess, a female whose significance lies, according to myth, in her founding the Japanese race. Early reports by Chinese visitors to Japan speak of reigning female empresses or chief priestesses. A titanic struggle occurred between some tribal blocs (or at least between elite clans from the various tribes) wanting to preserve traditional arrangements as against those wanting to institute a mainland cultural system with male rule.

The change from female to male dominance may have begun with the shift to sedentary agriculture. But introduction of a mounted-warrior orientation, possibly more than even the introduction of Chinese governance arrangements, facilitated male ascendancy. Everywhere the horse has given men an aura and mystique that translates into power. Nowhere was this so evident as in frontier life in northeast Japan. Simultaneously though, in Kyoto females continued to exercise great cultural influence and creativity into the thirteenth century or later.

While men strove to master Chinese writing (and to gain compliments for imitating Chinese literary expression), high-born women evolved an alphabetic system called *kana* to express thoughts of Japanese in the Japanese vernacular. They achieved such brilliance that they, not men, effectively chronicled what we now know about court life in Heian days. Murasaki Shikibu's *Genji Monogatari* (Tales of Genji), written in the early years of the eleventh century, has achieved wide recognition as the world's first novel quite capable of standing on its own merits along with literary accomplishments anywhere in the world in any era.

Even with the rise to power of frontier clans, women did not suddenly drop in status. Women continued to hold posts usually thought of as male prerogatives, such as constable and warrior. Reports exist of women who out-performed men in the martial arts as late as the fourteenth century. Only when civil war during Ashikaga times grew utterly pervasive did women, responsible for protecting and nurturing their families, shrink into the background. Only then did they become known as the "person in the rear."

As the rough and uncouth frontiersman came to wield predominant power, women became a liability, something true macho men did not consort with as social equals. Among samurai, as commonly occurs in warrior societies, homosexuality was not only accepted out of necessity; it was often preferred. (Jesuits' inflexible condemnation of this choice of sexual behavior provided a major irritant that led to the banishment of all missionaries in 1640 and the suppression of Christianity.)

Several shifts of conditions in recent decades might be at work reshaping the role and place of women in Japanese society. Females now have a better chance of getting an education, or at least better paying, more interesting jobs in the city. Consequently, rural men face a severe shortage of potential wives. Women hold a far better bargaining position than ever before in demanding better treatment from their husbands and more freedom. As McDonald shows, they may now work in the factories springing up in rural areas, rather than having ever to perform the monotonous backbreaking labor traditionally assigned them.

A different situation exists in the cities. There the cost of housing (and of living expenses generally) has risen so astronomically that families can no longer obtain decent housing on a single income. Moreover, more females want college educations. And since this investment is too expensive simply to ensure access to husbands with a potential for higher status careers, many women today want to use their educations for more than the customary (temporary) "office lady" job.

Regardless of what women might like, two recent factors may reshape the work scene for them. First, a burgeoning need for technical skill (such as with computers) faces Japanese industries; women are at least as competent as men in these fields. Second (and interrelated to the first) is Japan's strong aversion to inmigration in spite of severe shortages in the workforce. Either employers must change Japanese attitudes toward inmigrants or they must reassess their reluctance to tailor career employment acceptably to include women.

On the social side, the worsening housing crisis has forced three and even four generations of families to occupy a single tiny apartment. The inevitable tensions drive many young wives to escape the confined apartment by continuing to work, not only after marriage but after the birth of children. After all, the presence of a grandparent or great-grandparent provides a built-in baby sitter. And tiny apartments near convenience shopping leave too little work to keep one, much less several women, meaningfully busy all day without fighting.

The traditional tight bond between mother and son—a bond closer than between husband and wife—can only exacerbate family tensions in modern society. A flood of Western TV, movies, and cheap romantic novels, along with travel abroad, have made today's young Japanese wife expect far more out of marriage than her mother and grandmother ever dreamed of.

We cannot, of course, predict the future of females in Japan. Many continue to abide by traditional roles, perhaps because it gives them leverage over husbands, sons, and daughters-in-law, as well as a modicum of old-age security. Yet change does appear inevitable, whether sought or not.

Actually, much had already changed by this century, judging from a seventeenth century primer for women of high status. That primer, titled *Onna Daigakko* (higher education for women) and written by a man, saw women as inherently stupid. In this, men created a self-fulfilling prophecy by limiting women's realm of interaction to husband, children, and maids—not unlike preferences by large blocs of more recent Western males.

The primary message of this set of instructions to women, however, concerned their duties, that of total obedience without complaint to their father's, husband's, and father-in-law's every whim. The rationale given: since men owe absolute and unquestioning obedience to their feudal lord and a woman's feudal lord is her husband, her total obedience to him is only proper. Furthermore, upon marriage a woman "returned" to her new home since her home of birth served only as a transitional waiting place until she could accept the prime purpose of her life, that of marriage and procreation.

While much of this attitude may still prevail, it may do so only so long as a man's primary loyalty must go to his employer (his modern-day feudal lord) rather than to his family. This is changing, however, with increased educational levels, with affluence which allows less job devotion, and with exposure to Western modes of marriage and family. Also recent economic downturns have forced large Japanese corporations to start limiting their traditional lifetime employment practices.

Despite appearances to the contrary, many Japanese married partners do experience genuine love, albeit not expressed in Western gestures. Even the present emperor, Akihito, and his wife, Michiko, depart from the old ways. Theirs was a non-arranged love match thereby setting an example for others.

Another far more subtle process of change may be underway in Japan, especially in the cities. Where virtually everyone once lived in tightly confined villages and everyone knew everyone else, where everyone could evaluate how well each person fulfilled social expectations and participated in community reinforcing rituals (where one task of village headman involved keeping a record of *giri* owed between families), there social pressure could preserve the influence of *on, gimu* and *giri*.

But that social milieu no longer exists for the majority of Japanese. Instead, they live in teeming cities of faceless strangers. Here the intense competitiveness that has always churned just below the surface (and had ever to be controlled) now dominates each person's daily experience. Urbanites encounter rudeness more often today than traditional politeness, such as fighting daily to pack into a subway car to work.

They must put in long hours of unpaid overtime to hold their position at work. They must constantly guard lest they suffer others' one-upmanship. So long as Japan's economic miracle continues, they can rationalize their sacrifice of family for national prestige. But just let a major economic downturn deprive them of this rationalization; then painful social and psychological adjustments may become unavoidable.

Quite possibly an adjustment is already underway. Not only does Japan have the highest longevity; it has the lowest rate of births per woman of childbearing age (1.77) in the world. In a society which places such great importance on continuing the family, what could serve a more effective form of protest than for women to quietly stop being "baby factories"? Government officials are getting the message. Though they continue frantically to appeal to women to perform their patriotic duty, this appeal no longer wields its traditional impact.

COMMUNITY SYSTEM

Even this very brief survey of the processes of cultural change and persistency in Japan should have indicated that far more was involved than simply many generations of people, more even than a society with its own distinctive culture. The patterns of behavior and of change emerge too coherently to amount to only the sum total of innumerable individual events. We saw here quite clearly that Japanese society had an arena for action and almost a script for that action. It has enjoyed a bedrock process upon which it could adopt and digest all manner of cultural trappings and symbols from other societies over the centuries without losing itself; indeed, strengthen itself.

This phenomenon—this process occurring essentially as community cohesion—served as a living system. As an adaptive, multi-scaled, self-reinforcing, synergistic process, it met challenges, coped with its members' needs, and interacted with other systems, both natural and sociocultural. It was an evolutionary process with both consistencies and flexibility. Even during the horrible civil war era of the fifteenth/sixteenth centuries, even with the shock of impotence when faced with Western warships in the 1850s-60s, even in the assault on local community loyalty by militaritists in the 1930s, even in the aftermath of utter destruction by WWII, this living system re-acted with a distinctive tenacity, vitality, and verve.

We saw this as Japanese society/culture/community underwent an evolution—from matrifocal to patrifocal structure, from tribal to feudal to modern form—over a two-thousand year span. In so doing, it provides ideas for probing how less well recorded processes of change might have proceeded elsewhere. At least it might serve as a model for digging into how other societies/cultures differed in their evolutions. It might, then, throw light on the phenomena of community as a living system—as the arena/process of society acting out and also evolving its culture.

A question remains: Can the assault on community by modern forces of urban impersonalization, growing self-centeredism, and cosmopolital lifestyles combine to the point of overwhelming and hence shredding this strong traditional Japanese sense of community. If this happens, then certainly community as a system stands vulnerable throughout the so-called "developed" world as well as in so-called "developing" nations. If Emiko Ohnuki-Tierney's analysis is valid, even the shift among urban Japanese to a Western diet away from rice, the nation's soul, portends a dire restructuring of community system here. Perhaps.

Governmental reaction to the devastating earthquake which rocked and toppled Kobe in January 1995 reveals aspects of the inner workings of Japan's community system not normally so evident. Although tribal divisions within Japan may have died centuries ago, the integrated nationwide community exhibits a distinctly tribal orientation in its manner of dealing both with challenges and with outsiders.

The world has long noted Japan's resistance to allowing immigrants no matter how badly needed and to importing foreign goods, be they Detroit auto parts or Washington state apples. But even in this tragic Kobe crisis, not only was the ponderous governmental bureaucracy—like samurai of old—unable to abandon formalities and take individual initiative so as to react immediately to an horrendous catastrophe; the government refused to take on the burdens of *on* and *giri* inherent in accepting (much less of asking other nations) aid for its victims. What's more, American emergency medical teams had to negotiate for days with Japanese bureaucrats before being granted an opportunity to contribute their help—even though Kobe faced a threatening flu epidemic that would compound the people's stoic misery.

A rigid community system may bring stability under usual circumstances and, in the process of adopting orderly change, actually reinforce itself. But it can become a burden in the face of a severe challenge when responsive flexibility is so vital, as we shall observe in the next chapter about nineteenth century Hawaii.

BIBLIOGRAPHY

Allyn, John. *The 47 Ronin Story.* 1970.

Beard, Mary R. *The Force of Women in Japanese History.* 1953.

Bellah, Robert. *Tokugawa Religion.* 1957.

Benedict, Ruth. *The Chrysanthemum and the Sword.* 1946.

Blackner, Carmen. *The Catalpa Bow: A Study of Shamanistic Practices in Japan.* 1975.

Borton, Hugh. "Peasant Uprisings," *Transactions of Asiatic Society of Japan.* 1938.

Boxer, C.R. *The Christian Century in Japan (1549-1650).* 1951.

Brown, D.M. *Money Economy in Medieval Japan.* 1951.

Clement, E.W. "Chinese Refugees of the 17th Century in Mito," *Transactions of Asiatic Society of Japan,* 1896.

Collcutt, Martin et al. *Cultural Atlas of Japan.* 1988.

Edwards, Walter. "Event and Process in the Founding of Japan: The Horserider Theory in Archeological Perspective." *Journal of Asian Studies,* Vol.9, No.2, 1983.

Embree, John F. *Suye Mura: A Japanese Village.* 1939.

Fallows, Deborah. "Japanese Women," *National Geographics,* Vol.177, No.4, April 1990.

Hearn, Lafcadio. *Glimpses of Unfamiliar Japan.* (n.d.)

Hall, John W. *Japan: From Prehistory to Modern Times.* 1968.

Hisamatsu, Shinichi. *Zen and the Fine Arts.* 1971.

Ishida, Eiichiro. *Japanese Culture: A Study of Origins and Characteristics.* 1974.

Kornhauser, David. *Urban Japan: Its Foundations and Growth.* 1976.

Lebra, Takie S. *Japanese Patterns of Behavior.* 1976.

Levy, M. "Contrasting Factors in the Modernization of China and Japan," *Economic Development & Cultural Change,* 1953.

McDonald, Mary. *Displacing Rice: Factories in the Fields of Farm Power in Tohoku.* 1990.

Michener, James A. *The Floating World.* 1954.

Morris, Ivan I. *The Nobility of Failure.* 1975.

Morris, Ivan I. *The World of the Shining Prince: Court Life in Ancient Japan.* 1969.

Murakami, Yasusuke. "Ie society as a Pattern of Civilization," *Journal of Asian Studies.* Vol.11, No.2, 1985.

Nakane, Chie. *Japanese Society.* 1970.

Ohashi, Taro. "Uji Society and Ie Society from Prehistory to Medieval Times," *Journal of Asian Studies.* Vol.11, 1985.

Ohnuki-Tierney, Emiko. *Rice as Self.* 1993.

Okimoto, D.I. & T.P.Rohlen. *Inside the Japanese System.* 1988.

Pearson, Richard J. *Windows on the Japanese Past.* 1986.

Prestowitz, Clyde V. Jr. *Trading Places: How We Allowed Japan to Take the Lead.* 1988.

Reischauer, A.K. *Studies in Japanese Buddhism.* 1917.

Reischauer, R.K. *Early Japanese History.* 1937.

Reischauer, Edwin O. *The Japanese.* 1981.

Sakai, Saburo, et al. *Samurai.* 1957.

Sansom, Sir George. *Japan: A Short Cultural History.* 1943.

Sawada, Sho. "Financial Difficulties of the Edo Bakufu," *Harvard Journal of Asiatic Studies.* 1936.

Scalapino, Robert A. *Democracy and the Party Movement in Pre-War Japan.* 1953.

Shinoda, Minoru. *The Founding of the Kamakura Shogunate, 1180-1185.* 1960.

Smith, Thomas C. *Native Sources of Japanese Industrialization, 1750-1920.* 1988.

Spurr, W.E. "Business Cycles in Japan Before 1853," *Journal of Political Economy.* 1938.

Suzuki, D.T. *An Introduction to Zen Buddhism.* 1934.

Takizawa, M. *The Penetration of Money Economy in Japan and Its Effects Upon Social and Political Institutions.* 1927.

Takeyama, Michio. *Harp of Burma* (a novel).

Turner, Christie G. II. "Teeth and Prehistory in Asia," *Scientific American*, Feb.1989.

Vlastos, Stephean. *Peasant Protests and Uprisings in Tokugawa Japan.* 1986.

Vogel, Ezra F. *Japan as Number One.* 1979.

Weber, Max. *The Protestant Ethic and the Spirit of Capitalism.* 1905 (Talcott Parsons's translation, 1930).

Yoshida, M. *Requiem for Battleship Yamato.* 1985.

Zachert, H. "Social Changes During the Tokugawa Period," *Transactions of the Asiatic Society of Japan.* 1938.

CHAPTER SEVEN

HAWAII UNDER STRESS

At the same tropical latitude as Guadalajara Mexico on the eastern side of the Pacific Ocean and Hong Kong on the western side, Hawaii is the most isolated place with a large population of any in the world. This isolation, coupled with the prevailing patterns of wind and ocean currents, made it late in "discovery" by Western explorers. Captain Cook dropped anchor at Kona on the western slopes of the Big Island concurrently with the American Revolution and founding of the US government. By then, Hawaii had had at least a thousand years of independence.

Although some debate remains whether perhaps other groups reached Hawaii in the fifteen hundred years before Capt. Cook, people identifying themselves as Hawaiian are essentially Polynesians who arrived as colonists from the South Pacific. I say "colonists" because they came prepared to settle and continued to maintain contact with their origins for hundreds of years thereafter. Polynesians could and did regularly and accurately sail for thousands of miles across open ocean long before European sailors would hazard much beyond sight of land.

Given Hawaii's limited size, population, and isolation, its society evolved a quite elaborate organization and structure dominated by a large class of warrior chiefs known collectively as *ali'i*. This elite, itself divided into eleven ranks, continually widened the gulf that marked it off from commoners (*maka'ainana*), in contrast to Maori Polynesians on New Zealand whose chiefs and commoners continued to work together.

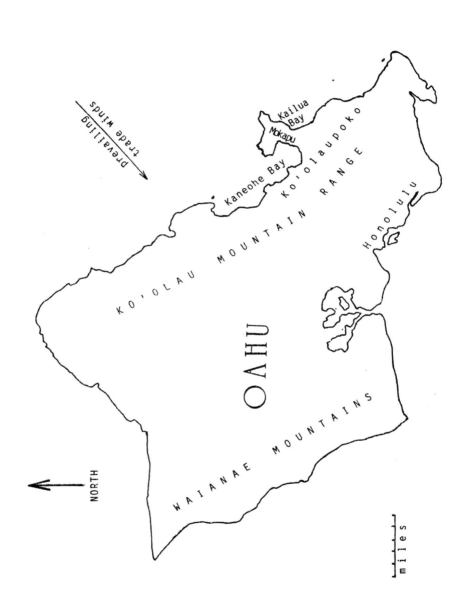

In this respect, Hawaii resembled Japan which also saw the emergence of a dominant warrior class after the eleventh century. Similarly too, Japanese and Hawaiian warrior elite would eventually constitute superfluous superstructures that would specialize in administering the realm, increasingly through an absolute control over the use of land and over who could use it.

Unlike their Japanese counterparts however, Hawaii's power elite continued to occupy priestly positions and hence exerted an additional power leverage over those subservient to them. Over time they would construct their *heiaus* (those truncated pyramids of huge boulders as hallowed sites for religions ceremonies) larger and higher until commoners outside could no longer observe. By the time Capt. Cook arrived at the end of the eighteenth century, commoners were denied not only participation in, but even visual contact with their own religion. They simply suffered, along with the *ali'i*, under the increasingly burdensome taboo (*kapu*) system upon which the political structure rested.

Hawaii's ruling class had grown so autocratic through the compounding application of the kapu that for a commoner merely to touch a high chief's shadow called for an immediate death penalty. Some elite women ranked so high—and hence possessed so much inherent "magic/power" (*mana*)—that they could not raise their own children lest that inherent "raging blaze" attributed to them cripple their offspring. Kapu also prohibited men and women of even the highest rank from eating together in the interest of ritual purity. For the same reason of "purity," men not women did the cooking.

With everything social and political encrusted with religious connotations, religion exerted great impact. Yet the same gods held different rank on different islands, and religion could be and was manipulated for political purposes. By excluding commoners, the elite made it their prerogative and tool. All of which made both that religion and *ali'i* use of it quite vulnerable when Europeans arrived and blatantly ignored the taboos with impunity.

Commoners and elite alike could not do other than notice the apparent impotence of their gods in the face of sacrilege by the newcomers. Internal inconsistencies and taboo burdens further added to Hawaiian doubts. Women in particular, especially those of highest rank, suffered from the system and took the lead in "lobbying" for change.

In 1819, King Kamehameha the Second (Liholiho) openly broke the *kapu*. He ate with women in public and thereby overthrew the central religious basis for his own political preeminence. We might liken the cultural impact of this act to a Pope in Rome decreeing the non-existence of God and the US Supreme Court on the same day declaring the US Constitution null and void.

In one of those coincidences of history which unexpectedly affect so greatly the fates, a band of New England missionaries would arrive soon after to find an entire society, whose religion lay in utter disarray, not unwilling to adopt a new one. Inadvertently with the new religion came all manner of cultural practices and morés ethnically linked to the missionaries' New England background though not necessarily Christian, including a view that saw Hawaiians as primitive savages. Missionaries even disdained the Hawaiians' far better hygiene so essential in the topics, such as bathing several times a day.

We now recognize that Hawaiians did not deserve such pejorative characterization. For instance, faced with a slow but steady growth in population over the centuries, they had to increase food production. Land managers among the elite devised their own quite sophisticated irrigation systems and terracing which were sufficiently well built to withstand all but the very worst of storms. They also constructed large fishponds in shallow bays where they could store living fish until needed.

To resolve tensions in commoner villages (usually an extended family: *ohana*), Hawaiians developed an effective form of what we now call group therapy but known to them as *ho'oponopono* where everyone could let out complaints and anxieties, then all would enter the ocean to ritually cleanse themselves of defiling animosities. Keeping the village ohana running smoothly was most important. The ohana as a group, not individuals, had to meet annual tax obligations or suffer grievous consequences.

In difficult times, villagers' own ohana had to take care of crises and tragedies. It was really their entire world; they were bound to it for life. Everything else remained in aristocratic hands. While *ali'i* gorged themselves to gain massive weight, commoners (especially women) often went hungry.

The gaping chasm between elite and commoner (between *ali'i* and *maka'ainana*) produced a rigidity that grew into brittleness in the Hawaiian social system. This brittleness became quite apparent when it encountered a strong foreign culture which so blatantly flouted Hawaiian religion. Once the king had destroyed the basis of the system, little remained to provide cohesion and direction and to ameliorate tensions. The floodgate of change stood open. Only their *ohana* remained to provide economic and emotional support for commoners, and it was soon destroyed by forces beyond what little control commoners had over their own lives.

LAND MANAGEMENT

Upon arrival, Europeans found here a hierarchy of subdivisions for government and land management; the two were largely the same. Each of the main islands had its own king (later subjugated by Kamehameha I) who controlled all land for the gods. Each island was divided into districts which were in turn composed of units known as *ahupua'a*. Usually wedge-shaped running from mountain top apex and widening out to the coastline, an ahupua'a would encompass the full range of nutritional and construction resources needed for commoner self-sufficiency—from fish to taro to upland fruits and forest. Somewhat like indigenous tribes in what became the US, Hawaiian culture had no provision for true land ownership as we now think of it. Instead, all land belonged in effect to the king who allocated it to his chiefs in sections known as *ahupua'a*. A particularly worthy commoner might receive a small parcel (a *kuleana*) without owner-ship for family use, but only so long as he made productive use of it. The chief or his konohiki could take it back or assign it to some other more worthy family.

The extended family (*ohana*) within each ahupua'a was self-organized with its own headman (*haku*) responsible for gathering taxes and coordinating an equitable distribution of produce among ohana members some of whom might specialize in fishing, taro growing, or collecting mountain resources.

Ideally, everyone had a right to all resources even though the ali'i took theirs first. Everyone, then, had a responsibility for conserving resources by taking only what was necessary and wasting nothing; they recycled every-thing back into the land including human wastes and even cut hair. These practices constituted part of the religion-based daily life. For, all of life had become intimately and inextricably tied to the ever-present gods who un-mistakably symbolized the ecological system for the people.

Hawaiians had learned these conservation practices over the centuries the hard way: from earlier mistakes. For instance, in exploiting bird feathers for royal cloaks to meet ali'i demands, they had hunted some species into extinction.

Again ideally, no one would take a fish or a tree or work the soil without first asking the gods' permission and then apologize for any harm inadver-tently done. Although such practices might become routine, they never to-tally lost sincerity. But when the massive impact of foreign change struck in the 1800s, these traditional conservation practices went the way of most customs—as discredited and obsolete.

Until then, they had meant survival for people isolated on a few small islands in the middle of a vast ocean. Now a part of a much larger alien world which local people did not understand, conservation became a relic of a bygone era—especially when people saw neither their ali'i nor powerful *haole* (foreigners) practicing the old ways of conservation and recycling.

Western influence began to question this traditional view of land as it did virtually every other aspect of Hawaiian culture during the nineteenth cen-tury. At the same time, the aristocracy grew increasingly concerned about keeping up with aristocractic ostentation elsewhere in the world. They spent lavishly on gowns, palaces, horse racing and entertainment without regard for the needs of their subjects. Commoners literally had to work themselves to death cutting sandalwood forests for export to China to underwrite their rulers' extravagances. Some places (such as western Moloka'i) thusly turned into wastelands from the loss of trees and the subsequent overgrazing by goat herds; they have yet to recover more than a century and a half later.

Haole settlers gained positions of power in Hawaiian government be-cause they could bring Western know-how to help stave off imperialistic grabs by Western nations then actively colonizing much of the world. New ideas about the meaning of land circulated. Economic development by foreigners had already begun. Legal codes needed clarification before more "progress" could occur. Now atune to Western luxuries, the aristocracy came to agree with the foreign entrepreneurs that change could no longer remain in abeyance.

Under this Western influence, a truly radical idea gained currency among the elite, that of private land ownership. In 1848 the king acceded to pressure from his foreign advisers. He declared the Great Mahele to distribute large portions of his lands on a permanent basis. Contrary to later billing however, his much heralded Great Mahele and Kuleana Act two years later put very little land into commoner ownership. After keeping the majority for himself, the king assigned the preponderance of what was distributed to his fellow *ali'i*.

The consequences were tremendous. Commoners long accustomed by the severest of penalties to never question the ruling class now had suddenly to come forward, stand before the elite, and demand ownership in their tiny kuleanas. With no prior experience in these alien laws and legal procedures, with no foundation in democracy and citizen rights, illiterate commoners seldom even asked for land and less often received any if they did take advantage of the 1850 Kuleana Act. Worse yet, the aristocrats who did get title to the land had neither the experience nor interest in farming it.

Given the epidemic of aristocratic spending and hence indebtedness, the new owners quickly sold out to Westerners who did know how to put it to profitable use. Foreign buyers, of course, had no interest in preserving subsistence agriculture. They sought to establish centrally managed plantations like factories in the field. All of which meant that commoners not only lost the use of the land their ancestors had farmed for centuries; they would have to leave.

Either they had to convert into tightly organized production workers on plantations or flee into port towns. Either way, they lacked the skills and cultural motivation for such an alien life style. Some men became sailors who left home and never returned, dying alone of some strange disease on a distant shore. Many simply fell into drunkenness and (for women) prostitution for which port towns always had a ready market.

Probably the worst aspect of this transition came with the loss of their all-important *ohana* extended family system. Once removed from the land and dispersed, they lacked the social and emotional support the *ohana* had always provided. And nothing else evolved to replace it.

Their traditions and religious base gone, forced off the land their wellspring of cultural strength, with Westerners pressuring them to change their dress, life style, and mating practices, Hawaiian commoners lost hope. Missionaries had long suppressed native music and dance as lascivious and condemned surfing and games as wasteful indolence. Public education then consistently denigrated everything Hawaiian in preference for haole culture from America.

With the loss of hope, their immune systems further deteriorated. Diseases which once had taken a toll now became epidemics even more devastating proportionally than Europe had experienced in its fourteenth century Black Plague. The final blow came in 1893 with the overthrow of the monarchy by foreign planters and businessmen, then annexation by the United States a few years later.

Eventually—in 1920—Prince Kuhio, Hawaii's first representative (nonvoting) to the US Congress, managed to have legislation passed to establish an Hawaiian Homes Commission through which Hawaiians would supposedly once again have an opportunity to return to the land. Two-thirds of a century later, only a fraction of eligible Hawaiians have ever experienced the promise in that legislation. Some have had their names on the list for decades without success.

Soon territorial governors saved funds in building airports and other public facilities to serve non-Hawaiian interests by usurping large amounts of the best land set aside for Hawaiian use. Commissioners always claimed a lack of front end funds to provide the requisite infrastructure for homestead development. Yet even after statehood in 1959, governors continued to protect their budgets by refusing to pay rent to the Homes Commission for the land seized illegally from it. So too did federal agencies occupying Hawaiian Homes land. Until the 1980s, Hawaiians remained too intimidated and too divided to demand their rights.

Once foreigners held the agricultural lands and found the indigenous population ill-suited for their ideas of workforce performance, efforts to bring in foreign workers began. First came Chinese; though hard workers, they tended to leave as soon as their contracts expired so that they could go into business and own land themselves. Japanese workers, the next imported group, might remain longer but similarly sought to enter the professions and set their children on an upwardly mobile track.

With the overthrow of the monarchy by restive haole business interests at the end of the nineteenth century, Hawaii's educational system became increasingly oriented toward maintaining a marked cleavage between all working-class people (whether Hawaiian or the children of imported Asians) on the one hand and the Hawaiian elite and upper-level Westerners on the other. Instilling obedience and diligent work habits took priority; definitely not aspirations for higher education, professional careers, and intellectual pursuits. Children of the elite went to private schools with a markedly different orientation.

The traditional honor associated with literacy and white-collar professions, coupled with a strong sense of family among Chinese and Japanese, had them push their children ahead even against heavy counter-pressures by the dominant class. Hawaiian children had no such tradition of upward mobility. Their culture had always emphasized social harmony where an acquisitive spirit met disapproval as highly disruptive.

Not surprisingly, Hawaiians became victims not only of their own elite and of a foreign entrepreneurial class; they fell behind the immigrant workers who, as they rose in the professions, especially teaching, looked down on them also. Forced to endure an education system that judged individuals by their individual performance instead of on cooperative effort among peers as traditional among Hawaiians, they became lost in the early grades. Polynesians still have the lowest educational attainments, highest morbidity rates from poor diets, and highest welfare and criminal records.

While their public school experience during this century denigrated their social and cultural roots, tourist interests exploited and twisted their artistry into forms more Hollywood than Hawaiian. Never having had a tradition of land ownership, few Hawaiians could perceive land as a means for ordinary individuals to amass wealth by monopolizing control of its use and exploiting those who needed it, a prospect previously open only to their ruling class.

Ironically, the state motto of Hawaii still proclaims the old Hawaiian value—that the life of the land is preserved in righteousness—in a society where Hawaiians long ago became dispossessed of that land and thereby lost their souls.

Kaneohe Bay Region

Located on the windward side of Oahu across the Ko'olau Mountains from Honolulu, Kaneohe Bay is this state's largest enclosed body of water. Although it would appear on a map to lie almost indistinguishable from the ocean, in reality a barrier reef effectively separates it from open water, thereby making it a lagoon. It is also a composite estuary where sea waters meet freshwater discharge from numerous streams.

The bay, encompassing 11,360 acres, runs for eight miles in a northwest/southeast direction and is 2.6 miles wide. Only a ship channel at the north end and what is called a sampan channel at the south end allow passage between the bay and ocean. The north channel was dredged to a 34 foot depth; the south channel is only some ten feet deep.

In addition to the barrier reef, two other kinds of coral formations occur within the bay. A fringing reef hugs much of the shoreline. Scattered throughout the area in between, coral heads (known also as patch reefs) have grown nearly to the surface.

Surrounding much of the bay only two or three miles away, deeply fluted cliffs rise dramatically one- to two-thousand feet. *Pali* in the Hawaiian language, these nearly vertical cliffs clearly delineate the Kaneohe Bay Region and force the warm, moist, prevailing tropical trade winds to rise, cool, and drop their heavy loads as rain on nearby mountain tops.

Rain runoff on the windward side is short, swift, and readily laden with silt. More significantly, rains can fall in horrendous diluges of eight to ten inches within a single 24-hour period on a small segment of the region yet drop barely an inch only a few miles away. The disastrous 1969 flood followed a one-day 20-inch downpour on top of a week of heavy rain.

In pre-Western times, Kaneohe's fertile lands, good supply of fresh water, and abundant fish gave this enclosed region what appears to have been the largest concentration of population anywhere on this island and one of the larger populations throughout the archipelago. This situation would change dramatically after Westerners arrived.

Kualoa at the north end of Kaneohe Bay enjoys the distinction as one of the first locales (if not the first) on Oahu settled by exploring Polynesians from the south. It retains particular historic and religious significance as a result. With a spectacular sweep of the bay and mountains, it has become a popular park in recent years even though badly eroded due to wave action after the Parks Department cleared all sand-retaining scrub vegetation for greater recreational use.

Other places in the bay region hold high religious significance, too. For, it was on Mokapu Peninsula where the Hawaiian god of creation, Kane, created the first man and woman. At Kaneohe, Kane taught humans to practice circumcision, hence the name Kaneohe. At Waikane—"the water of Kane"—Kane struck the land with his staff and brought forth water. Hawaiians built a *heiau* on He'eia Kea Peninsula, now a state park, dedicated to Kane "the giver of life," the one god to whom they never made human sacrifices.

Long a favorite locale for residence by Oahu kings, Ko'olaupoko district (of which Kaneohe Bay region comprised half) had perhaps the largest fish pond reserved exclusively for royalty, that known now as Kawainui Marsh. Once he had conquered Oahu, King Kamehameha retained much of Kaneohe for his personal use. Later, he bequeathed this area, including Kahalu'u and Kualoa, to his sons Liholiho and Kauikeaouli.

Some two-dozen fish ponds once lined Kaneohe Bay's shores. A few, such as the one at Kualoa, remain in operation for raising seafood. The largest one, Loko I'a O He'eia with 88 acres halfway up the bay, ceased production due to repeated flooding during the heyday of nearby urban development in the 1960s when development controls were minimal at best. Once slated to become a private marina, it remains in Bishop Estate ownership. Despite the Estate's avowed educational mission for the Hawaiian people, Bishop Estate trustees have yet to utilize this great fishpond as an educational resource.

Determining how many people lived around the bay in the early decades of Western contact defies exactness, estimates ranging from six to twenty thousand prior to 1830; consensus: about 15,000. What is certain is the marked decline thereafter. By the 1835-36 census, only 3,000 people lived here. This number had halved by 1849 and would not rise before 1870. It never reached its 1830 level until 1920. Only after WWII when tunnels pierced the Koolau Mountains to provide easy commuter access to Honolulu would population increases accelerate to 40,000 by 1980.

What happened in the Kaneohe Bay region typifies the Great Mahele land distribution in the 1850s. Only 460 kuleana awards went to commoners, none of them for more than ten acres. Some as small as .15 acres, they averaged only two acres. After the preponderance went to chiefs, three alone sold 29,700 acres to foreigners. Chiefs actually refused to sell to commoners even when they offered to pay for the land they had always farmed.

AGRICULTURE

One report on Ko'olaupoko in 1789 described productive farms of taro, sweet potatoes, and sugar cane. An acre of wet taro then could supply food for 20 to 30 people throughout the year without having to lie fallow. Though still cultivated as late as the 1940s, taro (the base ingredient in the Hawaiian staple, *poi*) suffered its demise with the introduction of the destructive grayfish.

Hawaiian families had grown sugar cane for their own enjoyment, but never as a commercial crop. Newcomers dramatically changed that. By 1865, three sugar mills had located in this region: at Kualoa, Waihe'e, and Kaneohe. Foreign planters vigorously sought a reciprocity agreement with the US and finally achieved it in 1876 At that point, sugar gained major importance in the cultural as well as economic life of Hawaii. Eight plantations suddenly springing to life in just the Kaneohe Bay region alone underscores this observation. But the optimism was short lived. Only two plantations remained here by 1885; none after 1903 even though a railroad had been built around the island to serve them.

Made a commercial crop in the 1860s by Chinese who had left plantation labor, rice retained its importance until rice birds, pests, less expensive rice from California, and a lack of Chinese laborers brought its demise in the 1920s. Other crops flourished for commercial purposes at various times—such as: cabbage, radishes, onions, turnips, beans, and lotus root. But farmers grew lichi, mango, lungan, pomelo, and banana mostly for home consumption, as they previously had done with sugar cane.

Begun at the start of this century, pineapple production reached commercial significance between 1910 and 1925, then declined on this side of Oahu. But in those years, it wrought havoc with bay corals because the extensive straight-line plowing practiced then encouraged heavy runoff of topsoil and hence heavy sedimentation. No longer could the neglected ancient Hawaiian irrigation works check this abundance of silt as they had for Hawaiian agriculture.

By the 1840s, livestock raising got underway. Judd's Kualoa Ranch turned to cattle after sugar proved uneconomic; it still conducts cattle operations. Dairies made their appearance in the 1880s and remained until forced out by urban development in the 1970s. Over the decades, livestock occasionally got loose, turned feral, and contributed (along with overgrazing of domestic herds and feral hogs) to serious deforestation and thus to further sedimentation in bay waters.

Under natural conditions, Windward Oahu had an abundance of fresh water whereas the central Oahu plain had too little. It took little imagination for Hawaii's haole business elite to see what windward water transported leeward could accomplish for profitable agriculture. Between 1913 and 1916, a system of 27 interconnected ditches and lesser tunnels, 37 stream intakes, and a major tunnel through the mountain made possible a flourishing agricultural industry on the dry leeward side for the first time. After that, pineapple and sugar cane production on Oahu proved quite successful with yields per acre not attained anywhere in the world for decades.

But that act, and subsequent additional diversions of Windward Oahu water, took a toll on traditional Hawaiian agriculture. Waiahole Stream, for instance, would only receive two-fifths of its previous water flow, too little for taro and rice. The Haiku tunnel in 1940 had a similar impact on Kahalu'u and Ioleka'a Streams. A tunnel at Kahalu'u in 1946 and another at Waihe'e in 1955 further reduced freshwater in the Kaneohe region, with commensurate ecological effects on wildlife as well as agriculture.

BAY WATERS

In pre-Western times, Hawaiians made excellent use of the bay. The ahupua'a rimming the shore ran out across the waters to the barrier reef thereby guaranteeing each local community a share of the protein supply contained in this estuary's then abundant fish life. Despite the extensive changes on land mentioned above, bay resources continued to serve local people. When major changes did occur, however, they were devastating.

First came a neglect of fishponds and serious sedimentation from plowing for pineapple cultivation in the 1910s. Then large-scale dynamiting and dredging began in 1939 and increased with the approach of WWII. This was done to create a ship entrance and to clear a 38-foot deep lane down the center of the bay for ocean-going ships to reach the south end's military installation. Further blasting of coral heads sought to create seaplane landing areas here. (When attacking Pearl Harbor on 7 December 1941, Japanese airplanes hit the observation flying boats at Kaneohe so that they could not scout for the aircraft carriers which brought the attackers.)

Some of the dredged materials went to fill in what is now the runway portion of the Marine air station on Mokapu Peninsula. But much dredged material was simply dumped, thereby smothering those corals not removed by dynamiting. After the war, continued dedging provided materials to fill in ancient fishponds as sites for new homes. Only in 1968 did tougher restrictions finally authorize U.S. Army Corps of Engineers enforcement to effectively end further dredging.

However, that involved only one kind of insult to the bay ecosystem. With large stretches of land exposed by extensive bulldozing in the 1960s for residential tracts, even small rains could turn the bay a sickening red with silt. Just then this region received a series of record-setting rainstorms.

Previously the corals had managed to shake off storm-created situation; and traditional land-use practices by the Hawaiians had absorbed rather than aggravated flooding conditions.

But now, bulldozing went on with few checks or controls. Nothing held back the silt, and the region's top soil flowed into the bay. It washed away in such quantities and frequency as to overwhelm the coral's recuperative capabilities. Stretches of former beach sand turned into bogs of ugly mud.

About the same time, another traumatic impact struck the bay's ecosystem, that of high concentrations of nutrients in the form of sewage. The Marine Corps Air Station began discharging untreated affluent into the bay in 1951. At the same time, increasing population in Kaneohe town generated a need for a wastewater plant with secondary treatment.

Inadequate analysis of the bay's replenishment flushing capacities led the Honolulu's City Public Works Department in 1963 to construct the outfall into the bay—and to do so at the most southern end where the least amount of flushing can occur. Instead of the four-day flushing cycle estimated by engineers originally, actual experience revealed the cycle took up to ten times that long.

Soon scientists at the University of Hawaii's Institute of Marine Biology (HIMB) on Coconut Island (made famous on television as Giligen's Island) grew alarmed at the rapid devastation occurring to what were once world-famous corals and the focus of their research. Not only had the ecosystem undergone stress and change; *Dictyosphaeria cavernosa* (commonly known as green-bubble algae) had increased in abundance and begun devouring what corals had somehow remained alive.

In response to HIMB cries of alarm, the State Department of Health conducted a detailed study of Kaneohe Bay in 1969 but found no problems. Concerned with health dangers to humans, DOH had not thought in terms of an ecological system in trauma. Its staff and officials could not see the problem because they were looking at the wrong thing.

But this was a time when Americans first became aware of ecology in their environment and to the dangers of pollution in general, thanks to Rachel Carson's best-seller, *Silent Spring*. Working together, various citizen groups—such as the Outdoor Circle, Kaneohe and Kahalu'u Community

Councils, Windward Citizens Planning Conference (Hawaii has no local municipalities)—joined by numerous university professors, began to mobilize in 1970. They formed a united organization known as "Kaneohe Bay in Crisis" to get the attention of public officials.

First, they blocked construction of a planned power plant along Kaneohe Bay's shoreline that would have added thermal pollution on top of the other problems plaguing bay waters. At this point the City and landowner abandoned, without a fight, any idea of developing the fuel storage and industrial complex designated on the official land-use plan for the area now containing the Valley of the Temples cemetery.

Then this coalition of citizen groups undertook to draft a much needed grading ordinance for the City. Eventually such an ordinance, when adopted by City Council, began to check what had been unrestrained disturbance of the land without respect for those normally heavy rains of winter. Mayor Fasi gave public recognition to the citizen input, even though civil servant technicians in his administration haughtily denied in a letter to the newspaper that they had need for outside assistance.

In concert with this citizens movement, Governor Burns appointed a Kaneohe Bay Task Force in 1971. Along with persons chosen from the aforementioned groups, it included the Marine Air Station commander and a prominent developer who was a longtime Kaneohe resident. This task force, chaired by the director of the newly established Office of Environmental Quality Control (himself a federal expert in the this field on loan to the State), built a case for diverting the sewage outfall from Kaneohe Bay to the open ocean.

The Governor's Environmental Council (which included the editor of the state's largest newspaper, the chairman of the dominant Democratic Party, several distinguished university professors, a labor leader, a spokesperson for the Bay Task Force, and other individuals of influence) proved effective in getting the appropriate political and administrative wheels in gear and moving concertedly. And the task force, on a person to person basis, overcame objections by nearby Kailua residents against running the outfall from their shore where it could go out further and deeper and thereby disperse its effluent safely below the thermocline.

Eventually the State and City obtained the needed funding. With a sewage outfall diversion constructed, the principal source of sewage ceased flowing into the bay in 1978. Scientific studies at the time determined most convincingly that nutrients in the sewage had brought on the bay's degradation. Turbidity cleared quite dramatically in only a matter of a few weeks, to a large extent in only days. Longtime boaters experienced shock to discover how close the previously unseen coral heads actually came to the surface.

Yet not everyone was happy. Some fishing interests claimed that less sewage meant less nutrients for fish food. While scientists could not prove such claims wrong, they did demonstrate with a preponderance of evidence that bay waters had improved for fish. They had improved because clearer water would mean a revival of corals, and corals would provided a requisite safe habitat for fish.

What became quite apparent from the related studies was how exceedingly complex estuarine ecosystems, such as Kaneohe Bay, really are. Not only complex; they are exceedingly delicate as well. They operate by their own system and not according to human preferences. The Hawaiians had learned that lesson; Westerners came to that understanding much later. Both had to learn from their myopic mistakes.

In Conclusion

According to his journal entries for the 1770s, Captain James Cook took particular note of the exceedingly good health evident among Hawaiians. He observed their graceful way of walking, their strength in work, and their athleticism in play.

Research by Dr. Richard Kekuni Blaisdell, a physician and University of Hawaii professor of medicine, accords with Capt. Cook's assessment that ancient Hawaiians (before the arrival of Europeans) had no epidemic contagious diseases and few dental problems. Commoners did not drink alcoholic beverages or take drugs whereas they did eat a high-fiber, low-fat diet rich in minerals and vitamins. They also got plenty of daily exercise through work and play. Moreover, they practiced a culture oriented toward personal hygiene and sanitation. The absence of tobacco and mosquitoes helped, too.

As Dr. Blaisdell demonstrated, even low-ranking Hawaiians had something more important than life-style for healthful living. They had a sense of belonging to the cosmos, a state closely tied to parents and family group (*ohana*) to be passed on to future generations. Each person sought to achieve *lokahi*—harmony with one's physical, emotional, and spiritual self, with others, and with the universe. Disruption of this encompassing harmony meant loss of the spiritual power known as *mana*. Loss of mana, in turn, brought shame, illness, and eventually death—exactly what did happen to them when their community system crumbled. And with their loss of community went their beneficial interaction with the ecological system they had felt themselves an integral part of.

Since the 1980s, some people of Hawaiian ancestry have sought to revive their culture and identity, even to demanding governmental recognition of Hawaiian sovereignty. Unfortunately for this effort, too few individuals with sufficient prestige to serve as influential role models are fluent in the Hawaiian language. And too few can agree on what would denote a true Hawaiian renaissance and sovereignty, much less agree on the most practical strategies for achieving them.

While interest in traditional dance and chants has grown, much of the music has succumbed to non-Hawaiian influences and many students are ethnically not Hawaiian. Moreover, few if any young people undergo the rigorous years of disciplined training necessary for true mastery of what ancient culture does remain. For most people, this effort to reestablish a sense of Hawaiian community goes no further than a similar effort among African-Americans on the mainland: a change in hairdo or shirt, possibly a change of name. Physical dispersion, overcrowding, industrialization, and a very different form of governance run by ethnically non-Hawaiians simply make a fully reconstituted ohana system unworkable today.

An occasional luau or hula festival might invigorate nostalgia for a long-lost era —only to produce a woeful letdown when reality returns next day. Try as they might, a viable, functioning, emotionally supportive community for ethnic Hawaiians cannot rise out of the flood of non-Hawaiian culture which continues ever increasingly to inundate them. Indeed, intermarriage now makes it impossible even for Hawaiians to decide who is ethnically

Hawaiian for inclusion if they could somehow resurrect the spirit and practicalities of *ohana*.

In the rescue of Kaneohe Bay from total degradation—despite its great historical significance for Hawaiian culture—virtually all the key players were non-Hawaiian. Hawaiians had lost too much of their once personal, communal, and sacred linkage to the lands and waters. Others would determine either destruction or preservation, on economic or political grounds. Indeed, the grounds for such decisions too often lay beyond the emotional and political grasp of most ethnic Hawaiians. They had become aliens in their own land because they had lost the force that could have preserved their sense of effective (rather than nostalgic) identity and concerted will. They had lost their community and with it went their collective soul.

ANOTHER CANDIDATE CASE, VIETNAM

Vietnam provided for me another type of case for probing into the essence and process of community. During 1967-68 as a consultant to Stanford Research Institute (now SRI International) for a USAID sponsored research project on land reform in that country, I has an opportunity to travel throughout, venturing everywhere from farming villages to industrial places and even remote hill areas while conducting the peasant and landlord surveys. For the purposes of this book, I relate in capsule form only one pertinent aspect of my observations.

Entering one hamlet I might find well mended houses, clean roads, men and women working together industriously. The next hamlet might appear dishevelled, the women wielding picks and sledge hammers to build a road while the men sat around with guns supposedly guarding. Members of the first hamlet displayed a sense of cohesion, as evident in their self-defense record, while the people in the second hamlet frowned suspiciously at each other, ever ready to accuse each other as a VC or government collaborator. The first kind of hamlet convincingly demonstrated relative prosperity despite the war, whereas the second epitomized the breakdown of infrastructure and of public administration so typical of on-going civil wars.

What obserable factor might best account for, or at least indicate, what underlay such marked contrasts within a single ethnic groups? (The other ethnic communities visited displayed still other indicators of their community identity and commitment.) The single must telling factor was whether hamlet members belonged to one religious persuasion or to several. Be it Cao Dai, Hoa Hao, or Roman Catholic, a single strongly held religioug commitment did unifyor at least focus communal energies and made cleavages cut through the hamlet mutual suspicions and hostilities eroded a sense of border responsibility among all residents. They became distinct communities which just happened, uncomfortably, to share the same locale.

To fully probe these divisions and the cultural milieu that gave rise to this diversity in communal experience, we would have to explore the cultural history of Vietnam as we did for Japan over the same time frame. Certainly both were heavily influenced by China. Like the Japanese expansion and conquest of aboriginal peoples, the Vietnamese only achieve full dominance within the last two hundred years. Yet they evolved quite differently—as evident at the basic scale of local hamlet and village.

A long-held adage in Vietnam saw the emperor's rule ending where the village began. And the communal processes of village life—however oriented, and for better or worse—still go far in shaping that culture and society, even when people move into urbanized locales.

BIBLIOGRAPHY

Atlas of Hawaii. 1983.

Bushnell, Oswald. *Ka'a'awa.* 1972.*

Bushnell, Oswald. *The Return of Lono.* 1971.*

Bushnell, Oswald. *Molokai.* 1963.*

Cooper, George & Gavan Daws. *Land and Power in Hawaii.* 1985.

Daws, Gavan. *Hawaii: the Island of Life.* 1988.

Devaney, D.M. et al. *Kaneohe: A History of Change.* 1976.

Fuchs, Lawrence H. *Hawai'i Pono.* 1961.

Goldman, Irving. *Ancient Polynesian Society.* 1970.

Kelly, Marion. *Loko I'a O He'eia.* 1975.

Kolb, Michael J. "Monumentality and the Rise of Religious Authority in Precontact Hawaii." *Current Anthropology.* Vol.34, No.5. Dec.1994.

Smith, Stephen V. et al. "Kaneohe Bay Sewage Diversion Experiment," *Pacific Science.* 1979.

State of Hawaii. *Hawaii Water Resources Plan.* 1979.

US Army Crops of Engineers. *Kaneohe Bay Urban Water Resources Study.* 1978.

Windward Citizens Planning Conference [Oahu]. *Planning for a Total Community System.* 1971.

---

* Historical novels written by an eminent biologist, each with a medical theme.

Part Three

Community as Coaction

Introduction

So far we have looked at human behavior as the manifestation of culture or culture as the sum total of what people do and what tools they use. So long as we limit our vision to people's ways of interacting with each other (their customs and morés) or to their beliefs and technology, simply identifying a people as a society because they practice a particular culture or identifying a culture because many people behave similarly may suffice. But the functional operations of large, complex societies appear to go far beyond the behavior of individuals, beyond even the influence of institutionalized organizations.

The cases examined so far suggest, at least to me, that more is involved. Without allowing for an underlying "force" of coaction, I find it difficult to envision the process that coalesced large-scale societies. How could so much apparent self-organization occur? In this awareness of a seemingly hidden (undifferentiated) force, I am not alone. For thousands of years societies have felt compelled to invent all manner of spirits (goddesses and gods, totems and demons) to help them effectively organize their world view and thereby come to terms with the driving force behind their own society.

This book and particularly this section of it asks whether community might not constitute a "hidden force." Please do not see in this analysis a reification of community as something akin to organic life. Too many conceptual dangers lie in that analogy. But in seeing community within a trinity along with the more tangible ingredients of culture and society, we may have a more apt, or at least a more workable analogy.

As you take the grand tour of change revealed in the next four chapters, try to use the details—try to see through the details—to the flow of change. Question what all of the interactions cited add up to and what they reveal about the society and culture participating in these events. See if they do not suggest the presence of both an arena for interaction and a process in those interactions. See if you can detect how functional interactions translate into symbolic meaning and how symbolic meaning affects functional interactions.

The grand tour of change examined in the next four chapters occurs in a real context of time and place: Orange County California between the 1860s and 1960s. The fifth chapter of this section extracts from our case details the essence of a self-organized complexity: a connected community, a concept with wider applicability. For, we see here what happens elsewhere: community as both the arena and the process of interaction and hence as the principal catalytic agent of adaptation to change. And that interaction takes on characteristics of a system—in particular, a living system—to be examined in Part Four.

CHAPTER EIGHT

ORANGE COUNTY CALIFORNIA IN SEARCH OF COMMUNITY

Gertrude Stein once said of Oakland in northern California, "There is no 'there' there." It failed to convey her expected sense of place. She must not have visited Orange County in southern California back then.

Entering Orange County along the Santa Ana freeway in the early 1960s felt like going from a blah into a punctuated void. The Los Angeles basin had become inundated by miles of look alike residential subdivisions and nondescript commercial or industrial plants. That same spread of housing tracts (they appeared as tracts, not as individual homes) occurred in Orange County, with one difference. Here they had not yet managed to blanket the entire landscape. Urban edges appeared occasionally, separated by unconverted farmland either still in production or merely awaiting crews of house builders.

Less than two decades earlier, skies would have presented a visitor's eyes the same hazy, whitish blue most any time of year. (I had lived there four months before discovering on one of those rare, utterly clear days that I could see snowclad mountains in the distance.) But one's nose would surely have encountered a definite "bouquet." In spring, the syrupy thick aroma of orange blossoms would have drenched and permeated as a visitor drove through miles of orchards. In other places, the sweet smell of hay-fed dairy cows and their swamp of excrement would have imposed an unforgettable impression. Still, farther one could see cowboys watching over their glacially slow-moving herds, as if a set for a Hollywood production.

By 1960, despite the tidal wave of urbanization, no true urban centers had yet emerged. Flying into Orange County by helicopter when a thick tulle fog rolled over it, one could see a vast stretch of white with lines of utility poles, frequent television antennas, and only an occasional building sticking out of the wool-like fluff. Only Anaheim's Disneyland and Newport Beach's harbor full of expensive yachts lent any marked sense of distinction from the rest of Southern California. And they served a national (even international) clientele.

Before freeways arrived in the early 1950s, a visitor to most any inland Orange County town from the American Midwest would have felt completely at home. Other than the absence of towering grain elevators, the sleepy pace along tree-lined streets where neighbors wished each other a good afternoon and old-folks rocked on porches would certainly have seemed familiar. After all, a major segment of Orange County's early settlers had come from the Midwest. For decades they continued to hold giant annual picnics to reaffirm links with the state—whether a Nebraska, Iowa, or Kansas—of their roots.

There were, of course, observable differences: palm trees instead of elms, for instance. Instead of an occasional tornado or hail storm in summer, Orange County had its winter "Santa Anas" when mild ocean breezes give way to unrelenting, bone-dry winds that drive tumbleweed from inland deserts, topple outdoor theater screens, and jolt people with static electrical shocks when touching metal or another person. A week of "Santa Ana" wind may plunge humidity lower than scientific instruments can measure, even forcing postponement of hospital surgery due to its dangerous effect on hemorrhaging.

Unlike New Orleans (described so well by geographer Peirce Lewis in 1979) or unlike San Francisco and Boston, Orange County would not have impressed a first-time observer as inevitable. It had no majestic river or teeming harbor, no center of great historical significance, not even a central city to dominate the social, economic, cultural, and political life.

Orange County then offered nothing romantic, nothing to rhapsodize about, nothing obviously unique. Unlike every small town in Hawaii, places in Orange County (excepting San Juan Capistrano) had no popular songs to memorialize them. It even lacked award-winning restaurants, other than Knotts Berry Farm with its home-style meals which set the general tone.

Still people flocked here in unprecedented numbers. Some sort of magnet lay below the surface, for surely it did draw new residents. Perhaps some of its attraction lay in its being so indistinguishable from "back home" wherever that was. Instead of a structured community, many people sought new choices—an opportunity to find their romanticized dream home in a simple setting so often fantasized by Hollywood as a "good" (a safe) neighborhood where they could raise a happy family. Not surprisingly, the higher their expectations, the more traumatic their eventual disillusionment and explosive frustrations.

Perhaps, too, they sought a new sense of freedom—the freedom of mobility accorded them by their personal automobile on a nearby freeway. They could go in any direction to shop, recreate, worship, and work. Indeed it now seems impossible to visualize Orange County when it did not have a weave of freeways, post-WWII America's most significant public monuments.

Orange County did not escape the bigotry so typical then in towns all across America. Olympic gold-metal winner and professional dentist, Sammy Lee for instance could not buy a home in Garden Grove. Anaheim made a big thing of welcoming the California Angels baseball franchise, then refused to sell homes to its million-dollar-a- year players of Latin derivation. Newport Beach police blatantly harassed Blacks, especially servicemen from nearby US Marine bases, to discourage their visiting public beaches with bikini-clad white girls. Much earlier, Santa Ana's city council decided to rid the town of Chinese by burning down their homes.

Yet voters in another Orange County town (Fountain Valley) elected the first Japanese-American mayor anywhere in America. And this county's largest newspaper, the Santa Ana *Register* (usually thought of as radically conservative), alone among major papers in the US opposed the Army's herding Americans of Japanese ancestry into WWII concentration camps. It even supported UC Berkeley students' rights to protest certain campus bureaucratic decisions in those tumultuous days of the 1960s.

PROTOTYPIC ORANGE COUNTY

In the quarter century from 1966 to 1991, Orange County doubled its population to two and a half million people, incorporated three more municipalities, unified several more school districts, and completed construction on several more freeways. Now high density, high rise buildings accent the landscape and buildable open space is hard to find. A University of California campus already renown for its research breakthroughs next to a booming high-tech industrial park and bustling airport (named naturally for John Wayne): these now typified the new wave of urban configuration and society emerging here. What's more, the magnitude of economic activity would swell by the 1990s until it ranks Orange County among the top dozen in this country and exceeds that evident in a majority of entire countries throughout the world.[1]

Yet this new kind of urban world (made famous in the 1990s by Joel Garreau's *Edge City: Life on the New Frontier*) had already gelled in the 1960s. Its patterns of development and community evolution had become established. Orange County gave birth to "edge city" where it matured over these last three decades and would emerge in other American urban centers.

In looking at these patterns of change we can discern the factors and forces—the driving aspirations and social order, the economic and political processes, the self-perceptions and linkage webs—that operated through time and in space to create both the physical place and interactional networks that characterize what we have come to think of as Orange County. We look at habitat, functional activities, and even the emotions that made Orange County far more than a geographical setting or set of jurisdictions.

More even than these, what we see here telescopes in time and space much of the evolutionary processes and patterns which characterized America's transformation from rural to urban over that century from the

1860s to the 1960s. Indeed, Orange County presents in perspective a digestible composite of American culture restlessly on the move. What we can learn from the 1950s and 1960s still holds much value: not only for its historic dimension, but for the insights it can provide into our unrelenting human movement toward ever greater and more complex urbanization and resource exploitation—and their impacts on emotion-driven people as social, economic, political participants.

From this temporal distance of several decades we may more readily see what to look at and discern more meaning than possible by examining only current situations. This detachment allows us to operate on the subject more clinically. Moreover, Orange County's rapid rate of growth made the strains and tensions, the adjustments and coactions more obvious than evident for community seen under less stressful conditions.

In effect then, Orange County of the 1950s and 1960s provides us a crystal ball for what was less obviously underway throughout urban America and, to some extent, in a post-industrial/information age society elsewhere. To many outside observers (academic and journalistic) back then, though, Orange Co. seemed an anachronism.

Lacking a central city, they saw it as just an oversized suburbia run by "local yokels" for intellectuals to sneer at. They failed to see that Orange County was ahead of its time. (The Census Bureau fell into the same blind hole by refusing to name this SMSA by its county name, insisting on a collection of city names in keeping with its antiquated image of how a metropolitan area must be structured.)

Establishing the Facts

To gain some useful insights, we explore detailed time and place factors and events. We begin by establishing the record of settlements, economic activity, infrastructure development, school district formations, municipal incorporations, spatial distribution of land use, transportation and communications, water limitations, and social cohesion. What all of these happenings really mean comes out later when we can interrelate them and see what linkages emerge. Obviously these aspects of Orange County involve a vast range of interactions provisioning necessities for human survival in a modern-day setting.

I started with the standard sources: census figures over the previous eighty years, then histories of local jurisdictions (especially municipalities and school districts), publications by county and local units of government, and whatever printed sources reported on any part or aspect of the county. Attendance at many County Supervisor meetings and other agencies, then interviews with the five members of that governing body and several department heads provided insights into the range of issues and strategies used here in resolving issues.

I then embarked on an extensive interview schedule, spending anywhere from a half hour to three hours (depending on the issues and availability of interviewees' time) with every city manager, then school superintendents of the larger districts. Already a member of the countywide professional planners association, I could readily arrange for interviews with all planning directors and with section heads within the large county planning department.

Directors of several important special districts (water, sewer, harbor) granted me useful interviews. From these I went on to interview mayors, city council members, and newsworthy politicians throughout the county. Only one (out of the many dozens asked) refused an interview and that one because she was engaged just then in a rather dirty recall campaign. The controversial editor of the county's largest newspaper, the Santa Ana *Register*, gave me an entire afternoon packed with interesting inside information.

After digging through local records and picking memories of old-timers and newcomer activists alike, I could put together a picture of change over some sixty years of people who headed county and municipal departments or who succeeded in bids for elected office. A questionnaire survey of contemporary professionals and elected officials then revealed the process of transformation from "local old-boy" cronyism to a highly professionalized, well educated public servant, a large portion of them originally not local and hence known as "hired guns."

Eventually I sought more particularized data, such as auto registration and daily trips, phone call patterns (from the two telephone companies serving the county), and newspaper circulation. One long-time community leader and professional engineer turned over his office to me for an entire week to comb his extensive collection of newspaper clippings about almost every aspect of life in Orange County over the previous half century.

Several other exceedingly well versed local residents provided their own unpublished histories and essays about such topics as the 1920s' KKK upheaval and 1950s' John Birch turmoil. My position with the university opened information about the Irvine Company and nonprofit organizations. Contacts with the region's largest developers brought more insights. I even sat in (most uncomfortably) on several meetings by extremist groups.

Chapter five probes these collected data on functional activities and resulting emotional spinoffs. It uses the evident web of mutually symbiotic dependencies and the internalized reactions to and identification with this web of relationships as it constructs a picture of community. (We might name what emerges a "comsystem" for short since it is the cultural equivalent of "ecosystem.") Here we recognize a systemic dimension to community for it has relevance at a range of scales, from family to town to region and on to nation. To that extent, it offers a useful tool of analysis and therein lies its validity.

CHAPTER NINE

SETTLEMENT PATTERNS

Overshadowed by Los Angeles, Orange County's rectangular 796 square miles run northwest by southeast along the Pacific Ocean; the coastline curves in between Santa Barbara and the Mexican Border. Mountains to the east and southeast further delineate Orange County from its far larger neighboring counties of San Bernardino, Riverside, and San Diego.

Only its northwest side (next to Los Angeles) provides no natural delineation, other than a concrete flood-control channel. Not surprisingly, it was originally (until 1889) a part of Los Angeles County. And from that direction would come most of the forces for developmental change. Try as its leaders might, Orange County never could escape the gravitational pull of, and reaction to, its much larger neighbor—at least through the time data were collected for this study in the mid-1960s.

THE SPANISH

The first permanent non-Amerindian settlement occurred in the 1770s at San Juan Capistrano, later made famous in song and legend by the yearly punctual return of the swallows. Despite scant rainfalls typical of a desert, this Spanish mission lay in what was then a sufficiently watered, narrow valley astride the most obvious route between other early missions at San Diego, Los Angeles, and on up the coast.

When Mexico gained its independence from Spain and secularized all mission lands in the 1830s, the indigenous population already lay crushed by brutality and decimated by calculated starvation and alien diseases. Mexican citizens of Spanish ancestry could carve out huge ranchos for cattle-raising with the help of Indian labor, such as it was. The first change to hit this region, then, was colonization by missionaries. The second change occurred through secular feudalization by Spanish cattle barons.

From all first-hand accounts, the society of the great Spanish families must have exuded color, despite their remoteness from urban life. They had bull fighting, fiestas, horse racing and gambling, gracious living and hospitality among the elite. There also came a feudal system of distinct caste cleavages, male dominance, and peonage for Indians and lower class half-breeds. Gentlemanly honor among the landed and fear among the Indians meant that, according to legend, a wagon load of supplies could stand in the street all day without its owner worrying about anything being stolen. (Richard Henry Dana provided a glimpse of cattle operations here in his *Two Years Before the Mast;* one town would be named Dana Point for him.)

Then the Anglos (as Americans were called) arrived. The first ones, coming while California remained under Mexican control, married into the ruling class and lived by its standards. Their land holdings would eventually run into the hundreds of thousands of acres. The Spanish baron's days were, however, numbered when the Treaty of Hidalgo ceded California to the US in 1846 and the discovery of gold in 1848 set off a tidal wave of Anglos who would begin to move southward as settlers after their gold fever wore off.

The newly appointed Senator for the new state of California, William M. Gwin, had Congress enact a law establishing a land commission to adjudicate land titles. According to historian R.G. Cleland, Mexican landowners suddenly had to operate in a legal process they did not understand with a language they did not speak and to produce long-since destroyed documents or departed eye-witnesses to sustain their vague land titles.

Here was a case of men, whose honor had (in their own culture) stood beyond question, having to prove ownership to land which everyone knew was theirs. To fight for their land, the basis of their social, economic, and political status, they had to hire Anglo attorneys. But their capital lay in land. They would have to mortgage the very thing they were fighting to save. With interest rates exceeding two percent per month, they soon lost their land to pay lawyers to defend their claims.

All twenty claimants in Orange County won their cases. Yet most of the land moved into Anglo hands anyway. Ironically, many an Anglo who thusly acquired the land fared no better. Ecological conditions simply could not support increased cattle operations; drought, so common here, finished them off. When the Civil War curtailed the availability of cotton back East and in Europe; the demand for fibre changed Orange County's economic equation again. Ranchers shifted to sheep raising—for a few years, at least.

Onto this scene of uncertain markets and ownership turnover came James Irvine, a Scotch immigrant and successful San Francisco entrepreneur, in 1874. The 110,000 acres he assembled (the central fifth of Orange County, running from the ocean to the mountains) launched a land "dynasty" that would exert lasting impact on the future of this region. It would once his son, James Jr., inherited and ran it. Until James Jr. took control and moved the family base from San Francisco to Orange County (after the great earthquake), the Irvine ranch had remained in the wool business. It would now change into a giant producer of oranges.

THE FIRST ANGLO SETTLEMENTS

A group of German immigrants established the first Anglo town in the future Orange County at the junction of the principal wagontrails, one paralleling the coast and the other connecting a Mormon settlement at San Bernardino to its ocean port These Germans had prospered sufficiently in San Francisco to have some investment capital, yet not enough to do well there.

Although they were musicians, locksmiths, shoemakers, and assorted craftsmen rather than farmers, they took a gamble on a site they named Anaheim near enough to the Santa Ana River for irrigation. There they laid out equal plots and drew lots for their ownership. Before the new owners arrived in 1859, a crew using imported Indian labor built structures and planted the grape vines. Wine would form this colony's economic base.

A decade later various developer/settlers would begin to lay out and promote new towns: Columbus Tustin founded one which bears his name. William Spurgeon established a rival named Santa Ana, the future county seat. Little happened until the Southern Pacific Railroad arrived from Los Angeles in 1875.

It took Anaheim residents much debate to make up their minds whether or not they wanted the tracks to go through their town and thereby diminish some settler's vineyards. Seventy-five years later Anaheim would experience the same turmoil over the issue of whether the first freeway, similarly from Los Angeles, should enter or remain outside of town—with identical results. They elected to have it by-pass their town.

Spurgeon had no hesitation, however; he anted up what the SP wanted and so secured the rail line for Santa Ana, leaving nearby Tustin a tiny village for the next eighty years. He had done the same maneuver earlier in garnering the stage coach station for his town. (Santa Ana would later welcome the freeway as close as feasible.)

Collins P. Huntington, president of Southern Pacific, intended to push his Los Angeles line on from Santa Ana to San Diego. He had successfully bowled his way over everyone else throughout California and expected to do the same here. But Huntington did not reckon the likes of James Irvine, once his shipmate on the journey around the Horn.

First he had the Solicitor General challenge Irvine's land titles. When that failed, he had his construction crew try the usual fiat accompli of constructing the line on a weekend before the landowner could get an injunction. Irvine, however, had his ranch hands and tenant farmers line up along the property line, their rifles at the ready. In that showdown with all the drama of a Western cinema, it was the Southern Pacific which backed down. Huntington's railroad never did reach San Diego. Instead, the Irvine trustees made a deal with Huntington's rival, the Santa Fe Railway in 1887.

The Santa Fe's arrival in 1886 touched off the first of several land speculation "wars." With fares as low as a dollar for passage from Chicago to California, settlers poured in. Santa Ana's population grew five-fold in just the 1880s alone. During the two-year land bubble of 1886-88, "cities" of Fairview, Carlton, McPhearson, San Juan-by-the-Sea, St. James, Olive,

Richfield, Aliso Bay, Aliso City, Crestline, Catalina-on-the-Main, and Earlham were surveyed and promoted nationwide. For the most part they died aborning, the chief cause of their demise: a lack of water. It is next to impossible now to determine exactly where most of them once were, except where a later discovery of oil generated law suits over clouded land titles. Only Fullerton and Buena Park, among this crop of promotional towns, survived the speculative bust of the 1890s.

Meanwhile Anaheim faced a crisis in 1885 after prospering quite well as a wine center. Suddenly their vines shrivelled; a blight wiped out some 25,000 of them. Not only the wine industry but raisin production ended too. (The same thing happened to walnuts around San Juan Capistrano just when Orange County billed itself the walnut capital of the world.) Large farmers in other nearby towns, desperately searching also for a substitute crop, eventually would discover the affinity of oranges for the growing conditions here. The valentia orange, brought from the Azores, did especially well.

Unfortunately, no sizable local market existed. To the rescue came the timely development of refrigerated railroad cars. Citrus ranchers, an appellation they came to prefer, could now realize substantial profits by safely shipping their harvest to East Coast markets. Ironically, the county's name did not come from the fruit that would later make it prosperous. Orange County had already broken away from Los Angeles and had its prophetic name selected, according to legend, through a card game. A different cut of the cards could have made it "Lemon County."

THE BIG RED CARS

Soon after the turn of the century, Orange County experienced a new wave of settlements in small towns ("village" more accurately describes them). These accompanied construction of H.E. Huntington's interurban rail lines fingering out from Los Angeles. Blocked from succeeding his uncle as president of the Southern Pacific, he formed the Pacific Electric and drew anti-SP men to his organization. Soon known affectionately for its Big Red Cars, the PE opted for standard gauge tracks, unlike most interurban lines which used narrow gauge. This way it could haul freight in off-hours to otherwise unserved locales.

Three PE lines reached Orange County. The first one ran through the central farm lands, planting farming towns at Cypress, Stanton, and Garden Grove in 1904. Almost immediately, another line ran along the coast and gave considerable impetus for growth in resort towns at Seal Beach, Sunset Beach, Huntington Beach, and Newport Beach. The third line, this one in the hills to the north, fostered suburban developments at La Habra in 1908, Brea in 1910, and Yorba Linda in 1911 for professionals who commuted to Los Angeles centers of employment.

By 1911 then, the western two-fifths of Orange County held a rather evenly spread dot-pattern of settlements, everyone of them on a rail line, and all of the rail lines linking Orange Countians to a hub in Los Angeles. Even so, these settlements definitely did not fit a single model. Three belts of differing land-uses grew increasingly distinct in their social and political characteristics as well.

The coastal strip produced resort towns often associated more with Hollywood than with the rest of Orange County. The next sector inland we might call the farm belt for it involved dirt farmers. Further inland came the larger and older towns of Anaheim, Fullerton, Placentia, Orange, and Santa Ana on the intercontinental rail lines. Here there located whatever manufacturing Orange County had then, along with the principal commercial and banking centers. The northern-most tier consisted of suburban subdivisions for commuters. The last two of these community clusters jointly constituted the citrus belt.

This differentiation of economic orientation of each belt went a long way in setting the developmental histories of their communities. It fixed them so firmly that decades later (long after their economic functions had changed and a blanket of urbanization had made them mutually indistinguishable), they would continue to respond to challenges differently and view each other by their earlier characterization. For it shaped how community leaders perceived and responded to challenges.

REGIONAL DISTINCTIONS

One example of community-related differentiation in this small region shows up in geographical distributions of county leadership. Over the decades, much of it would come from the landed citrus ranchers who doubled as oil-field owners and as bank officials in the major towns. Other (rival) leaders lived along the coast, especially in Newport Beach. As post-WWII development changed the distribution of status-giving jobs and prestigious neighborhoods, regional influence shifted from the citrus belt to the coast, as we shall examine more closely in a later chapter.

Struggling dirt farmers, caught between the two prosperous citrus and coastal belts, experienced resentments not unlike Mid-West farmers in debt to East Coast bankers. They leaned toward a populism, had the only section of the county with a majority of voters registered as Democrats, and gave Orange County its reputation as the Bible belt of California. The coastal towns, in contrast, gained notoriety between the world wars for wide-open gambling and rum running.

The pattern of municipal incorporations reflects another facet of distinctions manifested by differences in community identification, aspirations, and boosterism. The towns of Anaheim, Santa Ana, and Fullerton on main rail lines inland, and Newport Beach, Huntington Beach, and Seal Beach along the coast had incorporated before WWI. La Habra, Brea, and Placentia did so soon after that war. But none of the farm-belt towns would incorporate until well after WWII.

Yet another example occurs in their differing patterns of population growth over the decades. Between 1930 and 1950, Anaheim would increase 33 percent; Santa Ana by 50 percent; Fullerton, 29 percent; and Orange, 24 percent. In contrast, Seal Beach would experience a 210 percent growth; Coasta Mesa (then unincorporated and linked to Newport Beach), 225 percent; Laguna Beach, 250 percent; San Clemente, 325 percent; and Newport Beach, 450 percent. Only Huntington Beach had a natural hinterland and only it, of the coastal towns, followed the inland pattern by increasing a mere 41 percent.

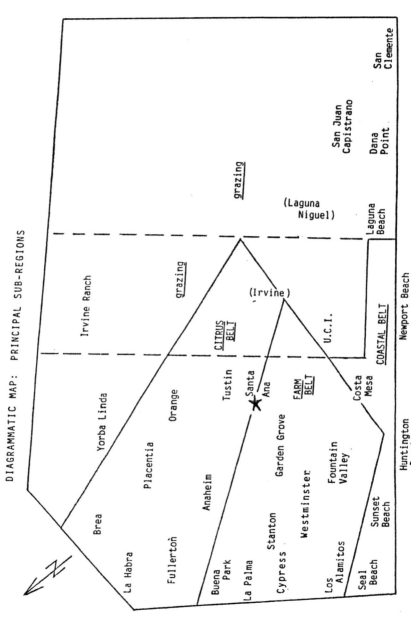

DIAGRAMMATIC MAP: PRINCIPAL SUB-REGIONS

During the 1950s the comparison switched. Coastal town growth would remain rather constant while that for inland towns would skyrocket. Fullerton would see a 325 percentage increase in that one decade; La Habra, a 407 percent growth; and 616 percent for Anaheim. Increases in some farm belt centers ran even more spectacularly: Stanton, 535 percent; 716 percent for Buena Park (in the seven years of 1953-60 alone); 722 percent in Westminster; and 2139 percent for Garden Grove.

In just the first six years of the 1960s, Westminister would doubled its population again. Placentia and Tustin would reach two and half times their 1960 populations. Huntington Beach would hit a sevenfold increase; Fountain Valley, seven and a half times larger; and Costa Mesa, eleven times.

Many other aspects of Orange County's evolution require review, particularly what lay behind these growth data. Only then may we look further into the geographical dispersion of community characteristics over time—especially the growing pains that would accompany this urban boom among erstwhile sleepy farm-belt communities. Space permits our only glancing at what happened to the other three-fifths of the county: the central fifth encompassed by the Irvine Ranch and the balance, the southeast segment. Their era of change had to await the end of World War II and the filling of the western portion.

OIL

For now though, consider the affects of just one geographical variable—the presence or absence of oil—in shaping pre-WWII communities in various parts of Orange County. Although an oil industry had existed for thirty years in Pennsylvania, no one had looked into the black ooze seepages in California until E.L. Doheny began digging it in 1892. By 1894 he had struck and a new "gold" rush was on: for "black gold." Wildcatting began early in this century in Orange County and soon produced large operations around what is now Brea.

Within a few years, oil production made the newly incorporated municipality of Fullerton prosperous. Indeed, for the next half century, oil would, on average, pay an estimated forty percent of all of Fullerton's taxes. Discovered in Placentia in 1919, oil played a role in impeding that community's development as it would later keep Yorba Linda from incorporating. Orange County's greatest oil pool and one of the largest in California was found in Huntington Beach in 1920, much of it under the ocean but close enough to allow slant drilling to reach it from shore. Soon travelers would remember Huntington Beach for its miles of praying mantis-like heads on oil rigs bobbing up and down in a never-ending non-synchronous dance.

For the next forty years oil generated more taxes than any other industry in the county. Not surprising, little happened in Huntington Beach that was not tied to (and usually controlled by) oil interests. Originally laid out in 1901 by P.A. Stanton, a power in the Southern Pacific-dominated state legislature, this town began as Pacific City, "the West Coast's answer to Atlantic City". Soon the Huntington Beach Company, a subsidiary then of H.E. Huntington's Pacific Electric, took it over. Later the PE became a subsidiary of Standard Oil, itself a dominant power in California politics nearly equaling the Southern Pacific of an earlier era.

For several decades, Huntington Beach had served as a resort for the elite of Los Angles whose duck-shooting clubs (the "social register" of southern California) used the Bolsa Chica swamps nearby. So powerful were those members that even the locally influential Farm Bureau found it difficult to obtain an ordinance barring, for duck-pond replenishment, the use of a woefully inadequate freshwater supply so critically needed for agriculture and residential life.

When oil field development began on the bluffs above fashionable Newport Beach, that municipality would run a one-foot wide annexation strip for several miles around the field so that the more contiguous community of Costa Mesa could not capture it. Not for lack of exploring, neither Newport Beach nor the Irvine Ranch ever found oil within their boundaries.

Death came to PE's interurban lines soon after WWII. It was not simply a case of "progress" in the form of automobiles replacing trains in a natural market process. Oil interests and automobile interests joined forces to buy out and then dismantle these beloved trains. Orange and Los Angeles Counties have tried every since to resurrect such a service, their chief obstacles of course being the horrendous costs faced to acquire rights-of-way and to serve a clientele now spread rather evenly like a blanket across the land, everyone wanting to go in all directions rather than between high density centers.

Oil and citrus in Orange County would greatly impact the life and outlook of a future US President. Born in an area of stony poor soil known as Yorba Linda, Richard Milhaus Nixon heard as a child the bitter feelings by unsuccessful farmers and small-time entrepreneurs (such as his father) over what they perceived a grave injustice. Here they were, God-fearing, Bible-loving, law-abiding, teetotaling, White Anglo-Saxon Protestants seeking out a living by hard work while just down the hill they could see wine and beer-drinking Catholics of Mexican ancestry in Placentia growing wealthy without work simply from the oil under their lands.

Nixon's father could not accept the situation and moved to Whittier just across the county line. Nixon would begin his political rise by representing this part of Orange County in Congress and would launch his successful presidential campaign with a rally at Anaheim. More than just coincidence lay behind President Nixon's acquiring a mansion in San Clemente, another part of Orange County. Ironically, the first cracks in his administration's sandbagging on the Watergate scandal would also occur in Orange County: those starting revelations by Martha Mitchell, wife of the Attorney General.

In many ways Nixon appears to typify Orange County as a whole: ambitious yet eclipsed by a bigger Los Angeles, proud and determined yet self-consciously awkward and at times a bit paranoid. And as in the case of Nixon, these conditions and characteristics had their bases in fact. Of particular interest here, Orange County—despite its markedly differing parts—has a far higher self-identification as a county than any other urban center in California, if phonebook listing have any indicative value.

CHAPTER TEN

ONSET OF
REGIONAL IDENTITY

World War I marks a major change in Orange County. Actually the war had little to do with it; the change would have come even without a war. We can see it in numerous activities, even in such things as where circuses would stop. Before the war, they would pitch their tent and perform at almost any little town along a rail line. By the early 1910s, only the largest towns could attract a circus.

School district formations and school attendance abruptly changed their previous patterns at that time, too. Just about the first act any new settlement undertook was to establish its own school as provided in California law. Until the mid-1910s, communities kept forming new school districts: 54 established, 6 lapsed or unified. After WWI, the number of districts began to decline and would continue to do so: only 2 new ones formed but 24 would consolidate by 1966 with more headed that way.

Before the war, attendance in both rural and town schools fluctuated in sync: up in prosperous times, down during recessions. Post-war enrollment took the opposite pattern. It increased in urban schools while decreasing in rural schools during prosperity, then decreased in town while increasing in rural schools during recessions.

Something else happened. Where local settlements had fought bitterly (reportedly exchanging gunshots) over access to water before 1910, in the 1920s the major towns of Orange County pulled together to form a joint water district. They then joined cities in Los Angeles and San Diego Counties to form a unified metropolitan water district and lobby for a dam on the Colorado River from which they could import water to an almost always dry southern California. In the 1920s, the former bitter rival cities of Fullerton, Anaheim, and Santa Ana also created a unified sewage outfall system to take their wastes to the ocean where before the war they had undertaken some rather immoral tricks to dump their sewage in the vicinity of their neighbors.

Why so abrupt a change? And why at this particular time? We will analyze more fully in the last chapter what processes of change underlay these events. Suffice it at this point simply to note what community leaders back then recognized had changed the world they lived in. It was the advent of paved roads and the subsequent proliferation of automobiles.

With a favorable vote in 1910 on an eighteen-million dollar bond issue for a sixteen foot-wide paved highway from the Mexican border to the Oregon border, California inaugurated its Division of Highways, then called the Department of Engineering, the outgrowth of a three-man study bureau created in 1895. Orange County benefited directly. The route of that first highway ran through the Orange County towns of San Juan Capistrano, Tustin, Santa Ana, Anaheim, Fullerton, and La Habra.

The year 1911 saw California voters elect a Progressive, Hiram Johnson, governor to break the political stranglehold the railroad interests had long enjoyed. In 1912, Orange County voters, by a plurality of 5290 to 2236, approved bonds to pave local roads. A special issue of the Santa Ana *Register* in 1913 could proudly state that road improvements made it possible at last for any rancher in the county to get to town and home again in the same day! Until then, travel over horribly rutted roads (either impassably muddy or blindingly dusty) limited visits to other towns to only the most urgent business. People found it far easier to catch a train into Los Angeles than to visit another Orange County town only a few miles away.

But by 1920, Orange County could boast all of 721 miles of paved roads with voter approval of two additional bond issues. Already in 1916 the Southern California Auto Club Magazine declared that Los Angeles had more cars per population than anywhere in the world. Orange County quickly acquired its share. By 1966, vehicle registration in Orange County stood at 670,000 and thereby exceeded the totals in more than a dozen states.

With roads, local booster groups began hosting picnics and festivities to which community leaders in other towns were invited. They formed a countywide chamber of commerce that took a leadership role in promoting all communities collectively. People began to desert their little local churches in preference for the fine churches with full-time ministers and choirs in the larger towns. Saturday night in town became the big weekly shopping event—to the demise of their traditional "cracker barrel" stores back in the villages.

Demand for travel between towns within Orange County grew so large, Pacific Electric built connector tracks between its three radiating lines. People could go by rail from Huntington Beach to Santa Ana or to Anaheim and on to La Habra without having to detour by way of Los Angeles first.

With paved roads, parents could now forsake the local one-room school house and send their children into the more modern schools in the large towns. At least they did when prosperity made it possible; when depression limited their economic resources, children returned to their village school. Interviews with retired teachers from that era extracted this explanation for the otherwise strange switch in school attendance patterns noted earlier.

THE COMING OF THE FREEWAY

If a shift from wagon to rail and from rail to auto on paved roads made abrupt changes in the scale and structure of community here, it should come as no surprise to find the post-WWII freeway would exert tremendous impacts. Not only did the density of urban development change radically; the scale and hence the nature and quality of community experience metamorphosed in ways quite unanticipated.

The first freeway to reach Orange County (1950), named for Santa Ana, began to push out from the center of Los Angeles in 1947. Like a bow-wave in front of a ship, suburban development spread out before the on-coming freeway. This rapid conversion of farmland, however, did not stem simply from greedy farmers anxious to sell out at a profit. Nature had an important hand in it, particularly in the citrus belt. There, landownership had always accorded status, far more than could any amount of ostentation possible with money. Selling old family ranches did not come easily, despite prospects for huge profits.

We noted that valencia oranges became associated with Orange County after a plant blight destroyed the once thriving grape industry in the 1880s. Blight suddenly struck again, this time devastating citrus trees by the tens of thousands starting in the late 1940s. Only the Irvine Ranch was largest enough (and debt-free enough) to remove all blighted orchards and replant with a blight-resistant sweet-root strain of oranges. Irvine would replant as many as 120,000 trees a year. Smaller ranchers, though, had little choice than to convert their land to some other use or go bankrupt. At that moment a surging demand for suburban housing came to their rescue.

By the time the first freeway had reached Santa Ana in 1951, other freeways appeared on drawing boards to weave a network across the northwestern two-fifths of Orange County. Anticipating this enhanced means of mobility, Stanford Research Institute surprised Walt Disney by recommending that he locate his new creation, a theme park, in what Southern Californians considered "out in the sticks" at Anaheim.

Disneyland (as well as the choice of site) did, of course, prove a tremendous success and a definite asset for Anaheim and Orange County right from its opening in 1955. Yet it did not immediately enjoy the embrace of Anaheim's cautious longtime mayor, Charles Pearson. Before he would arrange the necessary annexation, zoning, and permits, he made Disney prove it would not become a honkeytonk amusement park. Above all, Pearson felt a personal responsibility for Anaheim's image.

Success with Disneyland made Anaheim less hesitant about the city's next coup, attracting the California Angels baseball team. Indeed, Anaheim soon placed itself in a competitive race with Santa Ana to achieve premier status as Orange County's largest and fastest growing city in terms of population, business, and square miles of annexed territory. The competition grew so keen, it went on like a perpetual ball game with the two cities' newspapers publishing a running tally like a score. The 1950s had become an era of annexation warfare throughout the county, a city manager's prestige riding on rapid growth.

A municipality might incorporate one day so as to avoid annexation, then begin proceedings the following day to swallow the next subdivision down the road. It was not uncommon at that time for municipalities to run strip annexations a few feet wide for miles to cut off a neighbor municipality from staking out its claim to newly developing acreage, or wrap an annexation arm around another municipality's aggressive grab.

Between 1925 and 1928, five towns had incorporated. Each of the five did so primarily to gain improved public services. Only one, Tustin, had an additional reason: a fear of being annexed (by its longtime nemesis, Santa Ana). In contrast, all eleven post-WWII incorporations (between 1953 and 1962) had two concerns uppermost: They sought first of all to avoid being annexed; and they feared annexation because it would deny them land-use control over their own environment and future image.

Only two of these post-WWII incorporations (Garden Grove and Stanton) acted also because they had dire need for improved public services, particularly water. By the 1950s, county government could serve towns as well or better than municipalities. In fact, some towns, after incorporating, immediately contracted the county to continue to provide municipal services for them under what was called the Lakewood plan.

The wild 1950s game of annexation came to a head in the early 1960s when Santa Ana tried to plant a 300 foot-wide strip across the mid-section of the Irvine Ranch to take in a large (and presumably tax-profitable) retirement community more than nine miles away. It so blatantly disregarded sound growth management that the state legislature finally mandated creation of a Local Agency Formation Commission in each county to rule on the merits of every proposed annexation and incorporation.

Initially, urbanization involved new residents willing to make the long commute to jobs in Los Angeles so they might achieve their dream home in suburbia. Before the 1950s ended, major employers had begun to recognize that they could attract and hold a better workforce if they moved their plants out to where those employees lived or wanted to live.

Between 1957 and 1963, Hughes, Ford Aeronutronics, North American Aviation's Autonetics, Collins Radio, Douglas, Beckman Instruments, among others, had opened centers in Orange County, some of them with as many as 20,000 employees. Their employment (with families) alone accounted for as large a population increase as the county's entire 1950 population.

With two new university campuses and increasing cultural attractions, Orange County now had an image which the most prized economic multiplier—the high-tech, well-paying, aerospace industries—sought. Orange County had, in some ways, moved to the forefront in late twentieth century culture. In some other ways, it had a long way to go.

As we shall note later, more than Orange County's image changed. Its leadership changed, too: in composition and residential distribution, in style and aspirations, and in breadth of linkages and outlook. Yet patterns of civic action tended to run in ruts. Starting with Disneyland, but soon in many other ways, Orange County would gain a positive world fame. Yet other changes did not always prove so salutary.

THE SUBDIVISION CYCLE

In their scramble for growth, Orange County municipalities expected the much touted bonanza of economic and urban growth would center upon and hence enhance their old downtowns. Lord and behold what a surprise they experienced.[1] The mass of newcomers had no automatic loyalty to them. With a rapidly advancing network of freeways, people simply got in their cars and quickly reached stores or recreational facilities in any direction they chose.

Within a decade, major regional shopping centers mushroomed, and they did not locate in the old downtowns. They chose the junctions of these new freeways—in between the old towns. These new giant shopping centers, products of the freeway age, soon eclipsed the old downtowns in the 1960s, just like the downtown had eclipsed the village store in the 1920s with the advent of paved roads.

Immediately these giant new centers demanded an upgraded media for advertising. Where previously every little town in Orange County had at least one weekly or biweekly newspaper of its own, regional centers for a regional clientele required regionwide advertising in regionwide dailies. There followed a rash of consolidations (or demises) of local papers until only a few remained: those with a mass readership. The largest would eventually change its name from Santa Ana Register to Orange county Register.

This turn of events put local municipalities and local school districts in a serious bind. How could a local city manager or local school district superintendent get his message across about the great job his agency was doing for the people? How could he whip up support among voters when a bond issue desperately needed approval? Regional papers tended to deal with regional—namely countywide or statewide—issues. Local news drew less and less coverage.

The timing of this shift could not have been worse. Here had flocked hundreds of thousands of newcomers trying to escape the faceless big city and searching for a nostalgic sense of community. Yet the place they expected to provide them that sense of community lacked the traditional means to help them find anew a sense of hometown; it lacked a local newspaper. But that was not all.

The annexation wars further denied them anything to identify with because school district and municipality borders diverged so markedly. A family might live in an incorporated town named W, have children going to school in a district with the name of town X, get some public services from town Y (or from the county), and actually receive mail at a postal address named for town Z.

So what was their new hometown? Who were their community leaders, many began to ask. Finding no answer, they often conjured up images of secret cliques, a power elite, even at times a communist conspiracy. Most troubling for many, they now had the fine homes, good jobs, and ideal families which (back in their childhood hometown) should have spelled social status and recognition. Instead, they found themselves astonishingly now simply nobodies lost in a mass of nobodies.

Not only did the expected strong sense of rootedness elude them; they lacked support networks to help them make adaptive adjustments. They discovered themselves adrift and devoid of effective support groups. They may have acquired material objects but not a positive sense of identification.

Educated, professional-level Blacks, Asians, and Chicanos who made the move to suburbia often encountered discrimination. But few of them expected it would vanish here. Most were prepared for it and therefore had a built-in excuse for their disappointment. Many would move back to the ghetto or form new ones. White families had no such built-in excuse for their failures and disappointments. They had no ghetto to withdraw into. Some of them turned to ideological extremes or alcohol. Divorce rates soared; for a while in the 1960s divorces almost equaled the number of new marriages.

For most people, disillusionment worked its way out in a quite consistent three-year pattern within each new subdivision and in a five-year cycle in each newly developed town, from Buena Park to Costa Mesa, from Tustin to Seal Beach. During their first year, families tended to stew alone. Once neighbors found how fully everyone else shared the same frustrations and isolation, they would focus their anger at some readily available target. School and municipal administrators, overwhelmed by problems of unprecedented growth and always short of funds to meet exaggerated citizen expectations, unavoidably provided easy targets. And so the protest demonstrations would begin.

The cause célèbre might be some petty matter, even an unreasonable issue—such as the noise of chickens in a nearby farm or lack of police at every school crossing. New families came to Orange County in search of a bucolic life style yet immediately demanded all of the services and amenities of a long-established big city —and with minimum taxes.

Town after town went through bitter recall elections. Yet old-timers had the political connections to retain power though outnumbered by newcomers who lacked even social networks much less political organization. Developers who promised much and delivered less had long since disappeared; anger over shoddy construction could be assuaged by attacking city hall for not having regulated the builder better when in reality city hall had not existed then because the town had not yet incorporated when the subdividers secured official approvals.

After several years of almost constant agitation, families would begin to make their own networks of friends and interests. Activism became tiresome; neighborhoods would have shaken themselves down. Old-boy networks would no longer dominate local decisions. (Chances were the old-boy members, as typified by local merchants and service club members, would have moved to better suburbs elsewhere themselves.)

Decision-making would increasingly gravitate into the hands of professional administrators. And the quality of professionalism among those municipal and school district administrators went up while the problems of awkwardness inherent in a sudden burst of growth diminished. After five (at most seven) years, neighborhoods and towns would calm down to an almost monotonous routine.

In a few cases, however, this cycle got completely out of hand. It took on the dimensions of an extremist ideological crusade. Children were used to spy on teachers. Demands for Guffy Reader-type basic education and prohibition of any mention of evolution rose to a roar. One conscientious school board member, a decorated war hero who did not tout his record but who did stand up for the constitutional rights of free speech, was hounded to his death as a communist sympathizer by flag-wavers who had no such war record of their own.

This cycle of disappointment, alienation, outburst of frustration, political agitation and then social adjustment occurred in new subdivision after subdivision throughout the county. But how they were handled and their results were not so uniform. Indeed they varied greatly and with consistency of tactic according to their place context.

The wildest outbursts and worst extremism occurred in the newly incorporated farm belt towns. The least explosive cases happened in older towns where a sense of place and stability had had decades to mature, where community leaders knew each other, not as cronies but as people with considerable experience in taking responsibility and acting with stable fair-mindedness.

These leaders had had time to learn how to resolve problems before they became too hot to handle. They had learned how to co-opt potential leaders and isolate kooks. They also had an extra advantage: They had gone through it all before.

At the end of the first world war and the advent of paved roads, leaders in towns like Fullerton, Anaheim, and Santa Ana put together ambitious plans for urban growth and a local version of manifest destiny. Then they had seen it all destroyed by an outbreak of bigotry and wild agitation.

The resurgent Ku Klux Klan in its post-war urban format had grown so powerful that Anaheim police once (in 1923) actually directed traffic in their white robes. Long-time friends became deadly enemies. Suspicion and tension reached such a divisive fever pitch that civic and commercial activities suffered and Orange County acquired a disastrous stigma. Prospective industries chose to locate elsewhere.

Civic leaders, such as Anaheim's Mayor Pearson, had lived through that as young men. They vowed never to allow this to happen again. It did happen, but not in their towns and they succeeded in accomplishing after WWII what their parent's generation had failed to do with that earlier opportunity for development after the first world war.

ESSENTIAL WATER

In a region where rainfall is perennially low enough to qualify it technically as a desert, water commands major consideration. With other southern Californians, Orange County spokesmen participated in the political efforts, beginning as far back as the 1920s, to bring northern California's excess water to the south. After delays from the Depression and WWII, the California Water Project began in 1958—even before the plan's official adoption. Water would arrive in 1971, just 30 years after the first Colorado River water arrived.

A shortage of water did not always plague all of Orange County. At times and in some places, too much water became the problem. Every decade or so, a major flood might spread across thousands of acres in the farm belt. Other parts of the county had always had swamps.

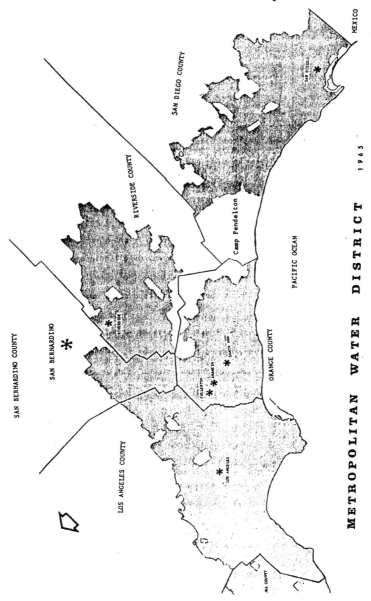

METROPOLITAN WATER DISTRICT 1965

Soon after WWI, a young agricultural engineer with the University of California Agricultural Extension Service detected a pronounced drop in the water levels of wells throughout the western portion of the county. Municipal engineers began making the same startling discovery. The county contracted for a full-scale study by a well-known water engineer.

His 1925 report shook the community. With less than a 100,000 population, Orange County already overdrew its underground supply by 40,000 acre feet—by nearly two billion gallons—annually. It shook Orange County leaders because a lack of water threatened their grandiose dreams for economic growth even more than the KKK had done.

Leaders in Orange County particularly envied Los Angeles, blessed as it was with water rights established by the Spanish pueblo settlement. Its municipal water system, started in 1901 and augmented by aqueducts constructed in 1913, assured continued urban growth. By 1922 however, Los Angeles's famed city engineer, for whom the Mulholland tunnel is named, began to warn that LA would soon run out of water. A 1923 conference in Fullerton with representatives from surrounding counties produced the Boulder Dam Association to promote the Swing-Johnson Bill that would dam the Colorado River. It also produced the Metropolitan Water District.

Conflict within the county over water did not cease, however. Newport Beach, lacking wells of its own, had depended on shipping water in by rail when it formed the first municipal water system in Orange County in 1909. Like Laguna Beach later in the 1920s, it piped water from the swamps near Huntington Beach. At first, Newport Beach felt it did not need to join the new MWD. Then people began to notice a drying of the swamps and the first signs of salt water intrusion.

When Newport Beach did apply for MWD membership in 1931, it was hit with litigation by Anaheim and Santa Ana. Allied with agricultural interests, they sought to prohibit all of the coastal communities and the Irvine Ranch from drawing out of those Huntington Beach swamps. Newport Beach incurred particular animosity because it had wasted 200,000 gallons a day to supply mud for Universal Pictures' filming of "All's Quiet on the Western Front" when water was in such critical supply.

Thwarted, Newport Beach determined to go it alone without MWD membership over the warnings of its own municipal engineer. By 1947 the inevitable was no longer deniable; salt water intrusion into aquifer-drawn water had become serious. It could no longer postponed an MWD application. Other coastal towns had already established their own water distribution district with membership in MWD in 1942. Even the small coastal towns of Dana Point and San Clemente would join by 1954.

A fundamental dilemma faced MWD officials. Growth-minded municipalities wanted to use MWD water as a tool for expansion the way Los Angeles City had done. But MWD, dominated by municipal Los Angeles which was now hemmed in by incorporated suburbs, decided against expanding MWD coverage. This prospect threatened to freeze Anaheim and Santa Ana in their race for regional supremacy. Their ally in gaining flexibility from MWD came from an unlikely source: agriculture.

The most active single campaigner for MWD membership in Orange County had always been the influential Farm Bureau. It had sought to have Orange County spread excess water on the gravel beds along the Santa Ana River which fed the aquifer. Opposition voices within the Farm Bureau, however, feared that high mineral content in Colorado River water would eventually destroy agriculture in the process of meeting its needs. They argued to allot MWD water to urban users while prohibiting anyone except farmers from drawing well water.

That argument encountered a counterargument from municipal leaders: Why should city users have to subsidize farmers? Fear of subsidizing others had long affected the internal politics of southern California water. (Municipal Los Angeles claimed it paid 30 percent of MWD's taxes for only 2 percent of its water.) It took some hard-bargaining by the Irvine Ranch to get permission for an MWD line to the southeastern three-fifths of Orange County so that urban development could begin there. (The new University of California campus on Irvine-donated land and its proposed surrounding new city gave the Irvine Company an argument difficult to oppose. Without water there could be no campus with all the prestige it would bring.) In the interim until the line was completed in 1963, Irvine had to share its limited well water with those awakening coastal towns.

Conflict with other counties did not end with the creation of MWD. Dependent so fully on irrigation, the Irvine Ranch brought suit in 1931 against the more flagrant misusers of Santa Ana River water upstream. Eventually a modus vivendi agreement emerged in 1937 between Irvine, Orange County, and the Orange County Water District on the one hand, and the Riverside and San Bernardino parties on the other. It guaranteed a flow of water to Orange County on a formula for Prado Dam openings, effective in 1942. By 1946, however, the litigants once again faced each other in court.

The difficulty of settlement lay in the fact that the original suit had not included all upstream users; loopholes had thereby developed. After years of litigation on this next round, a judge ruled favorably for Orange County in 1957 and restricted upstream users to 1946 production. One legal maneuver after another kept the decree from becoming effective until 1960 when a graduated cutback would phase in over the next three years.

Even this proved unsatisfactory. Until every upstream user fell under court control, water rights adjudication could not become effective. Therefore, Orange County Water District returned to court in 1963, this time to file suit against every upstream user—all 3500 of them. As of 1966, the end seemed nowhere in sight. Proposals by Riverside County for a tri-county authority met rejection from Orange County which had paid the bills for earlier mutual authorities while losing its water. Orange County particularly disliked the idea that San Bernardino had not joined MWD and hence would get a free ride at Orange County's expense.

Another major stumbling block: the disposition of waste water. Sewage flows down hill, which means sewage from Riverside and San Bernardino Counties comes toward Orange County. Yes, reclamation and use in agricultural irrigation can handle some of the waste water. (Via injection wells along the coast, it would served to block saltwater intrusion.) But not certain industrial "hot" wastes. Any settlement between Orange County and the upper counties would require not only minimum guarantees on amounts of water but an enforced level of purity for water entering Orange County. Construction of a sewage outfall seemed called for yet could end up polluting Orange County shores.

Despite all of these efforts to keep Santa Ana River water percolating into the Orange County underground basin, overdraft continued dangerously. Only some unusually wet years during WWII delayed the day of reckoning. Dry years after the war sent watertables plummeting.

In 1945, water in wells stood 10 feet *above* sea level in the middle of the Irvine Ranch, 20 feet above at Westminster and Buena Park, 30 feet at Anaheim and Santa Ana, and 60 feet at Olive. By 1956, those levels had fallen to 30 feet *below* sea level at Westminster and Santa Ana for a drop of 50 feet. Water fell 60 feet at Olive and stood 80 feet *below* sea level in mid-Irvine for a 90 foot drop in little over one decade. At an exaggerated vertical scale of about 500 to one, here is how Orange County appears in cross-section.

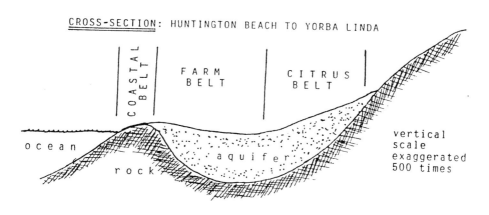

CROSS-SECTION: HUNTINGTON BEACH TO YORBA LINDA

COASTAL BELT · FARM BELT · CITRUS BELT · ocean · aquifer · rock · vertical scale exaggerated 500 times

Obviously, fighting court cases would not save this basin. In 1949, Orange County Water District began using its revenues to buy and spread MWD water into the aquifer during summer months. But its funds proved inadequate to meet the need. The countywide Chamber of Commerce and the Orange County Farm Bureau appealed to the County Board of Supervisors to levy a tax on all property through its flood control powers. A tax was instituted, even for areas beyond the basin. But it still fell short and began to generate political opposition.

The county then appointed a citizens task force to consider options, and they started by examining the 1937 *Pasadena* v. *Alhambra* water suit over the Raymond Basin. Courts had always adjudicated water cases upon prescriptive rights—what water an individual or agency had taken, even though illegally, for the prior five years forms the basis for what a person has a prescriptive claim to. In the Pasadena/Alhambra decision of 1945, all parties had prescriptive rights in excess of water available. Owners could not secure their full claim regardless of legality. There simply was not enough to go around. All would have to cut back.

This "mutually prescriptive doctrine" did not satisfy the Orange County committee because it rested on a "theory of scarcity" whereas members sought a solution based on a "theory of abundance." Instead of forced cut backs, they sought a way to secure enough water for all.

Out of their discussions there emerged a positive idea to tax the users of underground water according to the amount of water they used. This idea meant putting meters on private wells and charging landowners for water which tradition said was theirs. To city people accustomed to having their water line metered, this idea might seem only logical and far from revolutionary. But no jurisdiction had ever tried it before; it remained far from a foregone conclusion legally. The idea was "sold" to the public on the grounds that people would not pay for water actually under their property, only for water purchased to replenish what they had drawn from their wells.

From this distance in time it sounds like splitting hairs. Yet this subtlety proved crucial then and carried the day. Most city councils, the county Board of Supervisors, most sections of the Farm Bureau, the Chamber of Commerce, and Orange County Board of Water endorsed the replenishment concept: a "pump tax" in common parlance. Enabling legislation took effect in 1953.

At first, Santa Ana, Anaheim and Fullerton were excluded because they had already contributed so much to MWD. Then Newport Beach and Costa Mesa refused to pay and withdrew. Eventually Santa Ana, Anaheim, Fullerton and Costa Mesa ceased being exempt islands; only Newport Beach continued to draw water while stubbornly refusing to contribute to its replenishment. Naturally, long simmering resentment from people in the farm and citrus belts toward Newport Beach boiled more than ever.

Despite the internal politics with Newport Beach, Orange County Water District did pull off quite a feat. Between 1954 and 1965, it sunk 1,520,000 acre feet or 500 billion gallons of water. In one typical year, half of the water Orange County received from MWD—137,394 acre feet out of 277,447—went underground for basin recharge. By 1965, fresh water levels had risen above sea level completely out to the coast, except at Seal Beach and Los Alamitos. The overall table had risen more than fifty feet. By 1966, OCWD need not, for the first time, buy all the water available to it. Orange County had implemented the most successful large basin recharge effort in the world to that date.

Further Inland/Coastal Rifts

Obviously there must have occurred some effective salesmanship to convince farmers and municipalities alike to pay for underground water that had always come "free" as God-given. At the same time, though, coastal vs. inland differences continued to strain county harmony, no new phenomenon. When inland towns had pulled together to form a county chamber of commerce in the early decades of this century for instance, the coastal communities had formed their own rival joint chamber.

Or take the mental health hospital affair. Voters approved a bond issue in 1956 for a psychiatric facility and the County Board of Supervisors accepted federal funds to construct such a hospital. The existing "snakepit" dungeon had drawn too much criticism as medieval. Yet once completed in 1959, the new facility sat unused for years—its upper, hospital floors fully equipped with everything except patients and staff. Mattresses lay for years on beds still in their shipping cases. The obstacle: an ideological orientation opposed to mental treatment as potentially harboring a communist conspiracy.

It took some astute political maneuvering by the League of Women Voters, under leadership from Newport Beach residents working with the Coast Mental Health Association, to engineer a reversal by the Board of Supervisors. Unlike previous proponents of a mental health program, League members knew how political games were played (they did their homework) and had much to offer elected officials in return for cooperation. Board and League members agreed on a strategy. The Board would vote the issue a few days before Christmas 1963 when season's activities would keep inland opponents too busy to mobilize. Orange County at last had a mental health program and an activated hospital.

Or take the inland/coastal eruption over symphonic music. An Orange County Philharmonic Society came into being in the mid-1950s to sponsor an orchestra of Hollywood professional musicians who wanted to play serious music. Initially, society directors were rather evenly distributed between those with inland (mostly Fullerton, Anaheim, Santa Ana) and coastal (mostly Newport Beach and Laguna Beach) residences. The six annual concerts, too, occurred in evenly distributed locales around the county.

Then two changes occurred. Although each was understandable under its circumstances, coming together they generated conflict. First, financial complications (among other factors) eventually led to a decision to contract with the Los Angeles symphony orchestra then under its brilliant young conductor, Zubin Mehta, for all concerts commencing with the 1962-63 season. Second, constantly changing concert locations had created difficulties. So when the new Orange Coast Community College opened a fine auditorium, it became the permanent site.

Symphony lovers in Fullerton found, however, that they could just as easily attend concerts of the Los Angeles orchestra in Los Angeles as in Costa Mesa. Quickly the Philharmonic board changed from a geographically even distribution to one overwhelmingly dominated by residents of Newport Beach and Laguna Beach. Meanwhile, Disneyland had brought even more professional musicians to Orange County who wanted to play serious music. The Anaheim local orchestra soon took over the role played by the previous Philharmonic, that of Orange County's homegrown orchestra. In this way there now emerged a rival organization, the Orange County Symphony Association with boardmembers preponderately from Fullerton, Anaheim, Santa Ana, and nearby inland locales.

Although Orange County was large enough for two programs with two boards, the old coastal/inland tension erupted into heated words. By coincidence, the Los Angeles *Times*, a Chandler family enterprise, had purchased Newport Beach's newspaper, the *Daily Pilot*. Since Mrs. Chandler dominated the Los Angeles Symphony as its principal patron, inland Orange Countians charged a conspiratorial linkage in the symphony contract. Newport Beach people remained too closely tied to Los Angeles for the rest of Orange County to feel comfortable with.

HARBOR DEVELOPMENT

Many other inland/coastal incidents occurred. One more should suffice: the harbor development episode of the 1930s and its aftermath three decades later.

By 1963, only thirty years after a major federal harbor project, the Orange County Harbor District could proudly report that Newport Harbor had become the boating mecca of southern California. Some 7000 boats berth there and far more than that number regularly came on trailers to use its waters for recreation. An estimated 5.4 million visitors used Newport's beaches per year out of 17 million visiting all beaches in the county.

In a highly condensed format, here is how this came about. Involvement in Newport Harbor, starting in 1933, constituted the federal government's first venture into recreational boating. Since federal funding had always gone to commercial harbor development, Newport Beach promoters sold their project to voters elsewhere in Orange County on that basis. Hoping that a commercial harbor would create jobs during the depression, inland communities permitted themselves to be taxed to finance improvements on the coast.

Geologically, Newport Harbor is a quite recent phenomenon. As late as 1825 it did not exist. A flooded Santa Ana River that year shifted courses so that its mouth lay at the western end of today's lower bay. With huge silt deposits from floods, especially the flood of 1862, a peninsula grew out of a sand bar, and islands appeared out of swamps. In the 1870s, the McFadden brothers (who helped found Santa Ana) established landing operations inside what was then the harbor, eventually constructing a 1200-foot pier off the beach.

By the 1880s they had a railroad line between Santa Ana and Newport harbor. The future elite town of Newport Beach (where Rolls Royces could be seen drag racing on the main boulevard in the 1960s) had its beginnings as an unpretentious fishing village and small-scale shipping port. Known originally as "Cienega de los Ranas" (Swamp of the Frogs), it would turn into the handsome prince of Orange County communities. But by then the McFaddens (anti-SP men aligned with Irvine) had sold out in disgust when the SP acquired their railroad through the help of SP's supposed rival, Pacific Electric.

After decades of inadequate private funding and unsuccessful public efforts to make something of this potential harbor, the Depression provided a means for drawing federal and county funds. A poignant irony occurs here: staunchly Republican Newport Beach got its big boost from F.D.R.'s New Deal Democratic administration. After a countywide bond issue had failed for the second time, Newport Beach lobbyists in Washington managed to alter the Corps of Engineers' perspective into believing that this harbor actually could serve a commercial purpose and hence stimulate industrial development here.

With the help of Senator (former Governor) Hiram Johnson, Newport Beach even log-rolled the federal share up enough to cover part of county's legally required matching share. That accomplished, Newport Beach promoters secured a favorable vote in every town in Orange County for a bond issue. (This time the Irvines kept their distance which, reportedly, helped overcome inland people's skepticism.) During WWII, shipbuilding here did earn a record for turning out PT boats which won the Corps of Engineers' willingness to invest in further harbor dredging. The end of WWII, however, spelled the effective end of industry in Newport Beach.

With the 1950s' flood of newcomers into Orange County, recreational demand swelled. As high-paying aerospace jobs increased even more rapidly in the late 1950s, Newport Beach's earlier prestige, as home to movie stars and oil millionaires, made it THE fashionable place to be. And with that trend, inland resentment festered. They had underwritten Newport's success and received nothing in return except a coastal town that felt itself even more above the rest of the county than ever.

Not content with past success, the Coast Association and Harbor District in 1955 eyed a three-mile stretch of superb ocean frontage at Bolsa Chica near Huntington Beach. The owners cared only about their oil revenues and duck shooting for Los Angeles members. A rail line right-of-way complicated acquisition because the county feared that its abandonment would prompt the State Highway Division to grab it for still another freeway. That would preclude any chance for using ocean frontage as a beach park.

Meanwhile, however, it acquired the stigma of "tin can beach" for its unkempt, derelict condition. Only when Dow Chemical ceased operations there in 1966 did the owners join the county in asking the Public Utilities Commission for an abandonment authorization. At last progress could occur.

Soon after, a complicated set of political and economic moves brought an eventual development of another luxury residential development nearby. It became possible through County Harbor District efforts to work out agreements with the State Highways Division, the U.S. Navy (it had a major ammunition storage facility nearby), the landowners, and a developer backed by a Texas oil company. Congressman Hanna, a Democrat who happened to live there, secured Corps of Engineers' blessings and assistance in the requisite dredging.

By 1965, inland town officials had begun to object to the county's expenditures on a harbor district that so blatantly brought prosperity to coast towns. To inland eyes, those towns were never really Orange County in spirit and commitment. But little beyond talk happened.

Just then, however, one woman in Santa Ana raised quite a fuss about alleged political shenanigans by Santa Ana's long-time powerful clique (which called itself the Good Government Committee from an earlier day when its members had led a reform drive). She had raised enough clamor to attract the State Attorney General's attention. The mayor promptly appointed her to investigate the County Harbor District—thereby taking her off of his back.

She proceeded to investigate it so conscientiously that she drew a following throughout the inland towns. She articulated with a vengeance what they had long felt. Her brother-in-law happened to be a Fountain Valley city councilman and Fountain Valley was the first town to petition the Local Agency Formation Commission for withdrawal from the countywide district. Neighboring Huntington Beach then petitioned for withdrawal also. But LAFC ruled that the taxes affected individual property owners, not municipalities, hence petitions could only be made by individuals, not governmental entities.

When this women and her brother-in-law tried to withdraw their property, they met rejection on a Catch-22 rationalization that LAFC lacked empowerment to judge the efficiency and appropriateness of actions by a public agency. The Harbor District then came to an agreement with Huntington Beach which withdrew from the fray. Anaheim's Mayor Pearson, who served on LAFC, acknowledged that the lady had made her point quite effectively. It was time for all public agencies to undergo evaluation, he opined, largely to soften tempers.

The Harbor District, however, at this time became involved (a) with Irvine Company attempts to build a truly elite residential tract in upper Newport Harbor that would have yachting facilities in front of each house where presently water skiers from all over Orange County enjoyed their sport, and (b) a new recreational harbor even farther from the bulk of taxpayers, this one at Dana Point in the county's southeast corner.

To get federal design funds for the Dana harbor, county officials had to recruit the two Congressmen from this county (one a Democrat and one a Republican) along with Senator Kuchel who was born and raised in Anaheim and whose brother served on the Harbor Commission. Their campaign succeeded in getting the needed 9.4 million dollars. The Irvine plan, involving a long-haggled swap of land with the county, drew sharp attacks even from as far away as California's then most powerful Democrat, Jesse Unruh, Speaker of the State House.

CHAPTER ELEVEN

SHIFTS IN LEADERSHIP

O range County seems never to have lacked enterprising leaders with vision, drive, and an ability to rise above the local scene—to maneuver at regional, state, and even national levels as necessary. When, for instance, town promoters felt Los Angeles County ignored their needs and crimped their prospects, they managed to carve out their own county. And they did so in 1889 with a population of only 14,000. Santa Ana boosters then successfully sliced the boundary line to exclude Whittier so that they could be assured of a majority vote for Santa Ana over Anaheim as county seat.

The social backgrounds and linkages, primary economic activities and forms of political leverage, effectiveness (or "weight") in civic affairs and scales of involvement: these differed greatly over the decades among Orange County's most prominent leaders. At the same time, a leader's residence or base of operations frequently correlated with certain patterns or styles of behavior and with particular strategies for playing political games.

In some cases, the locale may have determined who played the game which an aspiring leader might seek to enter as well as limiting strategic options and maneuverability. In short, the rules and roles might already exist; each new player simply had to find a fitting role and then learn the rules.

This chapter examines leadership in several contexts and scales. We start with a few selected cases at local level for towns not dealt with thus far, such as the anomalous "agricultural cities," a municipality without a community, a miniature incorporation, and for comparison a town with a strong sense of spirit. Moving on to county scale, we take one instance of progressive leadership by county officials vis-à-vis their municipal counterparts.

We glance briefly, too, at changes in political process stemming from a professionalization of public administration. Leadership encountered unexpected twists when participants tried to interact simultaneously at differing levels and with diverse worldviews and responsibilities. This takes us into consideration of varying scales of region as determined by major modern-day challenges. With this base of observations, we start to recognize how diverse the realm of leadership can be. Still, an identifiable set of classifications do emerge for analysis.

LOCAL CASES

After WWII, a group of dairymen, mostly of Dutch descent, moved across the county line from Los Angeles to Orange County. For most of them, it was their second or third displacement by urbanization. This time they set their minds on remaining. Soon though, they found themselves isolated along the county line by a rapidly urbanizing and expanding Buena Park.

Residential tracts mushroomed helter-skelter wherever developers could talk a farmer into selling. Having little more than a one-man planning staff, the county could only give these farmers A-2 zoning which provided no protection; it all too readily changed into some urban designation.

Until threatened by urbanization, no recognized community existed in this agricultural corner of the county. The fifty dairy families and the few additional farmers, some of them of Japanese ancestry, found themselves segmented by three elementary and two high school districts. Not so much as a village center, much less a post office, ever existed to give this locale an identifiable name. What did exist was a determination among all dairymen and most of the small farmers to stay.

This common determination and anxiety pulled residents together. In 1955 they organized an incorporation drive that successfully gave them zoning control over an area of 1.35 square miles. Since they intended to remain in farming, the new "city" named Dairyland had only one zoning classification, agriculture. But therein lay its Catch-22.

Agricultural zoning kept land values exceedingly low. Meanwhile in neighboring Buena Park, residential development had sprung up so pell mell that school districts could not keep pace; they had not reserved enough sites for schools. What land remained, had gone sky high with speculation. Naturally, school district boards eyed that low-priced open ag land in Dairyland. Soon Dairyland's continued integrity became threatened mostly by condemnation proceedings from other public agencies.

To counter this condition, Dairyland's city council changed all zoning to industrial so that land value would become too expensive for condemnation. But doing that meant county assessments (hence taxes) on farm soared and threaten their continued existence anyway. Then there came the increasing conflicts between an agricultural environment (flies, dust from plowing, animal noises, smells, sprays, etc.) and what exurbanites in nearby subdivisions expected as their moral if not legal right, even though they came more recently and had sought a rural setting. Political pressures continued to foment.

Dairyland had come to a juncture. Its residents could simply give up on their dream and let landowners take their chances. Or, they could stick together and replan for an eventual conversion to urban uses. The first option meant some might get rich while others suffered. The second option would require everyone to wait until they had something worth their dreams and cost of moving again. They then would all get out at the same time, thereby all sharing the burdens and profits.

With plenty of examples of disastrous growth management all around them, they decided on the latter option. In 1964 they contracted with a planning consultant for a totally new plan and arranged with one of the region's foremost real estate companies to program the entire citywide project. Having hired a quite capable professional city manager in one of their first decisions, Dairyland leaders moved methodically, even in selecting a new name for their municipality. They would rename it La Palma.

By Spring 1965, residential construction had begun. Within four years the human population would increase fifty fold to 20,000 while the cow and chicken population would drop to zero. Nearby another locale with much the same ethnic mix also had depended extensively on dairy operations. But it went through a drastically different political experience. Even though it had a history as an identifiable place dating back to the previous century, back a decade before Pacific Electric put a train station there on its central line, it failed to gel successfully when under pressure.

When the post-WWII urban boom headed that direction, local leaders met with their counterparts in Los Alamitos and Stanton about pulling together into one incorporation large enough to make a go of it. When those talks broke down, residents incorporated themselves in 1956 as Dairy City with the principal objective of protecting local agricultural enterprises.

Dairy City should, in theory, have had a better chance of succeeding than Dairyland. Unlike Dairyland, it had long had its own elementary school district. And it had more tax base in the form of some commerce and even a famous race track. But events did not unfold that way.

Within a year, voters changed the town's name to Cyress and the greater diversity of interests present began to bicker over objectives and means. City council soon fired its first part-time city manager. (He was the one who, as manager, would play a key role in Dairyland's successful transformation.) Soon pro-development forces in Cypress openly fought the agriculture preservationists, and the second city manager resigned out of frustration with his council.

With so much profit beckoning from rezoning ag land for urban uses, it is not surprising that bribery occurred. What is amazing is how seldom it happened, the most notable case involving all the councilmen and city administrator of nearby Westminster. They were convicted and imprisoned. By 1960, charges of bribery (no convictions for lack of evidence) brought recall action and wholesale turnover among elected officials in Cypress. Chaos then took over.

Cypress provided Dairyland its most graphic example of what turmoil and selfishness Dairyland leaders sought to avoid. Where Dairyland's leaders took a big view, Cypress usually lacked the statesmanship and patience necessary for political compromise just when those attributes seemed most sorely needed.

Leaders in Fountain Valley, the third "agricultural city," never intended to preserve farming. They simply incorporated in 1957 so that they could control the development themselves. A mixture of various ethnic backgrounds, the voters chose a local farmer of Japanese ancestry as their first mayor, the first Nisei so elected in America.

Urbanization came rapidly. Population shot up sevenfold, almost as fast as land values. School attendance increased 1400 percent in only four years. All of which meant an urgent need for new public facilities and services such as police and fire units with all of the equipment they require. It meant parks and dozens of totally new schools—the most extensive school building program of any district in all of California until then. An horrendous need for taxes became inevitable.

But Fountain Valley did not sit on a rail line and had no existing industry. Worse yet, the county as a whole already had a 20-year supply of industrially zoned land all served by rail awaiting unused. Unavoidably, property taxation became burdensome, and skyrocketing taxes drove farmers to sell out at a profit before they were driven out by bankruptcy.

Until then, developers did not have to contribute to the infrastructure and municipal operating expenses they generated. Yet without front-end money, a municipality and school district found themselves hard pressed to meet their responsibilities, even if residents expressed a willingness to pay the bills through taxation later.

To accomplish what everyone knew had to be done, Fountain Valley's city manager pioneered and council instituted a service fee on developers. Soon developers challenged this front-end fee in court and forced its abandonment. Only later would this kind of fee, then upheld in the courts, become rather standard practice elsewhere, albeit too late to help Fountain Valley through its hour of crisis.

Not surprisingly, given this financial situation, Fountain Valley experienced various tugging and pulling among its population, some wanting smaller lots for quicker, cheaper housing development while others fought hard for controls on development to achieve a higher-class image. It took considerable diplomacy by the mayor, city manager, and school superintendent to keep affairs on a relatively even keel.

Another nearby incorporation, Stanton, never managed that miracle. Of course, Stanton had several strikes against it from the start. Originally incorporated early in this century when the PE trains arrived, it then covered the largest area of any city in the county. Within three years Stanton's dreams had vanished and the town had disincorporated. By the time the post-WWII urban boom hit, Stanton contained a totally bifurcated population—Mexicans segregated from Anglos. (The few farmers of Japanese ancestry fell into the Anglo classification since they were independent ranchers, not peasant workers.) As in Dairyland, several school districts sliced up Stanton which, moreover, had three postal designations other than one for Stanton.

Dissatisfied with available public services, a long hybernating chamber of commerce (composed of residents, not businesses) and a Lions Club began to discuss reincorporation. To win a majority vote in 1956, the Anglos talked a Mexican-American into joining them and made him the town's first mayor so as to disspell the inevitable charges of Anglo owners protecting their own interests. But that ploy generated rumors of plots anyway. Before long, suspicions and charges of sinister schemes became attached to whatever anyone tried to propose or do for the town.

Promising loose zoning and low taxes, city leaders sought to attract industry. At the same time they generated outbursts of alienation among newcomers. Twice, organized crime tried to make inroads without success because officials reported it to the District Attorney. Water, however, produced the most serious difficulty for Stanton as it would for Garden Grove.

Although private companies served Stanton, the city found itself caught in a fight between these companies and the Public Utilities Commission. When the water district tried to pass a bond issue to take over the private service, it lost as did the Mexican-American mayor who had backed the move. Along with that loss, bonds for parks also failed because opponents said it would make parks more accessible to Mexican-American children than to Anglo children.

With so much bickering, Stanton could not or would not keep a professional city manager long enough to remove from the political arena what other jurisdictions considered routine (non-policy) decision-making. Consequently, more issues here became politicized than typically happened elsewhere.

Placentia, like Stanton, had gained a negative image as a locale for Mexican-Americans. Unlike Stanton, however, Placentia had an exceedingly well structured community. It managed to unify its school districts (1936) before any other in Orange County. It could do so because the dominant oil and large citrus interests decided it would serve their interests.

These same old pioneer families (the ones who had brought the rail line here) also made the decision to incorporate in 1927—when it benefited them. When they decided that their packing plants and their town property needed fire and police protection, they arranged the incorporation boundaries to exclude their private estates, thereby minimizing personal taxes. That made Placentia an incorporated "city" of a mere .18 square miles (eleven and a half acres), a record even among Orange County towns.

Despite this tight control when it came to financial interests, these families did not form a ruling clique such as ran Fullerton. Placentia deeply split several ways: Protestants or Catholics, people of Anglo or Spanish descent, one faction identified with leaders in Anaheim while the other faction identified with Fullerton's elite, one side linked to one oil company while the other side held to a rival oil conglomerate. When rapid post-WWII urbanization overran Placentia, the tradition of an elitist control quickly broke down because it was so brittle. Soon every decision became a strain which left newcomers frustrated without knowing what was going on.

Laguna Beach presents an entirely different scene. Other than for anomalous Dairyland, Laguna Beach is the only town in Orange County whose growth never depended on a rail line. Indeed, Laguna Beach was the only town large or small to take on and stop H.E. Huntington from building a Pacific Electric line. That happened in 1905, and Huntington never did get beyond Newport Beach even though he planned to run the PE all along the coast. More than a half-century later, Laguna Beach would become the first town in California to successfully prevent the powerful State Division of Highways from ramming a freeway through it.

Laguna Beach did not have its first Anglo settlers until a few years after settlements dotted the western half of the county. Isolation stemmed not only from its geography—the craggy slopes walling the little town off by the ocean. Self-contained independence became a cherished tradition: a way of life.

Yet for all of its isolation, Laguna as a community probably included a wider variety of cultural orientations and life styles than any other in the county. With a population of only 6,000, it had two newspapers, one liberal and the other conservative. With its sizable retirement segment came everything from former high-powered executives to poor failures and young artists.

Instead of clique-dominated or class-run, Laguna Beach seemed continually to buzz with a wide proliferation of political, cultural and social organizations, each lobbying for its point of view and most if not all of them continually undergoing change. Laguna Beach characterized pluralism at its fullest and healthiest. In 1966 the local chamber of commerce counted 84 formally constituted local organizations among only 12,000 residents, the highest ratio per population in the county.

Operating their own famous summer-arts festival (the Pageant of the Masters) and their own opera, residents here enjoyed a strong sense of community identity. Even without industry (other than tourism), Lagunans managed to underwrite their public schools with both taxes and support. Consequently, the school system tended to take a lead in innovative education.

COUNTY LEADERSHIP ON GAS TAX USE

Since the early days of this century, Orange County has had a legislative body, the Board of Supervisors, composed of five representatives from five districts. For much of that time each Supervisor doubled as the executive director of a county department in keeping with the commission theory of local government in vogue before WWI. Only later would departments gain professionals as directors. In those early decades, each elected supervisor also had complete say on all road construction within his district.

The inherent duplications of effort and patronage grew so bad (as in all counties at that time) until Orange County created a single road department for paved highways even before the State legislature mandated a county engineer in 1919. In 1920, Orange County placed the construction and maintenance for all bridges and roads (unpaved as well as paved) under this professional engineer—even though it meant that politicians would have to forego the advantages of awarding patronage contracts.

Until the 1967 Supreme Court decision instituting our current one-person-one-vote system of political process, California's legislature represented counties over population. Since northern California had more counties, it secured more funds for roads than did southern California even though the latter had more population, more cars, and more highways. With the new political equation, a 40-60 split of gasoline tax funds between northern and southern California come into existence in keeping with their relative populations.

Despite the decades of tax-fund loss, southern California took the leadership in highway planning. Between 1927 and 1933 for instance, Orange County's planning consultant had promoted "superhighways." The first would not head toward Los Angeles; he slated it to connect Santa Ana and Newport Beach. Finally built three decades later in 1965, it little resembled the impressive 150-foot wide, foliage-lined parkway which Hugh Pomeroy had envisioned. Instead it amounted to a tiny part of a grid of uninspiring, standardized state freeways. Pomeroy's 1933 plan had, of course, suffered bad timing; the Great Depression kept the county from acting on it. Not until after WWII could the state and counties take up their earlier dreams.

Since 1927, the state had distributed some of its share of gasoline tax funds with the counties. By 1935 municipalities also began to receive a small slice of the taxes. As more towns incorporated and began to compete with each other, each wanted to go its own way, laying roads as it saw fit regardless of how well or poorly the sum total would interconnect into a workable network.

With the end of WWII when the day of more people in more cars and more road building loomed as inevitable, the county engineer had already started preaching a countywide master plan for highways. County leaders, until recently in charge of virtually all highway construction, took the leadership for a concerted planning effort. To gain municipal cooperation and coordination, they would have to make it worth the municipalities' while.

In the late 1950s they proposed sharing a larger portion of county funds with the municipalities than the law required if, in exchange, each municipality would agree to a concerted network plan. After all, county leaders could argue, people travel all over the county without thought about which municipality they might happen to be in at any spot along the way.

Not all municipal officials welcomed this gambit—particularly true in towns only recently incorporated. Having just gained their independence so to speak, they resisted having, in effect, to put themselves back under the county's aegis. Fortunately for the county's effort, it had recently brought on board two men who had that natural ability to talk sense at the level best understood by whatever their audience at the moment. They were the planning director and county engineer.

Their low-key approach and willingness to allow maximum input from the municipal representatives eventually reassured skeptics and brought every town into a fully concerted program of highways whether constructed within city limits or in unincorporated areas. A committee of professional planners and engineers would submit recommendations to a review committee composed of county and municipal elected officials. The caliber of both professional work and committee oversight during the first decade of this arrangement spelled its success in coping with a major public concern. In this process, Orange County led the way for all other California counties.

PROFESSONALIZATION

What the Linds described for "Middletown" (Muncie, Indiana) in the 1920s they could just as readily have observed in the way Orange County towns operated, not only in the 1920s but into the 1950s. Long-time observers would caricature local governance with such metaphors as "consensus by cronyism" and "high button shoes" administration. The large citrus ranchers and oil-field owners would run their towns through puppets who engaged in the plebian task of standing for election. In small towns, longtime cronies just naturally saw to it that decisions went the "right" way.

Drastic change in the late 1950s and early 1960s was not without precedent. From the 1910s through the early 1930s, local chambers of commerce and Farm Bureau groups had controlled virtually all communities. An attitude of rugged individualism and minimal government prevailed. The 1930s' Great Depression challenged these old-boy elitist-run alliances. It challenged them to find solutions to the terrible economic dislocation which had befallen their communities. Their traditional view of government, however, failed them; they could not resolve this horrendous crisis on their own.

There emerged then younger business leaders who did not oppose accepting federal assistance programs—if it would restore economic vitality to their communities. These men would succeed to dominance, particularly after they returned as veterans from WWII. Still, they were very much the creatures of their small-town backgrounds. They were no more prepared to cope with the challenges of massive urbanization than their predecessors had been in coping with the Depression.

There existed in several prominent towns and the county at large a festering sore which local leaders tried ever to deny. It had to do with corruption and violation of law by officials. Ingrown cronyism had bred a willingness for social and cultural leaders to look away from the illegal gambling, illegal rum running during Prohibition, bribery and blatant discrimination—so long as these did not disturb their lives.

Eventually in the late 1940s, circumstances threw together a handful of civic-minded leaders from around the county: a judge in Newport Beach, a grand jury chairman from Buena Park, a district attorney from Santa Ana, and a future State Governor, then the State's Democratic Attorney General. Together they drove out the gamblers and corrupt officials. Even the dog-catcher fled to Mexico.

Their timing could not have occurred more fortuitous for Orange County, coming as it did on the eve of the great temptations available from the lucrative windfall profits of rezoning to accommodate the wave of urban development just about to hit Orange County. As a result of this clean-up effort, mafioso did not gain control, although it was an exceedingly close call. They certainly tried to make inroads but with little success.

As relatively well educated families flooded Orange County with the advent of aerospace industries, expectations for professionally managed municipalities and schools grew into an undeniable clamor. While these newcomers lacked the organizational networks to mount successful municipal reforms on their own, there had long existed local residents who harbored the same aspirations for their communities but had lacked sufficient numbers to undertake a campaign. Once the newcomers found that they could not take over local government but had to depend on reform-minded locals, the two groups could and did bring about change. The change they brought involved the total professionalization of local government.

Going into the 1950s, local school boards would debate how many pencils and how many light bulbs and how much toilet paper their district should purchase for a coming year. Leaving such logistical management to a professional and focusing on policy issues simply lay beyond their vision. They drew superintendents, like city clerks and municipal "department" heads, from locals known as "good old boys." All played the local game.

Anaheim and Santa Ana had experimented with the new wave of "scientific public administration" even to creating a city manager slot in the 1920s. But they never really understood it and so soon dropped it. In 1946, Newport Beach led the way with the first appointed professional city administrator. Anaheim and Santa Ana followed suit in 1950 and 1951 respectively.

This prompted leaders in Orange, Fullerton, and La Habra to call for city managers, too. The first two succeeded with compromised city manager/administrator positions in 1952; La Habra made the move in 1954, along with Brea, Laguna Beach, and San Clemente. Seal Beach had to go through a decade-long battle against its powerful gambling interests before it could get rid of its archaic commission format and move into the modern era.

First Newport Beach in 1948 and then Santa Ana and Anaheim upgraded their city administrators to a true city manager. (A city administrator remains subordinate to the mayor whereas a city manager becomes the chief executive officer, the elected mayor only chairing council meetings and handling ceremonial functions.) Fullerton as of 1967 had still not changed the title of its chief professional from city administrator even though in reality he had all the powers and authority of a city manager.

The last of the thirteen old municipalities, Tustin finally made this change when growth overwhelmed its city council in the mid-1960s. Excluding tiny Villa Park (a contract city anyway), all municipalities which incorporated after WWII established a council-manager/administrator form of government. Even tiny Villa Park with a so-called council/mayor structure had its one full-time employee, its city clerk, operate in a manner not unlike a manager. Of 24 municipalities in 1966, 13 had managers and 10 had administrators, Villa Park being the twenty-fourth.

Without exception, city managers and administrators credit their councils with policy formation and claim that their own responsibilities lie merely in implementing that policy. Council members, however, looked skeptically at these reaffirmations of managerial theory. If they stopped to examine what transpired, they could and did sense that their CEO made the preponderance of decisions and that those decisions did tend to shape policy, whether intentionally or inadvertently.

Increasingly, part-time elected officials (who may commute to jobs elsewhere) became dependent on professionals operating on the scene all the time. Moreover, successful professional managers knew they must build their own constituencies among public interest groups to buffer and support themselves in the event their employer, the city council, decided to thwart the professional in whatever course he believed best. (In those days, females had not yet achieved municipal CEO status.)

Even the most skillful managers encountered trouble. Unable to fight big government at federal and state levels, local voters knew they at least had the power to block local government for such things as "palaces for politicians," their term for city halls. They could and often did vote down requisite bond issues intended to serve local needs for sewers, flood protection, or parks.

A manager would then prove his mettle by finding alternative funding routes to provide the public what it had said it did not want. The same evaluation applied to the management of school districts as they converted to professional superintendents brought in from outside. As outsiders, professional managers consciously address several audiences all the time: not only the city council which hires them currently, but potential future employers as well as other managers. "Success" in this context rests on expansion of staff which rests on an expanded population to be served and hence on an ever improved tax base.

Land-use planning graphically illustrates this phenomenal movement toward professionalization. In all of Orange County at the end of WWII there existed only one professional planner position: for the county planning commission. A decade later, county government had a small staff, and several of the larger municipalities had begun to create positions with the title of planner. By 1961, approximately half of the then 22 municipalities had hired professionals with educations and/or experience in land-use planning—as distinct from engineers or building inspectors who had previously worn a second hat as their town's "planner" (really meaning their zoning administrator).

This trend led the county planning director to establish a countywide organization of planners to meet monthly and discuss mutual concerns and innovations. By April 1966, the roster of this organization included 80 professionals in 20 out of the then 24 municipalities, in addition to a 22-member professional county planning department. Twenty-four affiliates, also professional planners but in private or educational organizations doing work comparable to those in local-level public units, brought the total to 126. And these did not include numerous architects doubling as planning consultants.

New Formats

As the giant aerospace industries moved to Orange County, they sought to demonstrate their civic mindedness and their desire to "fit in." Immediately their officials received invitations to participate in local service clubs and charities. Since their plant locations usually fell between towns, different officials from the same plant might serve on committees and head programs in several towns simultaneously. They did not belong to any one place-designated community.

Charities demonstrate people's transitional perception of their community. Since the 1920s, each of the larger towns had its own Community

Chest—13 in all. When people lived and worked in the same town and local industries hired mostly local people, donating to a local charity for local needs made good sense. As people began to commute between towns for work and residence and as charity needs took on a countywide scale, difficulties began to arise. Organizations doing the charity work had to prepare and make 13 different appeals.

In 1947, the 13 Community Chest organizations formed a loose confederation for pooling information, yet continued their individual campaigns. But when the large industries arrived with employees living throughout the county, the old system became obviously awkward. The messiness of having 13 collecting agencies make 13 presentations to solicit funds for 13 boards to give money to operational agencies that functioned on a countywide scale repulsed these ultramodern giants.

Since the money came from countywide industries for countywide purposes, why not, they asked, have a countywide Community Chest or (by its new name) a United Fund. Moreover, consolidation would benefit the charities because people could no longer claim they gave at work when contacted at home and claim they gave at home when contacted at work. Consequently a "blue ribbon" committee began the requisite exploration in 1965-66 to amalgamate the full charity effort. Nothing happened quickly, but the five professional Community Chest executives serving the 13 organizations expressed a feeling that they could all do a better job unified than separate.

Chief executives of the new aerospace and new university campuses brought with them experiences from many parts of America and other parts of the world. None of them owned the companies they ran; they were high-powered professional managers accountable to chief executives or boards of still larger organizations elsewhere. They thought in managerial terms and at a far broader scale than had typified local leaders.

They were, of course, welcomed for the jobs and hence for the economic prosperity they represented. But they did experience some exasperation (though expertly concealed, naturally) with local processes of decision making. In particular, they viewed weak environmental and land-use planning with alarm.

On 14 November 1963, John B. Lawson, General Manger of Philco Aeronutronics, proposed a citizens' organization to deal with countywide planning issues. He chose the Fourth Annual Orange County Economic Development Conference to make his call for a cross-section of conference backers to form a board to head an organization he named Project 21 for the twenty-first century.

Those invited included six executives from the largest aerospace firms, the University of California chancellor, three men in large-scale real estate development, a publisher, three bank executives, a philanthropist, two utility executives whose companies paid the largest taxes, the Irvine Company president, the local Marine Corps general, the executive manager of the Farm Bureau, the County Supervisor with longest tenure, and the then current local League of California Cities president.

In a handsomely designed PR brochure, Project 21 announced its intentions to "lend its services and support to help guide Orange County's growth into metropolitan greatness in the twenty-first century by: enlisting citizen participation in behalf of defining and clarifying Orange County goals and objectives; initiating and encouraging environmental studies of Orange County on a nonpartisan and objective basis...; organizing a reference center...; providing a forum where public and private enterprise can come together to study and discuss the problems, needs, and objectives of Orange County in a constructive and cooperative way; recommending improved planning standards and techniques...; sponsoring a biennial conference...; publicly honoring those corporations, activities, and individuals that contribute so nobly to the advancement of Orange County's living environment; generating citizen support for those objectives of the private and public sector that are compatible with the purposes and aims of Project 21."

Mr. Lawson hoped that Project 21 would become a "nagging conscience" for a rapidly developing Orange County, especially for the two-thirds of its area yet to urbanize. When President Johnson began to champion city beautification, Congressman R.T. Hanna submitted a speech into the Congressional Record for July 1, 1965, about this "ideal example of what farsighted, civic-minded Americans can do to insure that the growth we all know must take place will be a guided and orderly growth." Even President Johnson sent his personal congratulations to Project 21's leaders.

Then for two years these tycoons met month after month with little happening. Accustomed to formulating policy and having subordinates fill in details and carry out the program, they found themselves simply talking to each other. Project 21 had no staff because it had no money, other than what Aeronutronics spent on it out of its own public relations budget.

Members did agree it would take a million dollars to make the project workable. But no source existed for that kind of funding. After all, board-members could not come to grips with the crucial issues that constituted tangible impediments to the beautiful future they talked about—such as how tax assessing practice works counterproductively to the principals of sound land-use planning, to name just one of many troubling items. So what substantively would a lot of money accomplish if it had miraculously become available to them?

This outcome should not have been unexpected. Not one of its board-members had a political base from which to maneuver. Even the County Supervisor, the only elected official among them, expected to retire at the end of his current term. The others only had their institutional or positional prestige to lend—not give; they must shepherd that prestige for their career responsibilities. None had anything to bargain with even had Project 21 endeavored to take a positive stand on some goal. Perhaps more significantly, they did not conceptualize the planning of a beautiful environment as a political process requiring bargaining and horse-trading in a political arena.

The goals stated in Project 21's brochure typified the worldview of this new kind of leadership. They saw public salvation through education and gentlemanly discussion. They presumed that people only needed enlightenment since of course everyone acts rationally, a presumption which effective politicians know better than to operate from.

Actually, every one of its goals were so antiseptically non-controversial that none of Project 21's members could have been expected to stake much personal prestige on them. They were akin to being for motherhood and against sin--and about as effective. They were simply the same expressions, at county level, that appear in all the municipal master plans: an avoidance

of unpleasant realities in preference for platitudes which everyone can po-
litely agree to and promptly ignore.

Although Project 21 was ineffective precisely because it involved so
many high-level executives, the county chamber of commerce grew alarmed
lest it steal some of the latter's reason to be. To mollify everyone, Democrat
Hanna was called in to negotiate between these two overwhelmingly Republican groups which, to further the ironies, had overlapping membership.
Such was the antiseptically nonpartisan nature of the entire affair.

THE ROLE OF TAX APPRAISING PRACTICE

Having mentioned the impact of tax assessing as a crucial factor in land use,
it seems only appropriate to look specifically at its challenge to leadership in
Orange County.

Quite possibly every place in America has at least some people who view
tax assessments as inevitably unfair. Usually it never becomes much of a
political issue beyond an occasional property owner contesting a particular
assessment on his/her piece of property. Orange County, on the other hand,
had all the ingredients for the arcane art of tax appraising to touch off a
major conflagration.

There were lucrative oil fields and vast stretches of empty land, expensive mansions and impoverished school districts, an old social/political elite
whose status once derived from land ownership, and newcomers demanding
better public services. Into this scene came the rapid urbanization discussed
previously with all its disparate interests, social changes, and unstructured
accumulation of unintegrated people.

As in so much that happened to Orange county, there was the Irvine
Ranch, holding the entire mid-fifth of the county and undergoing an internal
fight among its family owners over the best use for that land. Its dominant
faction wanted to go slowly, keeping agriculture as long as possible in what
they presumed would be James Jr's preference. The largest stockholder,
James Jr's granddaughter Joan, however pushed hard for full-scale planned
urbanization.

One other factor: In Orange County the tax assessor stood for election independently. An assessor need only do what he/she interpreted the law to require, answering to no one except the voters. An assessor need pay attention neither to the planning process nor to what public officials at municipal and even at county level sought to accomplish in the way of growth management and environmental or economic protection.

Given this mix of ingredients, it was only a matter of time until tax assessing erupted as a political issue. By 1961 the mix began to boil. A group of almost five hundred Newport Beach residents challenged the County Assessor over alleged discriminatory practices. They charged discrimination in that their assessments rose faster than for property in Costa Mesa which meant Newport Beach residents with few children would have to pay for schools in Costa Mesa which had many children. Ironically, the protesters quickly drew the Irvine Company into the fray because they wanted the ranch with no people to contribute more taxes to support the many Newport Beach residents.

Technically, an assessor need say nothing at a hearing by a Board of Equalization because the burden of proof lay with each appellant. So the Assessor did not bother to appear for these cases, sending a deputy instead. But this flare-up was not an ordinary appeal by individuals; this was an organized mass political protest. While he won the initial skirmishes technically, he had not disarmed the revolt underway.

Indeed, his inability to enlighten and hence placate the public about the technicalities of assessing (and it is doubtful that anyone could have, given the archaic practices then employed) only fed the fire. The protesters had won in that they had made dissatisfied people all over the county aware that they were not alone. The legally prescribed set of requirements and procedures inherent in tax assessing—rather than individual properties—had become the burning issue.

As an issue, it had its diversity of perspectives, few if any of which felt comfortable with assessment procedures as then conducted. Each perspective had its particular objectives, complaints, and agenda. Single family residents, the most vocal bloc, wanted higher assessments on apartment buildings (as a way of keeping "undesirable" people out of their community) even though apartments paid proportionately higher taxes per child needing education than did single family homes.

Agricultural interests (such as the Irvine Ranch management) argued for preserving prime farm land, for several reasons. Since whatever taxes farms paid ran always higher than the amount of services they required, agriculture actually subsidized urban uses rather than the other way around as the protesters claimed. Preserving ag land meant preserving open space that at some future date can accommodate extremely valuable people-uses such as parks yet remain at a price public agencies can afford in acquiring it then.

Moreover, the Irvine Company was spending millions of dollars in careful planning, engineering, and marketing studies to ensure that, when urbanization did engulf its extensive land area, it would turn out exceedingly well. It resisted being stampeded into premature development due to excessive taxation on its remaining agriculture operations. Indeed, this agricultural base would provide the front-end capital to finance the eventual urban development in a manner everyone would take pride in.

Irvine management preferred to use agricultural production for front-end money, rather than selling off the land to developers, because it could in this way retain ownership in the underlying land. Retaining landownership would allow it to control future development into perpetuity. While planners could sympathize with this strategy (from their sad experiences with urban renewal), it made all other interests apprehensive about the horrendous wealth and hence power that would accumulate to the Irvine Company. Eventually (years later) the Irvine Company would recognize political reality and reverse its policy of only leasing land for housing; homeowners would gain clear title.

Professional planning circles and the forerunners of what would become the environmental movement sought legislation at state level around the country that would force tax assessments to reflect and support good land-use planning. In contrast, articles in the building industry's *House & Home*—pointing to the windfalls made by land owners who did nothing except raise the price of land—favored assessments which would open up land for development. Economists and planners have argued windfalls and "wipeouts" ever since.

Joan Irvine wanted increased taxes on Irvine ag land to force the conservative boardmembers to loosen their hold. (Her pressure on fellow boardmembers had caused them to donate a 1000 acres to the University of California for a campus that would surely attract high-valued industry and commerce onto Irvine land. And it did do exactly that—at a faster rate than even she anticipated.)

A somewhat bizarre twist emerged in this controversy. A countywide political brouhaha arose because politically conservative people in Newport Beach contended that the owners of undeveloped land had no right to profit from the sale of land because the community—by increasing demand and providing urban services—created the increment of wealth. None of them, apparently, recognized how accurately they espoused the nineteenth century "socialism" of Henry George.

As political agitation heated up, the long-time County Assessor decided to retire due to failing health. His successor won by promising everyone a favorable resolution. Some changes he could and did make, such as reassessing all property annually instead of every three or four years. In this way he could mitigate the shock owners felt when hit with huge increments which they might have tolerated if graduated upward yearly. What he could not do was clarify assessing practice as such to the public's understanding and then integrate it with community aspirations for orderly growth and land-use transformation.

The new assessor stated that the keystone of assessing "is found in the market place" and so should reflect market value. Market value, however, involves many aspects: income stream (rental or productive) discounted into the future, sales prices of surrounding or similar parcels, and potential use. Zoning, he said, was not a consideration other than as it affects the market. Value is a function of demand, a reaffirmation of nineteenth century "economic man" theory: no demand, no value.

Value, in this view, exists only to the extent it can be measured in monetary terms. Community aspirations have no place in reckoning property valuation since presumably the market fully and accurately reflects community values. Environmental, ecological, aesthetic considerations similarly may not be factored in. Only the economic equation counts because it alone can be measured with reasonable precision.

The on-going political tug-of-war, naturally, never bothered with such subtleties. The County Chamber of Commerce's Governmental Affairs committee in 1966, fearing the promotion of even worse sprawl, attacked the new Assessor. Even the Grand Jury became drawn into this tussle.

While it accepted the Assessor's explanation of appraisal by market value, the Jury concluded: "In view of Orange County's unique position as having the highest percentage of undeveloped land of any urban area in the United States, we strongly urge that the assessor give due consideration to the master plans of the Orange County Planning Commission and those of private landowners in exercising his discretionary powers in arriving at real property values, so that the county can develop aesthetically and orderly as it develops economically."

His response reveals the prevailing confusion over what planning should accomplish. "Because a piece of property has been zoned, we do not immediately go out and adjust the assessment. We wait to see the nature and extent of the market responses and then act accordingly; for value is not inherent in a thing itself but rather exists in the mind of man and is evidenced by him in his actions in the market place."

Orange County's struggle over the issue of the impact of property tax assessments on future community development did not happen in isolation. Counties throughout the state (and nation) faced it one way or another. In 1965, state legislators passed the California Land Conservation Act. It hoped to remedy assessment-induced premature conversion of prime ag land to urban sprawl.

Through a contract between landowner and county on a continuing ten-year basis, farmers could rest assured of taxes based on current use rather than on potential urban use. If an assessor persisted in raising the assessment in spite of such a contract, the county would have to compensate the agricultural interest. However, this conservation act applied only to land, not improvements. The assessor could make up for a lower land evaluation by assessing high other property, such as the trees the Irvine Ranch sought to preserve.

Where tried in other parts of the state, difficulties immediately arose. Not certain how well it would work, farmers chose the "agreement" provision instead of a binding ten-year contract—which left assessors off the hook. Simply keeping assessments down would do little good in checking taxes if the tax rate goes up sharply to meet the needs of newly urbanized lands within the same school district. Consequently, a year later, Orange County planners and officials still struggled to figure how to implement it. County counsel finally had to conclude that the law must be unconstitutional.

Several results followed what became an acrimonious fight between the Assessor and the Irvine Company. Instead of constructing the planned new city of Irvine on hilly land around the campus—on land otherwise good only for low productive grazing—Irvine took thousands of prime acres out of agricultural production on the flat central area. Not only was the best agricultural land lost, a valued future open space disappeared and the new university campus sat over on the hilly land isolated from the community it supposedly would provide a core and integrated theme.

A more immediate outcome occurred in the next (1966) election campaign for assessor. It revealed a political fact of life which few if any Orange Countians could have anticipated or believed.

A group assembled to plan a strategy for defeating the new assessor. This group consisted of what, not many years earlier, would have fit quite well Floyd Hunter's description of a power elite: oil men, agricultural interests, representatives of large commerce and industry, large-scale developers and major landowners. First they needed to find a viable candidate to oppose the assessor in the upcoming race, someone they could concertedly throw their collective weight behind.

After months of searching, they were shocked to discover that they no longer had control of the situation. No one with the requisite experience and stature would serve as their front. Furthermore, they discovered later that someone within that exclusive group was a Judas. Someone had informed the other side about all that transpired, possibly with recordings.

When these realities sank in, the group came unglued. For lack of a valid candidate, they could no long run a political campaign—even when their vital interests lay so directly exposed. A power structure no longer existed.

Pluralism had won at county level as it had already become abundantly evident at municipal level.

The fact that this assessor was later convicted and imprisoned for wrongdoing is really a minor footnote to this episode. Other changes mattered more: Power had diffused. The giant Irvine Company had to change its ambitious plans to fit mass economics. Lofty words about planning for a beautiful future by executive-class elites became exceedingly hollow.

LEADERSHIP CLASSIFICATION

During the first half of the twentieth century, certain families tended to dominate the social, economic, and political pecking order within Orange County. Most frequently these were citrus ranchers and bankers. Others, though resident in Orange County, reckoned their social status at a scale or in a realm which transcended the community functioning within Orange County. They operated economically at state level: the Irvines, for instance, and some of the oil operators.

As urban development altered the economic structure, the political process changed. Soon, some people had financial power, others had social prestige (and land), while yet others gained political influence without having to serve as fronts for the first two groups. Social, economic, and political influence no longer occurred in unison. Each had its own equations, processes, structure, and agendas. (This same transformation occurred dramatically in Hawaii after WWII, too, as well as in many parts of America.)

By the mid-1960s, positions of leadership took several distinct forms.

1. The **Wealthy Elite** continued to receive invitations to head or take prominent roles in charity drives and cultural institutions. Some of these came from the old landed families; others were oil, movie star, or industrial millionaires. They could contribute either glamour or an aristocratic aura to community efforts.

2. Positional Elites Non-locally Earned came from the ranks of top executives—the recently arrived outsiders who headed aerospace firms or universities. The University of California chancellor, for example, was quickly recruited to serve on the symphony, county chamber, Big Brothers, and Project 21 boards of directors. Having large organizations at their command, they could encourage subordinates to provide the legwork for charities and community endeavors, as well as rally subordinates to make donations.

3. Positional Elite Locally Earned consisted of elected representatives at county, state, and national level as well as managers of the county chamber, larger city chambers, some city managers, some school superintendents, president of the Orange County chapter of the League of California Cities, and president of the Farm Bureau. These became known as "the men who get things done." They differ from those in category #2 largely in that they were not automatic newsmakers (sometimes by choice), hence they had to prove their leadership capabilities by being elected or by demonstrating accomplishments on the job.

4. Earned Local included dynamic entrepreneurs, school board members, city councilmembers, and chief executives for smaller municipalities and school districts. No automatic mantel of leadership awaited them, yet their public service was quite essential. Their hope lay in moving up to classification #3 or in focusing on a specific issue in which they could, for a time, exert more impact than leaders in either #2 or #3 whose roles usually spread their attention widely.

5. Special Group Reps—for religious, racial, age, economic interests. By and large, their leadership strength remained strictly limited to one or at most two issues (such as race and poverty combined). For example: leaders of the War on Poverty Community Action Council or spokesmen (largely self-appointed) for senior citizens in the several quite large and politically active retirement communities.

The further down this list, the more evenly spread the members' geographical distribution. The first two categories and much of the third, however, tended to segregate themselves quite markedly. We noted, for instance, this among symphony backers. Of the 26 (out of 30) Orange County Chamber of Commerce directors whose 1966 addresses could be ascertained, ten (38.5 percent) lived within the corporate limits of municipal Newport Beach. That gave Newport twelve times its numerical representation.

Santa Ana and Anaheim, with four and five times Newport's population, had only three residents each on that board. Several municipalities with twice Newport's population had no representation. Eleven of 20 members on Project 21 resided in Newport. Even on the County Grand Jury where an effort was made to have geographical breadth, Newport had nine times its numerical share between 1962 and 1965. Tustin footills, Fullerton hills, Laguna Beach, and the new expensive marina development of Huntington Harbor also made disproportional contributions of members to countywide activities.

CHALLENGE OF SCALE

Thus far we have viewed the region of Orange County almost entirely within itself when in fact it is very much a part of a much larger region, that of southern California. Just as roads and water became workable when dealt with countywide rather than locally, the dynamics of mobility and water in this highly urbanized metropolitan conurbation called for an appropriately scaled approach, too.

Water was tackled in the 1920s with the creation of the Metropolitan Water District. With the demise of interurban rail service, regional mobility became the responsibility of the California Division of Highways with its freeway network plan. By the 1960s, scattered leaders in each of the counties of southern California began to recognize some of the other regional problems which massive urban growth generated.

They began to talk among themselves about the growing needs for mass transit, smog and pollution control, and regional parks—all matters which do not stop at county boundaries. Immediately they would face an obstacle, the lack of any jurisdictional entity to tackle regional problems on an appropriate regional scale. Only county and municipal governments existed then. But with Los Angeles City and Los Angeles County so disproportionately larger than the others, it became difficult to find a basis of parity upon which to negotiate the resolution of differences much less form a regional government.

During 1959-60, various agencies in southern California formed the Los Angeles Regional Transportation Study (LARTS) which imposed no membership fees, only the requirement that member jurisdictions contribute land-use planning information. Eventually 93 percent of all municipalities in Los Angeles, Orange, Riverside, San Bernardino, and Ventura counties did participate. LARTS then evolved into TASC, Transportation Association of Southern California, thereby losing its negative image of imposing Los Angeles on everyone else. TASC, a staff-based organization, would serve as a standing committee within SCAG, the Southern California Association of Governments whose constituent assembly could include only elected officials.

After the 1963 state legislature determined that any counties lacking regional planning would come under State planning, the County Supervisors Association pushed for locally created arrangements. The federal government sweetened it with an incentive: eligibility for "701 grants" for regional parks.

Although Orange County's Board of Supervisors played a key role in creating SCAG, only 13 of the county's 24 municipalities joined. It took the county two and a half years to join officially itself. The mayor of Costa Mesa denounced SCAG as a foot-in-the-door to regional government. He proposed to have a countywide organization of municipalities instead. Ironically, he was the last holdout against the county's proposed unified highway program earlier.

As SCAG began to function as a clearing house and coordinating assembly, it established RPPC, the Regional Park Planning Council in 1965 for channeling federal funds. Then came also SCPC, the Southern California Planning Congress, open to planning commissioners, professional planners, civic organizations and interested parties. It would provide a forum for constructive discussion toward stimulating greater cooperation and coordination among municipal and regional bodies. At the same time, RPA (Regional Plan Association) came into existence to provide a forum for nongovernmental interests to make their contribution to the ongoing enlightenment—or confusion.

The most immediate observation possible from a review of this alphabetic scramble of organizations concerns the difficulty of defining what constitutes a region. Orange County lends itself easily to delineation because
three of its four sides have distinct geographical boundaries: mountains and
ocean. Some of the other counties are at least partially recognizable too.
With a little imagination one can perceive all of southern California within
physical borders. But when one thinks in terms of functional issues—such
as transit, smog, land use—then "region" gets fuzzy indeed.

State Highway District VII for freeways covers three counties. TASC
and RPPC encompassed five counties. SCAG, six counties. SCPC, eight
counties. RPA, nine counties. Air pollution and rapid transit, however, remained structured by separate counties, each on its own. When the State
Planning Department drew its concept of regions, it ignored county lines
entirely, preferring geographical determinations without resolving how such
a region could do anything jurisdictionally.

Not resolved by any of these attempts at regionalism was how to neu-
tralize (and hopefully co-opt) each tax assessor's ability to implement the
unprinted, unreviewed, and unadopted land-use plan which exists within that
assessor's mind.

There remains one other aspect of this flush of regional mindedness seldom acknowledged. Until 1962, efforts to bring officials together from the
various counties and municipalities of southern California (northern California as well) made scant substantive progress. From 1963 on, progress
became surprisingly less obstructed. But why this marked change just then?

One particular factor appears to have made it possible for southern Californians to find a meeting of the minds as never existed before. That factor
was the playoff series at the end of September 1962 between the Los Angeles Dodgers and San Francisco Giants. As Governor Pat Brown stated, for
three days all of California came to a standstill as people everywhere sat
glued to their television sets, erupting from time to time with shouts of excitement or moans of disappointment.

After three days of intently shouting either "Los Angeles" or "San Francisco," people in both regions found a sense of identification that had never
really existed before. From so much emotional electricity, far more people

held a common perspective than they had previously believed possible. All of which leads into the next chapter where we look at the phenomenon of community as a complex system.

NEIGHBORHOOD ASSOCIATIONS

At the same time that issues of "local" governance encompassed more intricate problems at ever larger regional scales, politicization of neighborhood life became the norm. Urban development of the giant Irvine Ranch graphically demonstrated this trend, though it most definitely did not occur in isolation. A new approach to land-use planning emerged, that of "planned community" with a single zoning classification to cover as much as several square miles and for all of the diverse uses of land commonly found in a town. (Irvine's planner and subsequent president, Ray Watson, had extensively examined planned communities in Britain and the US East Coast.)

The difference now, from what transpired in traditional towns, lay with the ownership factor. Instead of multiple landowners requiring governmental regulation, a single large landowner would employ a coordinated team of engineers, architects, financiers, realtors, and infrastructure managers to produce not only an attractive, integrated, land-use and circulation layout but an optimally feasible strategy of staged development. Government planners now need only set broad policies, not details.

Initially the Irvine Company had hoped to avoid the frustrating problems which public jurisdictions then encountered in trying to renew old areas and the typical blight that accompanied obsolescence. It sought to do so by retaining ownership of the land and keeping all urban development on a lease basis. Then it would, hopefully, have far better leverage over both economic and political forces decades down the road.

By the time the Company read the political future—that residents, if unable to gain ownership rights in the land itself, would politically fight Irvine over every little issue out of fear for Irvine's colossal might—a potentially more powerful force already existed. This power lay in the neighborhood association theoretically controlled by residents themselves. They could directly control their own communal fate.

As much as homeowner associations might fear and resent giant development corporations which the Irvine Ranch had become, their individual interests for real estate values, amenities, property maintenance, and an upper-middle class life style turned out identical to Irvine Company interests and objectives. Moreover, as occurs in virtually all condominium or planned unit developments, the original owner/developer structures the unit's by-laws to ensure compliance with the originator's economic interests.

In this way, home buyers found themselves oriented toward conformity whether they initially wanted it or not. And where home prices run two or three times higher than average, residents tend to share a mutual interest in retaining their neighborhood character/quality and in controlling their common areas. Expressing individual idiosyncrasies—such as in choosing bizarre house colors, leaving yards unweeded, and parking pickup trucks or campers on the street—encountered severe social pressure and eventually legal action by local associations to impose conformity.

Except among the large blocs of retirees moving into Orange County, much of the informal policing of neighborhoods tended to fall to those women who spent more time at home than their husbands. Besides expected involvement in public school, library, and recreational programs, newcomer female residents often took on important (leadership) roles in neighborhood politics, more so than acknowledged where males continued to hold a majority of the positions on boards and commissions. Generally, newcomer wives had more opportunities to establish and hence to use local networks for political action (whenever mobilization became necessary) than did their husbands.

With the center fifth of the entire county, what happened under Irvine auspices would unavoidably have a sizable impact on community evolution throughout this region. But the significance of neighborhood governance predates the first Irvine developments. Already huge tracts of single-owner land on the southeast (Laguna) side had begun their transition from cattle ranges to planned community developments. Still earlier, housing tracts on the northwest side had tended to wall themselves off and then generate a base for the political upheavals we noted already. As far back as the turn of this century, tract developments like Yorba Linda, President Nixon's birthplace, had explicit deed restrictions to insure a prescribed life style, even to prohibiting consumption of alcoholic beverages.

A 1990s Update

Already by the 1970s new freeways wove a countywide fabric to an even greater extent. Without eliminating local jurisdictions and local identity, a distinct countywide landscape pattern of community functions emerged quite clearly for a population now doubled to more than two and a half million. Indeed, within its 796 square miles, little Orange County evolved fully into a new kind of city, one of the nation's largest albeit composed of a multiplicity of local jurisdictions and hence not recognized as a true city by the US Census Bureau.

The recreational centers at Anaheim (with Disneyland, a stadium for Angels baseball, then Rams football teams) and at Newport Beach's harbor remained. But the local airport, named for John Wayne and now greatly enlarged into one of California's busiest, came to provide a hub for the burgeoning aerospace and think-tank industries which located here to take advantage of spinoffs from University of California Irvine research nearby. The schematic map also shows the once localized spatial pattern of trendsetting residences for local leaders now distributed (largely for the top corporate strata) at a regional scale.

A touch of irony occurs here. After so many decades of a love/hate (or envy/fear) relationship between local leaders in Orange County's western two-fifths and the giant Irvine Company in the middle fifth, the emergent countywide community became focused largely within the Irvine realm—the airport, its surrounding high tech industrial center, the UC campus, a major corporate headquarters complex just above Newport Beach, one of America's largest shopping centers in nearby Costa Mesa, all circled by such new elite residential areas as in Laguna Niguel and Laguna Beach.

As in an earlier age when Irvine family members and oil interests living in Newport Beach did not limit their scale of influence to just Orange County, so now the residents of these elite residential areas live and interact

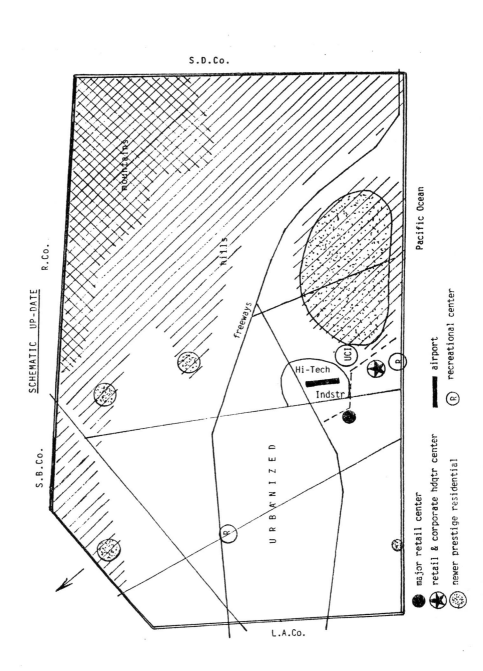

SCHEMATIC UP-DATE

S.D.Co.

R.Co.

S.B.Co.

L.A.Co.

Pacific Ocean

Mountains

Hills

Freeways

Hi-Tech

Indstr

UCI

URBANIZED

major retail center

retail & corporate hdqtr center

newer prestige residential

airport

recreational center

R

in networks predominately stretching globally far beyond the local scene. Even the ordinary Orange County resident lives in an interlinked world beyond his/her consciousness—consuming food and fiber grown in remote parts of the world, viewing electronically communicated news and entertainment from worldwide sources, working to produce goods or services destined for distant markets.

Nationwide news media attention on Orange County in early December 1994 revealed, unwittingly, not only the lead O.C. had taken in federating local public agencies to better serve an integrated, multiscaled community system, but a totally different kind of "leadership." Orange County, one of the largest, most prosperous, sophisticated metro regions in America jolted the Securities & Exchange Commission and other state/federal watchdog authorities by filing for bankruptcy protection. If this could happen here, what might be happening to other jurisdictions? Even bond markets overseas as well as on Wall Street felt the jolt.

It seems Orange County gambled the pooled cash reserves of 187 municipal, special district, school district, and county agencies—a total of some twenty billion dollars—on high-risk derivatives. With the rise of interest rates, this investment fund lost nearly two billion dollars in a few months, setting off a cascade of ramifications. Some immediate impacts: agencies unable to meet operating expenses; new schools, roads, and other needed projects put on hold and likely lost; their Standard & Poor's credit rating fallen to junk bond status thereby wiping out private bondholders. Then to top it off, public agencies had to discharge employees just when the worst storms in decades created a desperate need for emergency and public clean-up operations.

The long-run implications, however, may prove even more interesting in a region well noted for cynicism about government and for resistance to increased taxes even for essential services. Since these public agencies had felt pressured to pool their cash reserves, this fiscal crisis could reverse Orange County's pioneering trend throughout this century toward an integrated (though fragile) web of variously scaled local units. It could possibly ignite centrifugal forces to fly apart, thereby making local government even less reflective of the evolving community system we dissect in the next chapter.

More likely, this crisis could force local governments to do what people have long talked about doing but seldom tried, namely to privatize public services.

After Orange County had recently survived devastating fire storms in some of its elite new residential areas as well as weathering southern California's economic decline, this latest crisis might reveal more about its prototypic community system than any aspect reviewed here. It appears well worth watching in coming years, mostly for its social and political spinoffs long after the immediate fiscal storm has subsided. But Orange County leaders at least did do what all king's men and all the king's horses could not do: they put Humpty Dumpty back together again. They managed to get their fiscal house in order—and in only 18 months, much to the dismay of all outside observers.

CHAPTER TWELVE

A REGIONAL
COMMUNITY COMPLEX

O n that day in 1966 when Orange County's population topped 1,200,000, residents made 4.5 million vehicular trips, used over 250 million gallons of water for all purposes, conducted 6.3 million dollars worth of retail transactions, read approximately 400,000 newspapers, and made nearly two million phone calls, 92 percent of them between parties within the county, half of them within their immediate locales.

With a population in excess of that in 15 entire states, Orange County had no overall governing structure. The five-member Board of Supervisors dealt with some issues countywide, its jurisdiction limited to only unincorporated areas for a different set of decisions. Other functions came independently under 24 city councils, 26 elementary and unified school boards, 4 high school districts, 3 junior college districts, 49 water districts, 37 lighting districts, 12 fire districts, 9 community services districts, 8 maintenance districts plus countywide districts for flood control, harbors, mosquito abatement, and cemeteries, among others—a total of 436 entities with 1399 different tax rates. And all of them were governed by nominally nonpolitical (actually just nonpartisan) officials.

How did this welter of people, places, things, and interactions keep functioning so that humans could obtain the water, food, shelter, and protection they needed for family survival and the perpetuation of the species? Certainly laws and police enforcement operated within an institutionalized legal framework. But laws and police have not always prevented every aggregation of humans from experiencing chaos and strife.

At least a core of participants in Orange County had to believe in those laws and in those institutions for them to function as intended. Even though not all residents participated in setting societal values and norms and in running community affairs, at least the core had to feel satisfied. And they usually had—until the flood of newcomers tried to insert themselves into this core, especially after 1950.

Before the first world war, life in Orange County exuded Norman Rockwellism in its small town character. Life revolved around family, church, and school, all garnished with social events, patriotic parades, ladies' clubs, fraternal orders, and male business contacts. Everyone knew everyone else and watched everyone else. This portrait at least ran true for the middle-class Anglos, the self-styled "proper society."

By the 1920s when the local business entrepreneur clearly dominated local towns, young people gained recognition and began their move up through the ranks to town leadership by participation in school plays and orchestra, in sports, the YMCA, Boy Scouts, then junior social associations. Adult membership in service clubs (topped by Rotary), fraternal clubs (topped by Masonic Order), and ultimately the country club with communitywide recognition and comradery among the people who "counted" clearly indicated social strata. These determined who had contact with whom, hence which young people married each other.

But not everyone had this route open to them. Jewish merchants might be tolerated in business, but not in clubs or "Y" where their children would interact with (i.e., date) Christian children. Mexican families had no chance at all; if they were part of the old landowning elite, they distinguished themselves as Castilian, not Mexican, and then still might find themselves relegated to the Catholic segment of society. Japanese who owned their farms and whose children did well in school might occupy a marginal position: included with Anglos on some things (such as in farm organizations and

PTA) but never within church and country club society. Life was comfortably segmented—comfortably at least for those within the core.

Autumn Saturday afternoons were devoted to the communal ritual of high school football; Saturday evenings year around to a visit to the downtowns or, for the elite, to a country club dance. Mexicans and Blacks, on the other hand, risked their lives just venturing into a local public swimming pool.

Little changed for old-timers during the post-WWII influx. The problem lay with the newcomers, a large portion of whom brought better educations and an anticipation for naturally receiving an elevated status. They expected to move into town leadership roles, service club membership, and even country club membership. What a shock; they amounted to just so many more faceless newcomers who had yet to "pay their local dues."

Very quickly these newcomers did grasp local attitudes toward Mexicans to ensure a higher rung on the social ladder for themselves. When Anaheim school district proposed to name a new school for a Mexican hero (to help integrate Mexican children), the outburst of protest grew intense. Yet by the 1980s, certain sections of Orange County appeared more like a foreign country on the basis of store front signs; Vietnamese and other Southeast Asian lettering almost totally replaced English.

Rituals of athletic events still provided a major means for communal identification. More than likely, the newcomers brought their identification for a distant major-league professional team (not the local high school's) with them. Newport Beach at least had its special Christmas parade of gayily lit boats circulating around the harbor. Other municipalities tried to manufacture some sort of annual festivity to conjure up a sense of localness for their suddenly expanded populations.

What did all of these representative incidents and situations add up to? What held them all together? Certainly there occurred countless interactions which served functional purposes. People bought food from a retailer who had obtained it earlier from a wholesaler who had secured it still earlier from a processor or producer. People depended on water from their faucets—water that reached their home because other people operated the water distribution system. They could do so because still others administered the agencies which collected taxes and user charges and paid the water district's own bills. Police and fire units provided necessary protection, again because people organized public agencies with tax collections. All of these could happen because people had enough faith in the monetary system because they had enough faith in their political system, whether by conscious conviction or habit.

These and so many other services occurred in an unimaginably complex web of public and private sector interactions. What they all add up to is a system of life-sustaining functions. But whether a million or a hundred thousand or a hundred people lived in Orange County, the functions boil down to just about the same.[2] They ensure access to nutrition, protection, and training. Without these, humans cannot survive.

More is of course involved than simply meeting material needs. There is a spiritual dimension. It need not always involve religion, though that has played a central role in human societies throughout history and throughout the world, certainly for many residents of Orange County. The spiritual (nonmaterial, transcendent) dimension may take the form of artistic creativity, folk expression, pep rallies, company picnics, and whatever else imparts a sense of shared spirit or *esprit*.

Like people everywhere, Orange Countians sought a sense of communal foundation from seemingly nonfunctional rituals and customs and identifying signals. These can allow people to know whom to trust and whom to be wary of, to know how to interact and how to "read" each other, to know who should lead and who should follow. These rituals and customs ranged from religious or patriotic ceremony to festivities such as Christmas or cheering for the local ballteam, deferential treatment of others and paying tribute, even to shaking hands or bowing, laughing or crying on culturally designated appropriate occasions.

Apparently the Biblical observation held true here: People do not live by bread alone. They require more than that. They required a sense of identity, a sense of belonging, a sense of significance and worth: in short, a positive outlook and faith in the system that provides cohesion and direction. Normal people can experience those positive emotions primarily in terms of their relations and interactions with other people, starting in the family. To do that, however, the relations and interactions appear to require a structured process that can both provide the vehicle for interaction and guide how people internalize the resulting experiences.

The arrival of so many newcomers into Orange County in so short a time made the existence of the two basic societal dimensions—the functional and emotional—undeniably evident. Their importance was undeniable because they both came under such severe strains from time to time and place to place. Misinterpretation of signals, of expectations, and of values ran rife.

Virtually no one in mid-twentieth century Orange County satisfied all his/her functional needs alone. Everyone depended on other people in a gigantic web of symbiotic relationships most of which they were individually quite unaware. But to allow such a massive web to evolve, function, and continue, its participants had to do more than robotically perform their part. Enough of them had to want to believe in it.

Believing in it meant identifying with it. Identifying with it required symbolic indicators that it was a viable system and that it could serve participants with the spiritual (as well as functional) rewards they needed. Economic benefits, no matter how great, could not by themselves suffice. Newcomers and old-timers alike expected that local towns could continue to provide an effective rallying symbol for identification—that their emotional and functional experiences would prove both positive and identified by that place name. Disappointed, they seethed at first, then turned to other forums of interaction for the social reinforcement they needed as normal human beings.

This widespread process created a dilemma. Residents expected effective survival functions, whether from private or public providers. Doing so required an extensive and highly elaborate social, political, and economic organization of society. Achieving that requisite level of operational organization involved far more than chance happenstance. Participants needed some sense of stability and predictability upon which to make their individual plans and decisions.

Stability and predictability, it seems, rested largely on a mutual sense of responsibility. The difficult question to unravel here concerns a chicken-and-egg enigma: how did so many new Orange Countians achieved as much of a firm foundation as they did. Certainly they had to have basic functions to survive. To the extent they secured them, they would support the providers. But those providers had to have public support to undertake and accomplish their functions.

This circular formula presumes (1) an appropriate set of positive rewards—emotional as well as economic—for services rendered, and (2) a positive experience for those rewarding the providers. But how can enough organization evolve to establish these basic conditions? What medium or process—or system—sets the stage and gets/keeps the processes in motion?

Certainly newcomers to Orange County seemed to believe that "community" was important, given the frequency with which they used the word and given how stridently they sought it and how vehement they grew when denied it. But what is it? Is it simply a place? Social sciences have long tended to relegate this term to an identifiable location, fearing that any other use of the word would become confused with the term "society."

If community is only a place, then what was all the commotion about in Orange County? Newcomers found "place" aplenty and it did not satisfy. A "community," apparently, requires far more if we expect it to satisfy the symbiotic *and* the symbolic dimensions of human life suggested here. If community is a place, then what place was community in Orange County when people lived in one place, worked in another, did their major shopping in still another place, recreated somewhere else, and cheered intensely for a ballteam located in still another town? We must ask whether society can provide the requisite organization in and of itself. Or is community the key ingredient—the arena and process—of this requisite self-organization?

TOOLS OF ANALYSIS

Traditionally, we saw community as a place where most of a society practiced its culture over the span of each individual's life. Then Frederick Toennies a century ago recognized that this traditional concept did not cover everyone. Either more than one kind of community existed (he distinguished between *Gemeinschaft* and *Gesellschaft*, folk versus modern) or a major and ever increasing portion of society had to exist without benefit of community.

In the 1920-30s, the Chicago School began to make even finer distinctions, not only in the spatial configurations of demographics but in spatial distributions of functional activities. Following the Lynds' success in analyzing Middletown (1929 and 1937), the social sciences had a string of valuable studies of community as denoted by local places: such as Warner's Jonesville (1949), Hunter in Atlanta (1953), Seeley's Crestwood Heights (1956), Berger's working-class suburb (1960), Vidich & Bensman's Small Town (1960), Williams & Adrian's four cities (1963), Wildavsky's Small Town (1964), Lowry in Chico (1965), and Gans's Levittowners (1967), among others.

Until the 1950s, an observer of Orange County towns could readily employ the Lynds' model of community: a core of local leadership, surrounded by the majority of townsfolk who conducted virtually all of their interactions in that one town and who strongly identified with it by shopping and worshipping there, by socializing there, and by supporting the local high school and civic activities. The social periphery mostly involved people who simply lived and worked in the town but felt no allegiance to it and took no part in its affairs.

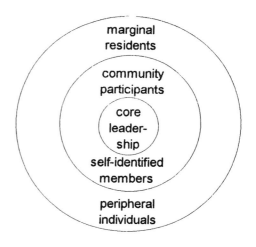

By zooming in on one town at a time, even post-WWII social scientists could continue to see community in terms of place only. They could do so by simply eliminating from their research all interactions which local town residents conducted with people, institutions, and service providers outside of that particular town.

But increasingly observers found it impossible to continue blocking out what really happened. We saw that interactions by residents in Orange County even as early as the 1920s did not remain bounded by their local town. First the interurban trains and then paved roads made this expansion of functional and emotional linkages both possible and desired. Post-war freeways drastically accelerated the proliferation and distance evident in those linkage networks.

Besides increased post-WWII daily travel, far greater electronic communication with heightened social and physical mobility spread networks far beyond local towns. A large portion, if not most, residents here already felt more sensitivity to friends, colleagues, relatives, and role models (e.g., sports heroes or entertainment stars) scattered all over America and the world than to neighbors down the block.

As more observers of urban America grew dissatisfied with the old limited concept of community, they sought a more realistic comprehension. Some social scientists focused on vertical structures since American life seemed increasingly organized hierarchically, whether in business, government, or semi-public sectors. More social scientists simply dispaired and came to doubt whether anything still remained that deserved the title of community.

A rather different direction of inquiry began among students of urban problems who, not being social scientists, were not so limited in their approach. Initially concerned with traffic engineering in metropolitan centers, R.B. Mitchell and C. Rapkin in 1954, followed by John Rannells in 1956, caused a few social scientists to take a new look at urban phenomena. They saw the flow of traffic as indicative of functional linkages and hence as indicating community in systemic terms.

Building on their work, Richard Meier perceptively began to think of traffic as a form of communication and argued so in his 1962 book on the theory of urban growth. Melvin Webber, also at UC Berkeley, went on from there to conceptualize community as a switchboard linking people to each other—linking people to activities and linking functions to other functions

(1963, 1964). From Webber's perspective, propinquity no longer constituted a requisite characteristic of community. This breakthrough subsequently spawned a new generation of analyses so completely focused on networks as sometimes to ignore spatial, physical, and functional factors.

We observed how each technological advance in human mobility—from wagon to locomotive to paved roads to freeway—brought marked changes in settlement patterns, in urbanization of culture, in scale of economic and social activities, and in the means of communication such as newspapers. No longer can we imagine community in Orange County as restricted to a set of distinct places. It was a thriving, teeming web of functional activities, communicative interactions, and identificational patterns involving many places linked together in a multitude of ways. Those ways included functional services such as essential water and waste disposal, police and fire protection, commerce in food and clothing, worship and recreation, all of which reached people in as many ways as there were people.

Yet already by the 1960s, even the basic social unit, the family, no longer belonged to a community delineated only by place. One parent would work in one place, the other parent either worked or engaged in activities in another place, while each child developed his/her own network of communicants in still other kinds or scales of place.

This burgeoning importance of networks in people's lives did not, however, spell the demise of everything place-related. Many functions essential for biological survival still remained place bound—water and sewer service, schools and parks, fire and police protection, to name a few—because they were provided by public jurisdictions as delineated by metes and bounds place descriptions and set into law. Commercial services, too, occurred in physically fixed places (such as in new shopping centers or older downtowns) known by locational names.

When newcomers arrived, they knew only the existence of a place, whether it be Anaheim or Tustin or Westminster, because they could see it and that was the locality cited on their home deed. Many of them soon discovered that that particular place did not command their loyalty as a community because they received services from other place-delineated jurisdictions and shopping centers elsewhere. And as urbanization sprawled all these place-based entities into an indistinguishable jumble and as cooperative agreements among municipalities and with the county became increasingly common, citizens no longer knew (nor cared eventually) where the services came from so long as they came faithfully.

This situation either shocked or disillusioned a significant segment of the population, old-timers and newcomers alike. Old-timers, though, had their long-established networks to provide emotional and social support. They also had memories of traditions set in simpler times for guidance not available to newcomers who came as a flood. Once the newcomers had established networks for themselves, they could settle in and come to tolerate the confused community scene. They could do so as long as the requisite functions remained fairly reliable.

Certainly by the 1960s, Orange County's community no longer resembled the concentric circle diagram, the one shown above as typifying the idealized, totally self-reliant, independent, and no doubt very isolated community—the conceptualization underlying Lynds' Middletown and subsequent community studies but not a reality after the American pioneer era. Instead a multiplicity of city service centers, public agencies, and

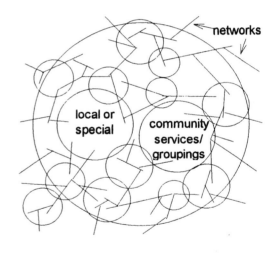

non-place related networks characterized the community scene. We might diagram its social space something like this.

Since no one had portrayed Orange County or its collection of towns this way, no one knew for sure how it all functioned or what it collectively represented. When needed functions broke down as happened from time to time (no water in Garden Grove, floods elsewhere), communal responses tended to reveal more brittleness than resilience. More significantly perhaps, an ambiance of anxiety prevailed over an increasing divergence between the two dimensions of community: between the functional and the identifical, between the symbiotic and symbolic.

A functioning community and an inspirational/identificational community seemed not in sync, or at least not to occur at the same scale. Life-sustaining functions did not evoke the expected sense of community identification. And it bothered people, often quite severely. As they became more attached to their networks, their hoped-for sense of place grew fuzzy. They lost their feeling of responsibility to identify with and hence support the providers of life-sustaining services. In moments of stress or functional breakdown, they would turn on those providers, sometimes conjuring up conspiracy charges.

This trend toward greater reliance on networks than on place for identification suffered from at least two significant factors: One, networks in an age of high mobility tended to be more transient (relative to the greater chance for permanence of place); they thereby failed to instill a hoped-for sense of roots. Two, the looseness of networks could lessen one's sense of personal responsibility, both for the network and for its members. Associational identity proved disquietingly shallow.

Together these factors could and did weaken commitments to community and its mainstay, a deep sense of mutual responsibility. Eventually, one way or another, most middle-class whites at least found a workable balance between place and network, and with that balance came a reasonable feeling of community—to the extent they felt their neighbors and network participants shared a similar sense of accommodation.

Community as a System

What we have seen for Orange County in the 1960s dramatically reveals the emergence of a new kind of life-sustaining and identificational mix. Despite emotional/political upheavals at times, it (whatever it was) continued to function. Out of seeming chaos at times, people did manage to live and thrive, to marry and raise children, and to gain some semblance of social, economic, cultural order. A system of some kind did exist and it has continued evolving, apparently adapting to more change—even when people began to wonder who really was "minding the store."

To the extent that community exists in practice (beyond mere nostalgic myth), we might reasonably expect it to exhibit some sort of structure—such as in leadership and hierarchy. Traditionally we saw a class structure where "old family" or "power elite" cliques ran affairs either directly or through frontmen. This seemed to characterize Orange County even into the 1950s or '60s, not unlike localities throughout America. But assumed reality and actuality do not always coincide here or elsewhere.

"Elites" did try to run Orange County but never with the thoroughness non-elites feared or favored. Through the 1920s and '30s, local elites felt defensive in the presence of so many Hollywood stars and oil millionaires in their midst who lived in a world quite unconcerned with local interests. And of course there always loomed those colossi of Los Angeles and the Irvine Company, making local elite's quite conscious of their limited economic base. Then the Depression and WWII imposed challenges local leaders could not solve on their own. The end of WWII saw the return of newly assertive veterans armed with GI Bill educations. A mass influx of better educated, more sophisticated newcomers in the 1950s along with a couple dozen world-renown aerospace industries hiring tens of thousands, two new large university campuses with national and international rankings, followed by a convergence of large concentrations of non-Anglo immigrants—these could not help but shake up any power structures left over from a rapidly passing era. (see Appendix E on class structure).

But as we noted in the preceding chapter, community leadership had become a matter of status (always an individual matter) instead of class (always ascribed collectively to a group). As class and its relative stability evaporated, its replacement, status by achievement, proved quite fleeting. Retirement, mobility, or momentary set-backs readily jeopardize status. So too do accellerating shifts in the fashions which dictate what merits an influential status. Moreover, advances in transportation and communications increasingly erased distinctive local identification.

When once upon a time people did receive virtually all of their life-supporting services and conducted virtually all of their interactions within a local place, the symbiotic functions did provide a basis for the symbolic reinforcement of allegiance, and the symbolic dimension reinforced (supported) the functional symbiosis. Residents back then may have conceptualized places and communities as coterminous. Most functional services did come from agents identified by a place designation. To the extent that people also participated in coterminal community-reinforcing rituals and associational networks, they identified them with a single place.

Although community was traditionally described as the concentric ring diagram, this does not mean the second diagram was totally new or that it replaced traditional community. Rather, the second depiction may have always existed but we simply failed to recognize it. We may have focused too narrowly on local place indicators (since most functions occurred within delineated places) and insufficiently on networks which also provide both functional needs (symbiosis) and emotional support (symbolic interaction); later the social science pendulum swung to overemphasize networks.

Comprehending community as a system may lie in fathoming the interaction between place and network—functionally (economically, administratively) and emotionally (socially, culturally, politically). Fathoming these interactions appears to rest heavily on comprehending the full system of communicative linkages, be they moving people or moving messages and the nature/strength of the linkages thus accommodated.

This dynamic Orange County experience suggests a rather intricate set of interactions that occur within a matrix structure as depicted below.

COMMUNAL INTERACTIONS	Symbiotic (functional)	Symbolic (emotional)
Place Based	basic infrastructure, services, protection for biological survival	patriotic/festival/sporting rituals for locational identity
Network Based	exchange of cultural info/learning for intellectual survival	creativity, religion, for personal & associational identity

Where parts of this community structure crack apart and break off, the system may operate as effectively as, say, a human organism without kidneys or limbs. (We saw this happen in Hawaii, as compared with Japan where it managed to hang together.)

Depicting how this (or any) community system works as a process, however, is far more difficult. Both the obvious and unwitting network linkages of modern-day community may already have ranked as complex as the synapsed linkages in our neurological system; the functional interactions, as complex as our metabolic, circulatory, and cellular operations. Community, in this perspective, takes on a systemic hue. Immediately we have made a quantum leap in complexity. The significance of this realization we examine in Part Four where we consider how to tackle living systems.

In Conclusion

While retaining its welter of political jurisdictions, Orange County's amorphous web of community has evolved what amounts to one of America's largest "cities," though still denied that recognition in census data collected on the basis of outmoded conceptualizations. A composite of smaller local communities and networks and a participant in conglomerates at larger scale, the community of Orange County is a process of adapting to change as change could be observed within the confines of both a regional complex and aspatial networking.

Every public act underwent interpretation, and people reacted on the basis of their internalized interpretations. Their interpretations, in turn, grew out of all previous communal experiences. Every interaction, no matter how mundane and functional, made some impact on each person's outlook and emotional response for subsequent interactions. To the extent communal experiences were positive, a sense of community deepened. To the extent such experiences were negative, a sense of community eroded and with it went mutual identification and mutual respect, further spiraling down the sense of community.

When a sense of community either eroded away or never did gel, there remained no organized alliance of functions and emotions binding people together with mutual responsibility. Some people sought ersatz community in other forms, be those ideological cells, fundamentalist religion, gangs, drugs or hedonistic dissipation. Or they may have simply withdrawn into themselves and their TV set.

For all the incidences of turmoil noted here, most people managed to establish supportive networks and to cope with the requirements of functional interactions. The net result, consequently, produced a positive impact—unlike conditions found frequently in inner-city ghettos today or in the chaos displayed by the former Soviet Union and in those other embodiments of communal disarray, Bosnia, Somalia, and Lebanon.

The vitality of mutual identity (whether positive or negative) may go a long way in influencing how positively or negatively individuals act toward themselves and then toward everyone around them. It would appear that, as networks and functional services diverged, a community-oriented sense of mutual responsibility tended to diminish. Where networks spread evenly among community members, a resilience to the challenge of change did tend to prevail. Where networks accentuated cleavages (such as by race, religion, class), there the community in its multi-scaled form more likely proved brittle exactly when flexibility and resolve become essential to meet challenges.[3]

In this perspective, community seems neither just a place nor just a network. Community, in essence, is the vital interaction between place and network and simultaneously between symbiotic and symbolic dimensions. It can, then, encompass several subsocieties/cultures, provided they share enough functional interests and enough symbolic rituals in common to bridge their day-to-day divisions.

It would appear that all members of society have stakes in the full connected community and that this community system is definitely not a zero-sum game. The more fully open it is for all members' participation, the more all members can benefit. So too, the more anyone suffers imposed disadvantages and denials, the less viable the entire system is for fulfilling the cultural needs of everyone; and we all suffer.

A system of community would appear to be an integrated, adaptive, self-reinforcing, multi-scaled, synergistic process for meeting challenges, for coping with its members' survival needs, and for interacting with other systems. The extent to which any particular interconnected community system fulfills this description rests on an intricate set of (seemingly chaotic) variables. Over time and place, Orange County has generally fulfilled these criteria—despite occasional troubles, political storms, and emotional uproars, often the concomitants of an anxious search for community.

No wonder so many social scientists have in recent decades dismissed community as a nostalgic myth. They were looking for the wrong thing. Community as a system was present all the time but too often not recognized because systemic details did not receive sufficient attention and probing. Nor usually was the scale of complexity under examination large enough to reveal patterns of systemic indicators. Community, the hidden force or underlying dimension of human life, remained obscure.

It will be interesting to see how the coming age of extensive computer linkages between the preponderance of families, individuals, and institutions reorders human contacts and hence our interpretations (expectations) of community. If the arrival of paved roads during the 1910s and of freeways after WWII could drastically change the scales of community and how people identified themselves communally, what might the electronic superhighway do—when people need no longer engage in face-to-face interaction for shopping and employment?

And what happens when computer literacy/illiteracy and computer ownership /nonownership markedly slices people between participants and nonparticipants? How much more strain will the requisite interaction between the place and network dimensions of community suffer from such a jump in networking capability? Will there emerge an even more chaotic looking arena/process than that depicted on page 214? Will the anxious, often strident search for a sense of community grow even wilder than what occurred in an Orange County inundated by growth?

Or, might we see more people pulling themselves into their own armored shells (or into drugs) as the age-old sense of support from community grows ever more unreachable? Might this anxiety over community-lost underlay the recent outbursts of religious fundamentalism within a diversity of religions around the world? To many people, today's material benefits and our communal rituals of entertainment and sports do not seem to fill a needed inner sense of purpose and belonging, any more than "bread and circuses" could maintain Roman vitality. Meanwhile the perpetual motion of modern industrial society seldom allows the maturation of deep roots.

Might we rightly ask whether our Industrial-Age community system stands on its last legs? Perchance then, might something new emerge—a new kind of community system—out of collapsed Industrial-Age communities grown beyond human scale? Might this new community system emerge, somewhat like a new ecological mix bloomed after the age of dinosaurs had crashed 65 million years ago and would eventually evolve humans? Indeed, might the ubiquity of interactive computers, in facilitating networking on an unimaginably vast scale, actually spread society back into stable human-scaled place-communities where society might experience the richness of personal interactions, mutual responsibility, and a shared sense of living systems?

Alas, the horrendous complexity of systemic factors generates far too many alternative possibilities to allow us to guess, much less predict, the future. We may only look further into this involved systemic complexity, as begun in the next section.

END NOTES

1. The 1991 book, *Postsuburban California* edited by Rob Kling, Spencer Olin, and Mark Poster, updates events in Orange County from where my narrative ended in the 1960s.

2. Please note that this term "function" used here differs from its usual connotation in social science "functionalism." Functions here relate to physical activities or processes that facilitate human biological survival. Function does not refer to social structures or whatever other social phenomena Thomas Merton, Talcott Parsons, et al might have focused on.

3. Dorothy S. Thomas's perceptive 1946 study of Japanese-Americans in Tule Lake concentration camp during WWII (*The Spoilage*) provides a well documented and most poignant case of community undergoing severe strain. The worse the strain, the more the internees' anxiety rose to achieve a united sense of community. (They felt they needed communal unity so as to weather their humiliation and wrenching of heretofore strong family cohesion, as well as to stand firm against official injustice.) Yet the more they strove for unity, the more the divisions among them emerged and festered.

Here were gathered people who represented the epitome of conservative rectitude and American values. They had the lowest crime and welfare rates and the highest education rates for children among all groups in the western states. Still, the strains grew so intense that riots, mayhem, and eventually murder erupted—not against the armed guardsm, but against each other. Ironically, some of the most pro-American families before the war felt the strains the worst and so left America after the war whereas more ambivalent families adjusted better and remained American.

Partial Bibliography: Orange County Related

Allen, A.E., County Supervisor. "Report to the Board of Supervisors on Assessment Practices in Orange County." 1963.

Allen, H.P. & W.S. Briscoe. *A Study of the Junior College Needs of Orange County.* 1960.

Ashly, T.J. *Power and Politics in Community Planning* [Anaheim]. 1962.

Banks, H. *The Story of San Clemente.* 1930.

Bergh, H.E. "The Diminishing County 'Myth'," *County of Orange.* 1961.

Bigger, R. et al. Metropolitan Coast: San Diego and Orange Counties, California, UCLA Bureau of Governmental Research, 1958.

Cleland, R.G. *The Irvine Ranch.* 1962.

Crouch, W.W. et al. *Agricultural Cities: Paradoxes in Politics of a Metropolis,* UCLA Dept. of Political Science. 1964.

Crump, S. *Ride the Big Red Cars.* 1962.

Doig, L. *The Village of Garden Grove, 1870-1905.* 1962.

Dunlap, S. "96 Years of Orange County Newspapers," *Orange County Illustrated,* Feb. 1966.

Freedgood, S. "88,000 Golden Acres Waiting for the Dust to Settle," *Fortune,* Nov 1963.

Friis, L.J. *Orange County Through Four Centuries.* 1965.

Hill, M. *One Hundred Years of Public Education in Orange County.* 1957.

Hinshaw H. 192 page unpublished report to the 1965 County Grand Jury, reassessing in Orange County.

Kernahan, G. "The Travail of Klanheim," *Orange County Illustrated,* July 1965.

Koch. A.S. "Arterial Highway Financing Plan, " California Highways and Public Works, Sept-Oct 1960.

Kroeger, L. *Urban Services for Irvine.* Dec.1964 (unpublished report).

MacArthur, M.Y. *Anaheim, 'The Mother Colony'.* 1959.

McWilliams, C. *Southern California Country.* 1946.

Meadows, D. *Historic Place Names in Orange County.* 1966.

Meyers, S.A. *Fifty Golden Years* [Newport Beach]. 1956.

Mowry, G.E. *The California Progressives.* 1951.

Pleasants, J.E. *History of Orange County.* 1931.

Plumb, H. "The Appraisal Program of the Orange County Assessor in Regard to Transitional and Fringe Areas." 1963.

Rinehart, C.H. "The Ku Klux Klan." 1928 (unpublished essay).

Saunders, C.F. *Capitrano Nights.* 1930.

Schrag, P. *Voices in the Classroom.* 1965.

Scott, S. & L. Keller. *Annexation? Incorporation? A Guide for Community Action.* 1953.

Scott, S. et al. *Local Governmental Boundaries and Areas: New Policies for California.* 1961.

Sherman, H.L. *A History of Newport Beach.* 1931.

Smith, S.C. "The Rural-Urban Transfer of Water in California." *Natural Resources Journal,* Nov. 1961.

Swanner, C.D. *Santa Ana: A Narrative of Yesterday (1870-1910).* 1953.

Talbert, T.B. *My Sixty Years in California.* 1952.

Thurston, J.S. *Laguna Beach of Early Days.* 1947.

Partial Bibliography, Public Documents

City of Anaheim. *Report to the Redeveloment Agency.* Oct 1963.

City of Anaheim. *Hill and Canyon General Plan.* May 1966.

City of Anaheim. *Anaheim Center City Study.* Apr 1966.

Bechtel Corp. *Engineering and Economic Feasibility Study for a Combination Nuclear Power and Desalting Plant.* 1965.

Bollens, J.C. & Assoc. *A Study of the Proposed Merger of Placential and Yorba Linda.* Oct 1965.

Blurock Ellerbroek & Assoc. *San Juan Valley Study.* Mar 1963.

City of Buena Park. *The Comprehensive General Plan.* Sep 1962.

State of California, Dept. of Finance, Office of Planning. *State Development Plan Program Progress Report and Summary Interpretation of Phase I Studies.* Feb 1965.

California State Board of Equalization. *General Appraisal Manual* (Assessors' Handbook). Jun 1964.

City of Cypress. *General Plan.* May 1964.

City of Dairyland-LaPalma. *General Land Use and Circulation.* Sep 1964.

Elliot, G.A., B.A. Etcheverry, T.H. Means. *Control and Conservation of Flood Waters in Orange County California.* 1931.

Economic Research Assoc. *An Evaluation and Projection of Industrial Land Requirements Through 1980 in Orange County,* California. Jun 1964

City of Fountain Valley. *General Plan of Land Use and Circulation.* May 1961.

Fountain Valley School District. "Professional Portfolio" (introductory materials for all newcomers).

City of Fullerton. *General Plan.* Jun 1965.

City of Fullerton. *A Municipal, Economic, and Land Use Analysis.* Jun 1966.

Hanauer, J.G. & Co. *Incorporation Study* [for Yorba Linda]. Aug 1963.

City of LaHabra. *General Plan.* Jul 1961.

Los Angeles Regional Transportation Study (LARTS). Summary Edition to Volume 1, Base Year Report 1960. Dec 1963.

Melbo, I.R. *Factors in Future District Planning: Huntington Beach Union High School District.* 1963.

City of Newport Beach. *Corona del Mar Study.* Nov 1964.

County of Orange. *Departmental Organization and Function.* 1964.

- Orange County's Diamond Jubilee. 1964 [reprints of earliest county documents]
- Zoning Code Reports. 1965, 1966.
- Annual Industrial Inventory. 1965.
- Recreaton, 65. Jul 1965.
- Master Plan of Regional Parks. Jan 1966.
- Master Plan of Riding and Hiking Trails. Jan 1965.
- Capistrano Valley General Plan. May 1966.
- General Plan, Mission Viejo Ranch. Nov 1965.
- Tustin Area General Plan. Sep 1966.
- Yorba Linda General Plan. Mar 1962.
- Orange County Sewer Survey. 1947.

Orange County Sanitary Districts. *First Annual Report.* 1955.

Orange County Superintendent of Schools. *Financial Report of Orange County Schools; for years: 1957 through 1966.*

Orange County Flood Control District. *An Investigation of Flood Control and Water Conservation Deficiencies within Orange County, California.* Apr 1964.

Summary if Engineer's Report: *Presenting a Program for the Control and Conservation of Flood and Storm Waters in Orange County, California.* Mar 1966.

Orange County Water District. *Engineer's Report on Ground Water Conditions; for years 1960 through 1966.*

Orange County Grand Jury Reports: years 1949 through 1966.

Patterson, R.L. *Improvement of Upper Newport Bay, Newport Bay Harbor.* Jul 1950.

City of Placentia. *Placentia General Plan.* Aug 1962 [and associated public plans, 1965 and 1966].

City of San Clemente. *General Plan.* Oct 1960.

City of Santa Ana. *Basic Studies Series.* Oct 1965.

City of Seal Beach. *General Planning Studies #3.* Aug 1966.

City of Stanton. *Comprehensive General Plan.* Oct 1964.

Stanford Research Institute. *Orange County: Its Economic Growth: 1940-1980.* Sep 1962.

City of Tustin. *Goals and Objectives.* Sep 1964.

University of California. *Site Selection Study.* Mar 1959.

University of California, Irvine. *Long Range Development Plan.* Jun 1963.
City of Westminster. *General Plan.* Feb 1965.

Partial Bibliography,
Comparative and Theoretical

Altshuler, A.A. *The City Planning Process.* 1965.

Altshuler, A.A. et al. *The Urban Transportation System: Politics and Policy Innovation.* 1979.

Andrews, R.B. (ed.). *Urban Land Use Policy.* 1972.

Arensberg, C.M. & S.T. Kimball. *Culture and Community,* 1965.

Baldwin, M.M. (ed.). *Portraits of Complexity: Applications of Systems Methodologies to Social Problems.* 1975.

Banfield, E.C. *Political Influence.* 1961.

Banfield, E.C. *Urban Government.* 1961.

Bender, T. *Community and Social Change in America.* 1978.

Bendix, R. & S. Lipset. *Class, Status and Power.* 1953.

Bennis, W.G. *American Bureaucracy.* 1970.

Berger, B. *Working Class Suburb.* 1960.

Besher, J. *Urban Social Structure.* 1962.

Blumer, H. *Symbolic Interactionism: Perspective and Method.* 1969.

Bock, K. *Acceptance of Histories.* 1956.

Bollens, J.C. & H.J. Schmandt. *The Metropolis: Its People, Politics and Economic Life.* 1965.

Boorstin, D.J. *The Genius of American Politics.* 1953.

Bossleman, F. *The Taking Issue.* 1973.

Boulding, K. *Ecodynamics.* 1978.

Burgess, E.W. (ed.). *The Urban Community.* 1926.

Chapin, F.S.Jr. & S.F.Weiss (eds.). *Urban Growth Dynamics in a Regional Cluster of Cities.* 1962.

Coleman, J.S. *Community Conflict.* 1957.

Conant, J.B. *Slums and Suburbs.* 1961.

Cox, H. *The Secular City.* 1966.

Crouch, W.W. & B. Dinerman. *Southern California Metropolis.* 1963.

Dahl, R.A. *Who Governs? Democracy and Power in an American City,* 1961.

Dickinson, R.E. *City, Region and Regionalism.* 1947.

Dobriner, W.M. *Class in Suburbia.* 1969.

Dobriner, W.M. *Social Structure and System.* 1963.

Drucker, P. *The Age of Discontinuity.* 1968.

Duhl, L.J. *The Urban Condition.* 1963.

Etzioni, A. *The Active City.* 1968.

Ewing, D.W. *The Human Side of Planning.* 1969.

Firey, W. *Land Use in Central Boston.* 1947.

Fischer, C.S. et al. *Networks and Places: Social Relations in the Urban Setting.* 1977.

Flynn, Charles P. *Insult and Society: Patterns of Competitive Interaction.* 1977.

Fordham, J.B. *A Larger Concept of Community.* 1956.

FORTUNE Editors. The Exploding Metropolis. 1958.

Freeman, A.M. et al. *The Economics of Environmental Policy.* 1973.

Friedman, J. *Retracking American: A Theory of Transactive Planning.* 1973.

Galbraith, J.K. *American Capitalism: The Concept of Countervailing Power.* 1952.

Gallion, A. *Urban Patterns.* 1958.

Gans, H. *The Urban Villagers.* 1962.

Gans, H. *The Levittowners.* 1967.

George, H. *Progress and Poverty.* 1878.

Glaab, C.N. *The American City: A Documentary History.* 1963.

Goldschalk, D. *Planning in America: Learning from Turbulence.* 1974.

Gordon, M.M. *Assimilation in American Life.* 1964.

Gottschalk, S. *Communities and Alternatives.* 1975.

Greer, S. *The Emerging City.* 1962.

Greer, S. *Metropolitics.* 1963.

Griswold, A.W. *Farming and Democracy.* 1948.

Haar, C.M. (ed). *Law and Land.* 1964.

Haar, C.M. *Land Use Planning.* 1976.

Hauser, P.M. & L.F.Schnore (eds). *Study of Urbanization.* 1965.

Haworth, L. *The Good City.* 1963.

Hicks, J.D. *The Populist Revolt.* 1961.

Hillery, G.A.Jr. "Definitions of Community," *Rural Sociology,* Vol.20, No.2, 1955.

Hillery, G.A.Jr. *Communal Organization: A Study of Local Societies.* 1968.

Hiltz, S.R. & M.Turoff. *The Network Nation.* 1978.

Hirsch, W.Z. (ed). *Urban Life and Form.* 1963.

Hoffer, E. *The Ordeal of Change.* 1952.

Hofstadter, R. *The Age of Reform.* 1955.

Hunter, A. *Symbolic Communities.* 1974.

Hunter, F. *Community Power Structure.* 1953.

Jackson, K.T. *The Ku Klux Klan in the City, 1915-1930.* 1967.

Jacob, P.E.& J.V. Toscano. *The Interpretation of Political Communications.* 1964.

Jacobs, J. *The Death and Life of Great American Cities.* 1961.

Janowitz, M. *The Community Press in an Urban Setting.* 1959.

Jennings, M.K. *Community Influentials: Elite of Atlanta.* 1964.

Kahn, A.J. *Theory and Practice of Social Planning.* 1969.

Keller, S. *Beyond the Ruling Class.* 1963.

Kornhauser, W. *The Politics of Mass Society.* 1959.
Krammerer, G.M. et al. *City Managers in Politics.* 1962.
Laszlo, E. *The Systems View of the World.* 1972.
Laurenti, L. *Property: Values and Race.* 1961.
Lane, R.E. *Political Life.* 1959.
Lane, R.E. *Public Opinion.* 1964.
Lee, E.C. *The Politics of Nonpartisanship.* 1960.
Levin, M.B. *The Alienated Voter: Politics in Boston.* 1960.
Lewis, P.F. *New Orleans: Making of an Urban Landscape.* 1976.
Lindblom, C.E. *The Policy-Making Process.* 1968.
Lindeman, E.C. *The Community.* 1921.
Locke, J. *Two Treatises on Government.*(1960).
Long, N.E. "Ecology of Games," *American Journal of Sociology.* Nov. 1958.
Long, N.E. *The Polity.* 1962.
Long, N.E. *The Unwalled City.* 1972.
Lowry, R.P. *Who's Running This Town.* 1965.
Lynch, K. *The Image of the City.* 1960.
Lynd, R.S. & H.M.Lynd. *Middletown: A Study in American Culture.* 1929.
Lynd, R.S. & H.M.Lynd. *Middletown in Transition.* 1937.
MacIver, R.M. *The Web of Government.* 1947.
Makielski, S.J.Jr. *The Politics of Zoning.* 1966.
McKelvey, B. *The Urbanization of America* (1860-1915). 1963.
Mayer, R. et al. *Centrally Planned Change.* 1974.
Mead, M. *Cultural Patterns and Technical Change.* 1955.
Meadows, D.H. et al. *The Limits of Growth.* 1971.
Mecklin, J.M. *The Ku Klux Klan.* 1924.
Meier, R.L. *A Communications Theory of Urban Growth.* 1962.
Meier, R.L. *Planning for an Urban World.* 1974.
Meyerson, M. & E.C. Banfield. *Politics, Planning and Public Interest.* 1955.
Meyerson, M. et al. *Housing, People, and Cities.* 1962.
Mills, W.E. Jr. & H.R.Davis. *Small City Government.* 1962.
Millspaugh, M. & G. Breckenfeld. *The Human Side of Urban Renewal.* 1959.
Minar, D.W.& S. Greer. *The Concept of Community.* 1969.
Mitchell, R.B. & C. Rapkin. *Urban Traffic: A Function of Land Use.* 1954.
Moffitt, L.C. "Highest and Best Use: A Concept Reexamined," *Journal of Soil & Water Conservation,* Sep-Oct 1965.
Moffitt, L.C. "Planning and Assessing Practice," *Land Economics,* August 1966.
Moffitt, L.C. "Value Implications for Public Planning," *American Institute of Planning Journal,* November 1975.
Moffitt, L.C. *Strategic Management: Public Planning at the Local Level.* 1984.
Monsen, R.J. & M.W. Cannon. *The Makers of Public Policy.* 1965.

Morrill, R.L. *The Spatial Organization of Society.* 1970.

Mowitz. R.J. & D.S. Wright. *Profile of a Metropolis.* 1962.

Mumford, L. *The Culture of Cities.* 1938.

Nisbet, R.A. *The Quest for Community.* 1953.

Overstreet, H. & B. Overstreet. *The Strange Tactics of Extremism.* 1964.

Owens, W. *The Accessible City.* 1972.

Packard, V. *The Pyramid Climbers.* 1962.

Park, R.E. et al. *The City.* 1925.

Park, R.E. *Human Communities.* 1952.

Perloff, H.S. (ed.). *Planning and the Urban Community.* 1961.

Pollack, N. *The Populist Response to Industrial America.* 1962.

Polsby, N.W. *Community Power and Political Theory.* 1963.

Popenoe, D. *The Suburban Environment.* 1977.

Pred, A. "Place as Historically Contingent Process," *Annals of American Geographers,* No.74. 1984.

Rannels, J. *The Core of the City.* 1956.

Reissman, L. *The Urban Process.* 1964.

Ridley, C.E. *The Role of the City Manager in Policy Formation.* 1958.

Robinson, J. *The Policy-Making Process.* 1971.

Rodwin, L. (ed.). *The Future Metropolis.* 1961.

Rondinelli, D. *Urban and Regional Development Planning.* 1975.

Schlesinger, A.M. *The Rise of the City, 1878-1893.* 1933.

Schneider, K.R. *On the Nature of Cities.* 1979.

SCIENTIFIC AMERICAN. Special Issue on the City. Sept. 1965.

Schnore, L.F. *The Urban Scene.* 1965.

Schnore, L.F. (ed.). *Social Science and the City.* 1967.

Seeley, J.R. et al. *Crestwood Heights.* 1956.

Spectorsky, A.C. *The Exurbanites.* 1955.

Stearns, F.W. & T. Montag [eds.]. *The Urban Ecosystem.* 1974.

Stein, M.R. *The Eclipse of Community.* 1960.

Sussman, M.B. *Community Structure and Analysis.* 1959.

Suttles, G.D. *The Social Construction of Communities.* 1972.

Toennies, F. *Community and Society* (C.P.Loomis translator) 1957

Vasu, M.L. *Politics and Planning.* 1979.

Vidich, A.J. & J. Bensman. *Small Town in Mass Society.* 1960.

Vollmer, H.M. & D.L. Mills. *Professionalization.* 1966.

Walker, R.A. *The Planning Function in Urban Government.* 1950.

Warner, S.B. Jr. *Planning for a Nation of Cities.* 1966.

Warner, W.F. et al. *Democracy in Jonesville.* 1949.

Warren, R.L. *The Community in America.* 1963.

Webber, M.M. et al. *Explorations into Urban Structure.* 1964.

Weber, A.F. *The Growth of Cities in the Nineteenth Century.* 1899.

Weber, M. *The City* (translated by Martindale & Neuwirth). 1958.

Wengert, N. *Natural Resources and the Political Struggle.* 1955.

White, M. & L. White. *The Intellectual Versus the City.* 1962.

Whyte, W.H. Jr. *The Organization Man.* 1956.

Wildavsky, A. *Leadership in a Small Town.* 1964.

Williams, O.P. & C.R. Adrian. *Four Cities: A Study in Comparative Policy Making.* 1963.

Wilsher, P. & R. Righter. *The Exploding Cities.* 1975.

Wingo, L. Jr. (ed.). *Cities and Space.* 1963.

Wirth, L. *On Cities and Social Life* (A.J. Reiss Jr. ed.). 1964.

Wood, R.C. *Suburbia.* 1958.

Yin, R.K. *Street-Level Governments.* 1975.

Plus consultation conferences during the 1960s within the University of California with professors Bauer, Bollens, Branch, Crouch, Fagin, Folley, Gallion, Hinderaker, Kent, March, Meier, Meyerson, Peltason, Scott, and Webber.

PART FOUR

CONTINUING CONSIDERATIONS

INTRODUCTION

My students in comparative government ask why people, living under totalitarian regimes in other countries, don't revolt. It is easy to go no further
than the obvious (and superficial) answer: that such repressive governments
control all the means of exercising power—through police, army, courts,
and regulators. Yet if this provides the whole story, then why do authoritar-
ian regimes collapse so soon after they begin to institute political reforms, as
happened for example under the Shah in Iran, with Gorbachev in the Soviet
Union, under Nicolas II in 1917 Russia, and in France of 1789, among others? Again a superficial answer seems at first to suffice: that people finally
have a chance to compare their gripes, thereby to see the dry-rot within, and
then to react at last.

While these ready explanations do, of course, correctly indicate reality as
far as they go, do they go far enough for us to grasp what really occurs?
Here the conceptualization of community as a living system just might allow
us to bring more factors onto the table for concerted examination. Especially
so since every human activity produces some sort of symbolic spinoff
which, when inevitably interpreted and internalized by people, generates

positive or negative linkages to the arena and process of a wider, on-going and future set of interactions.

Tyrants like Stalin, Hitler, and Mao not only commanded an awesome array of armed force. They controlled two core ingredients in the lives of people. They controlled: (1) the agencies which provided such necessary functions for survival as the means of producing and distributing goods, services, energy, water, sanitation, food, shelter; and (2) the manipulation of virtually all symbols to achieve emotional commitment—whether in the press, the arts, religion/ideology, or recreation. To the extent they could also determine how people networked and how fully people extended community loyalty from family and local place to a national scale, they had a stronger foundation for enacting their political agendas.

Does their frequent, unconscionable use of terror provide the full explanation for such monolithic regimes? On the surface the answer seems affirmative, but we should question it. The Shah in Iran, Pol Pot in Cambodia, the Kuomintung earlier in China, Marcos in the Philippines, Diem in Vietnam, Pinochet in Chile, and sundry dictators in Central America and Africa have pursued a draconian treatment of their subjects yet fell eventually. In contrast, regimes in the Soviet Union, communist China, Cuba, and North Korea did not simply suppress opposition. Exceptional longevity among these three may have rested at least as much from their operating at a level of community involvement with the most immediate significance to the vast majority of people.

Stalin, Mao, Castro, and Kim
-sung held power largely through the manipulation of symbolic spinoffs from the monopolistic dispensing of essential goods and services at a level where people could directly, personally, and communally experience them (as well as the co-optation or elimination of potential counter-leaders who might also manipulate those symbols for emotional commitment). Instilling fear and suppression alone may simply be too negative to achieve positive identification.

As observed in the preceding chapter, it would appear that services and symbols must either self-reinforce each other or they conflict toward self-destruction. Herein we might find the real nature everywhere of a connected community. To endure, a political system must offer something symbolically positive, something that can transcend its inadequate functioning. (So too for an economy, a prospect oft forgot by economists.)

The other dictatorial regimes cited above failed neither for lack of enforcement power nor will to use such power ruthlessly, but for lack of sensitivity to the workings of their society's community. Once Gorbachev admitted the hypocrisy of the soviet system, its hollow shell of political power became evident there too. The community system had for so long operated like a puppet at the Kremlin's tugging that it lacked sufficient indigenous vitality to adjust quickly. And so the entire edifice crashed down. People found themselves left to their own devices with neither adequate basic survival functions nor on-going viable symbols of community identification to rally around.

Similarly in the former Yugoslavia. Once the pervasive totalitarian umbrella of communism which held it together under Tito began to unravel after his death, the monolith had no real base at community level. Any sense of both local and national community had remained true to ethnic (tribal) traditions, be they Muslim, Serbian, Macedonian, Albanian, Croatian, or Slovenian. Yugoslavia tore apart, and long-suppressed ancient communal animosities quite naturally erupted into civil war.

A political subsystem (its economic subsystem too) appears to rest heavily on the structure, process, and vitality of its multi-scaled community system. Politics and economics may have a diminished chance to operate effectively by imposition from above where the places and networks of communal interaction and their functional (symbiotic) and emotional (symbolic) dimensions do not all concertedly reinforce each other. If this equation holds true for obviously repressive regimes with naked terroristic power to force compliance, it holds doubly so in a pluralistic, openly democratic, free enterprise culture.

The question before us concerns the "essence" of community that earns it the designation of a system. We now must address community's systemicity—not just to achieve knowledge for itself, quite interesting though that turns out to be. We do so in search of possible benefits to life on Earth potentially derived thereby.

A basic working premise underlying this book contends that we enhance chances for coping with challenges to the extent we can comprehend not only those challenges but the resources and strategies available to us. And community is not only a major resource; the extent of our familiarity with it may translate into perceiving effective strategies—strategies now often overlooked for lack of an understanding into a larger, systemic web of community: namely the connected community,

Another working premise here sees potentially grave danger in ignorance. This is especially true since people abhor voids in their worldview the way nature supposedly abhors a vacuum. Consequently we humans fabricate explanations for phenomena which we can feel but cannot understand. Which is permissible if all it produces are imaginative stories (myths) about, say, a geocentric universe or about spirits causing rain and drought or about why individuals and societies go to war with each other.[1] But when people (individuals and their societies) take action that imposes suffering and death on members of this and other species based upon those myths, then obviously ignorance is dangerous. It can even threaten the survival of our species.

This section suggests that current societal efforts to cope with modern problems (such as violence, economic strains, alienation, ecological degradation, and the demise of cultural values without the emergence of equally beneficial replacements) may suffer from inadequacies in how we conceptualize the systemic world these operate in: especially the connected community. Just possibly, a fuller appreciation of systemic complexity—to replace today's prevalent linear thinking—might open new vistas for decision-makers who manage our urban scene, our natural resources, and our intergroup/international relations.

Admittedly, approaching research through a new paradigmatic framework, such as that of systemic complexity, always faces the possibility of requiring some anguishing abandonment (by scholars and public decision-makers alike) of comfortable traditions, hence their entrenched resistance. This prospect should not however deter us. It has come with each new discovery in science and new stage in human history.

This section offers a set of working premises which conceivably might contribute to bridging formidable chasms of scholarship—in particular the chasms now separating diverse specialists on society, culture, and biology, whether in universities or public agencies. Just as constructing the Panama Canal required overcoming the obstacle of yellow fever first, so too do breakthroughs on issues involving both biological and cultural considerations depend on cutting through entrenched myopia in those fields as traditionally organized.

Science might then suffer less from its antiquated, parochial segmentation. Sociologists, for instance, might no longer fear allowing genetics to play a role in the human behavior they study; and biologists could allow for wider ranging processes of evolution without anxiety over the heresy traps of Lamarckism. But they need a common frame of reference, a common working approach, a common language; and these must be suited for communicating to the general public and its decision makers. A new nonlinear math might serve scholars well, but only when nonscholars can understand and use it too.

Accepting a world of complexity, instead of ever searching for simplicity, might actually open breakthroughs potentially worth the likely emotional travail involved. Hoping for this advance does call for at least a glance here at how science might address such matters.

The first chapter of this last section surveys the significance of a systems approach across the sciences, social as well as biological. The second chapter looks at some possible implications in how we pose questions and frame strategies in dealing with not only human problems but with threats to a highly integrated, living, systemic world. The third chapter returns to questions left dangling since Part One on the interplay of culture and genetics in the evolution of human behavior and its expression in a connected community.

Rather than chance our losing track of the flow of argument by detouring here and there to expand on particular issues, I have elected to make use of appendices. Into these go various germane and supportive but narrow discussions on such aspects as: whether consciousness provides an essential distinction between humans and other species; the dangers of propounding elegant structures in depicting systems; how legitimate are incest and altruism in undergirding sociobiology; the politics of sex as a factor in human life; and the question of obsolete social stratification theories.

Refer to these appendices if the main text arouses your curiosity; otherwise, don't worry about them. I also append a brief explanation, entitled "The Route Taken." It covers how I came to research and write this book, as well as what might have colored my vision.It might quell some of your dismay at the selection of case studies and paradigmatic range employed here and why this book took so many decades to complete.

CHAPTER THIRTEEN

SYSTEMIC SYMPHONY

Chances run quite high that your evening televised news program, your daily newspaper, some casual conversation today referred to acts of violence somewhere in the world: ten people blown up by an extremist's bomb in London, hundreds shelled to death in Bosnia, thousands of Kurds killed by the Iraqi army, tens of thousands butchered in Cambodia, hundreds of thousands killed in Rwanda, and (not all that long ago) millions massacred by Hitler and Stalin in Europe. Closer to home, muggings, rapes, spouse abuse, and drive-by shootings tax our police, our courts, our educational system, our hospital emergency workers beyond their limits—while making many people fearful of venturing out of their homes at night.

As technology improves in bringing us more news faster from even the remotest corner of the world, we can readily feel that violence has grown more pervasive. Whether it actually has or not is next to impossible to document. Certainly violence is not new to humanity. In the hope of keeping the populace pacified, Roman governments provided the edifying entertainment of feeding an assortment of "unwanted" people to lions in Colosseum spectaculars. Seven centuries ago, Mongol invaders into cultured Persia had great sport in decapitating prisoners and piling their bodies in huge mounds.

America, like so many other former colonies, won its independence on the field of battle. Old economic delineations along religious lines lie at the heart of Protestant/Catholic strife in Northern Ireland and Indian-Pakistani tension. Political delineations along religious lines have sparked Balkan wars for five hundred years or more. Azerbaijani/Armenian conflict has thousand year-old roots. Dutch trade in slaves from Africa expressed, to the extreme in barbaric cruelty, attitudes toward slavery that go back several millennia in Europe and the Mediterranean region.

In America, the 1930s saw pitched battles between workers, scabs, and police over union strikes. The 1940s brought race riots of whites against Blacks and Chicanos in Los Angeles and Detroit where police did nothing except arrest the victims for littering the streets with their battered bodies, an experience only slightly less violent than the lynch justice practiced in much of the South during the century after emancipation.

Why do humans so readily engage in violent behavior? Is it a manifestation of some primeval "survival of the fittest" drive or a concomitant of "civilization" and a politically organized state? Is the resort to violence linked to some sort of genetic predisposition or a result of "unhealthy" child-raising practices and environment? Are poverty, broken families, ugly neighborhoods, or high sugar diets and television to blame? These all certainly have drawn their share of accusers. Marx, for instance, used class exploitation to explain all human turmoil, though his "solution," that of communism, has generated some of the most violent of recent exploitation.

The shallowness of such simplistic "causes" becomes quite apparent when we note how many people raised and living in the same ugly environments or the same poverty, eating the same poor diets and watching the same violent TV, do not engage in violent behavior. Yet genetic explanations seem no less shallow and inadequate; behavioral variability within families and racial groups over time and across the board at any one time is too great to attribute totally to genes.

One question should immediately arise but seldom does in public efforts to address violent behavior: Do all scales of violence stem from the same set of "causes?" Is domestic violence—spouse on spouse, parents on children, adults on elderly parents, as well as date rape—the same as the violence evident in institutionalized war between nations? Does small group violence—as in gang warfare, racial bigotry, robbery and muggings by hoodlum bands, and the use of rape as a form of ethnic cleansing and terrorism evident in many conflicts—resemble more the massive violence of warfare between nation states or is it more like the personal expression of individual violence since individuals perpetrate them?

What acts one commits when under orders in the military may be deeply repugnant to that person and hence something such an individual would never engage in on his/her own. An irony arises here. The more sensitive a person is to social pressures, the more enthusiastically he might engage in the violence of war yet shun such behavior when out of uniform. The corollary: that those less sensitive to social pressure often make poorer law-abiding citizens and also less heroic soldiers. Apparently the sources of individual and institutional violence differ.

What then of small group violence? To what extent does gang violence approximate the institutional violence of "legal" warfare? To what extent does it approximate individual violence? Are we dealing with three different phenomena or a single expression in varying forms? Is the sexual factor, to the extent that it underlies each of these differing scales of human interaction, a constant or a widely ranging variable?

To what extent does the urge for violence stem from a need for power, control, dominance, and sexual prowess? To what extent does the impetus for that kind of violence differ from whatever underlies nonphysical violence (such as in hostile buyouts, one-upmanship, office intrigue, and sexist or racist jokes) by people whose strength lies in using words instead of fists— by people who get a high from "hanging others in the wind" but who would never shoot a gun or throw a brick or rape?

If individuals feel a need for power, control, dominance, and sexual prowess, what combination of more fundamental forces (genetic, psychological, and/or cultural) prompt this need? And after identifying those forces, we would need to ask WHY. We should ask why what generates those more fundamental forces does so. At this point we face the horrendous matter of comprehending what we commonly call "human nature" (more accurately: the human phenotype) as a factor in human interaction.

THE CHALLENGE

This book does not focus on violence. Violent behavior constitutes just one of myriad ingredients in the human experience. But what is the human experience? Now *this question is* central here!

We have identified the connected community as the arena in which we humans play out our economic, political, and culture processes? We saw, too, that those processes facilitated our human species—from an inauspicious genesis in East Africa millions of years ago—to eventually dominate planet Earth. The move to domination, however, really does not get underway until some forty thousand years ago and only achieves significance within the last ten thousand years. But what drove humans all along this route, increasingly as time passed?

That humans constitute a social species is so obvious, we readily fail to ask: WHY? Why do we of the *Homo sapiens* species act as we do, particularly in clustering together? Do our genes dictate this propensity? Or did our ancestors "learn" to live together. At some evolutionary point, however, our ancestors did "organize" this propensity for collective life into regulated affairs, a product of culture and eventually (at large scale) a manifestation of what we now like to call civilization.

But what brought on this change? What facilitated it? We risk blindness from myths if we simply presume that today's crop of cultures was inevitable. More to the point in this book, we ask whether this evolutionary process, if adequately comprehended, might perchance throw useful light on some of our current societal troubles, including violence.

Just these few questions have challenged scientists to a vast circle of concerted endeavor spanning many academic disciplines from social science to biology and back. Unfortunately in this human quest for answers, reality's complexity leaves clear-cut answers and hence quick-fix solutions wanting. The unfathomed web of genetic, biological, psychological, and cultural factors have forced scientists to probe ever deeper and hence into more specialized areas of penetrating focus until no one can comprehend the enormity of all we have uncovered.

Discoveries in each disciplinary field of science lead to ever more specialized concentrations of research. Over time, these inadvertent divisions have a way of growing into formidable chasms. No reputable scientist today would attempt a universal theory of human behavior on the scale tried by a Hegel or, even more so, a Marx in the last century. And if one did, such a global vision would immediately attract the scorn of all specialists, as happened to Toynbee.

An ever compounding deluge of literature makes it virtually impossible for a human today to keep abreast of happenings in one's own specialty, much less advances in all other fields. Eventually bureaucratization, competition for funding, and the physical dispersion of research make strangers out of scientists who might otherwise appreciate and so benefit from cross-disciplinary interchange.

In this situation, each discipline forges its own paradigm around which its adherents collect and (as true in social contexts generally) relate to each other in terms of this their common symbol and ritual of identity. Occasionally of course, segments in two or more diverse fields of inquiry recognize a shared concern and so break off from their parent disciplines to join and form a new specialty. But this simply creates new paradigmatic chasms without necessarily bridging old ones.

Sociobiology offers an interesting case in point. In attempting to fill-in the chasm between the social and biological sciences, Edwin O. Wilson's bulldozer produced barriers instead. While he never managed to replace sociology as hoped, he certainly did challenge social scientists to question the basis for their own paradigm. Leaving Wilson's hyperbole aside, sociobiology met resistance because he tried to go too directly from genetics to a grand explanation of life without reckoning adequately that large, added dimension of cultural drive.

Two decades after Wilson's bombshell of sociobiology, the issue still tends to cleave over which aspects of human behavior stem from genetic programming as against which from cultural programming. Since how one states a question goes far in determining what one looks at, this bifurcation of foci could become (and has proven) less than beneficial for the scientific study of human behavior in its highly complex context. It has generated more controversy than breakthroughs.

But suppose we phrase the question differently. Suppose we ask this: How does a genetically programmed organism of any species have its behavior modified by cultural directives?

No longer burdened with having to delineate prime causations, we can focus on possible interactions between genetics, culture, and the vast array of other factors in the behavioral equation. We can now probe this intricate web of interaction in its ever changing world—the way genetics could advance once scientists began to look at interaction between genes instead of trying to match individual genes to specific traits.

PHENOTYPE

The most useful concept (the most useful tool of analysis) here may well be that of phenotype. It regularly comes into play in biology, albeit often with a limited or biased emphasis on biological indicators; sociologists barely (if at all) recognize it. Yet it allows us to distinguish one species, genus, deme, family, etc. from another.

A phenotype encompasses all features about each type of living organism: its size, shape, coloring, mating and reproductive process, rearing of young, choice of food and habitat, disease susceptibility and autoimmunization, problem-solving intelligence, communications, conspecific recognition and interaction with other species. A robin, for instance, is not a robin simply because it weighs a certain number of ounces, has wings, a beak, red feathers in front, and lays blue eggs. It is a robin as much because it eats worms, prefaces mating with a certain ritual, and builds a prototypic robin's nest.

Phenotype, then, involves both biological and behavioral factors. And it is, apparently, the product of both a species' genetic inheritance and environmental conditions/experiences. Since *Homo sapiens* shares a common DNA system with all other eukaryotic species and even to some extent with all prokaryotic (bacteria) species, our species shares the basis of life on Earth with all other forms of life. We have no grounds for considering our-

selves exempt from a phenotypic classification applicable to all species—
nor exempt from the same evolutionary processes that generated such an
astonishing breadth of speciation.

Although we have not fully fathomed the complexity of evolution, we
can rather safely at least recognize a generalized pattern of factors which
contributed to that set of particular features distinguishing one species from
another, even one subspecies (race) or breeding deme from another. We can
diagram this web of factors with general applicability as follows:

Phenotypic Framework for Living Systems

Several aspects of this depiction stand out boldly. One, its great complexity: everything affects speciation. Two, the horrendous amount of interaction among the factors: everything affects everything else directly or indi-
rectly. Three, this vast variety of ways the factors can interact to produce
such a vast variety of species.

Until *H. sapiens* achieved sufficient intellectual capacity for sophisticated tools and organization (discussed in Part One) to meddle into and
muck up natural evolutionary processes, species probably did not evolve
strictly on their own. Other species had to have evolved so as to allow all the
other niches in the ecological system. Evolution may have rested on interspecies accommodation as well as on Darwinian competition. Probably too,
the more the entire system changed the more species could evolve—
especially so when the ecosystem reaches a critical degree of strain and

crashes. Although individual species might suffer, the system could regenerate through coevolution of its remnant and new participants.

Whether human interference will prove similar to a meteor strike or a sudden marked change in global climate in accelerating both speciation and species demise, we know too little to forecast now. (One need only fly low over almost any inhabited area to see how extensively humans have altered ecology.) The crucial observation to draw about phenotype is the immense importance of interactions among all of the ingredients—physical, biological, genetic, cultural—in determining what we humans are as well as what all species are. Since this array of interactions has occurred and itself evolved over the several billion years of life on Earth without a total demise of life, we really have no choice but to think of it in systemic terms.

Recognizing the challenge before us in this way places the spotlight on interactions. To the extent that observed interactional phenomena appear predictable, we expect the presence of some sort of system, inferring usually a homeostatic one. And since the phenomena explored by both genetic and social sciences involve living creatures, we reasonably think of the systems themselves as somehow "living" whatever that might entail.

In this light, any chasm between social and genetic sciences should pose no great difficulty. Yet it does. For one thing, the more we learn about phenotypes and the processes of interactional evolution, the more we discover how little we know. The enormous complexity involved grows awesome. The complexity demands more than we can now comprehend. For another, we need to uncover what constitutes "living" in a system.

CHAOS AND COMPLEXITY

Just as in art where the medium is a major (some experts argue it is the dominant) factor in the product; so in science it is difficult to separate findings from methodology used. The medium—the paradigm—determines what we perceive, hence what we probe, hence what we find. Our first obstacle, then, is paradigmatic, as Thomas Kuhn so effectively made us conscious of over three decades ago.

Frustration with traditional paradigms gave rise in recent years to new perspectives/methodologies and the beginnings of a new paradigm, that of "chaos" and "complexity" theories. Might these possibly assist our effort here, too? Perhaps; they seem worth a try—if we can translate their obscure mathematics into a more generally applicable form of communication. We might do well, though, to start with these terms in their customary usage before delving into their more esoteric meanings.

We humans have for thousands of years given names to tangible things. We have also found it easy and natural to name nontangible things which are observable—such as processes: running, thinking, talking, etc. A little more difficulty occurs in naming abstract aspects of our experience, such as love and honor; we usually have to think of them through readily observable cases that exemplify those concepts. Some languages may convey abstracts better than other languages, but people in all cultures must really stretch their imaginations to comprehend totally unobservable "things." The concept of infinity comes to mind; what finite human mind can envision actual infinity? (When physicists use symbolic equations to depict infinity, they must think equation rather than imagine infinity per se.)

Chaos falls within this realm. To deal with any concept we must fit it into some preexisting mental frame of reference. In effect, we order it into our mental organization of the world. But chaos means turbulence, the seeming absence of an order of our making. So how can we imagine true chaos if it cannot be fitted into the order we need to understand with? This is like imagining "an irresistible force meeting an immovable object." Trying to visualize and internalize anything absolute lies too far beyond our quite circumscribed human experience. All is not hopeless, however, though this portends some fundamental rethinking.

Exploration of turbulence in physics in recent decades (such as for weather and water flow) found that even a slight perturbation in even a subunit of a dynamic complex system can compound into such extensive change as to render predictability impractical. If utter uncertainly can result from even slight turbulence in the physical realm, how much more likely will turbulence affect predictability in the less concrete (messy) realm of sociocultural phenomena. This application of "chaos" from physics to other, even distant, academic fields could alter how we envision our world and hence we try to cope with applied problems.

We must widen the realm of factors whose play require an accounting. No longer can we presume to keep all other variables constant while we focus on a bare chosen few. Interactional processes now command center stage: especially how the many forces for stability interact with the many forces for instability (change). Order is far more complex than traditionally assumed by scientists as did as by society in general.

Out of this breakthrough comes an even tougher change for scientific (and applied) research to swallow: namely that there are no independent variables, other than such global factors as variation in the amount of energy reaching Earth from the sun or plate tectonics altering continental locations. Within the realm of human life, all actions are interactional. Social scientists may no longer look for and talk about "causes." We may only think in terms of "contributing" webs of factors/forces.

Traditionally sciences have sought to construct a chain of causation suitable for predicting future conditions and situations. We did this by detecting how one factor supposedly determines what happens to another factor. We liked to declare that observed phenomenon A causes observed phenomena B which will affect expected phenomenon C thusly. One spinoff from chaos theory has us seeing phenomenon A contributing to B which may contribute to C which influences both A and D, the latter sometimes contributing to B, and so forth in an endless web of influential interactions with no clear-cut, direct, cause/effect determinism. Indeed, we cannot even isolate for certain the sequences of influences. We may find ourselves limited to exploring patterns of occurrences.

In this sort of interactive world, the best we can do is search for potential processes of change. Accurate prediction, now, can no longer constitute the prima facie justification for science. The social and biological realms appear far too interwoven for accurate prediction—unlike physicists predicting a sun's eclipse or a satellite's trajectory. Yet even in nuclear physics, observing a phenomenon changes that phenomenon. How less structured are social and biological phenomena!

Obviously the world has suddenly become much more difficult for science. Or rather: we at last admit that the world is far more complicated than we have thus far envisioned and acknowledged. Instead of the arrogance of Western culture that presumed humans could comprehend and then could and should reorder the natural world (as in "conquering nature"), we may finally be gaining some valuable humility. Certainly the way we have mismanaged natural resources around the world and have spread human suffering (from wars and their resulting famines as our technology expanded) calls for a more humble worldview.

But the challenge of chaos did not end there. Complexity theory has sprouted and with it has come advances in mathematics needed to again find order in what seemed like chaos. It recognizes self-organization among all forms of reality within the universe: galaxies coalescing out of primordal dust, atoms joining into molecular compounds, molecular compounds forming amino acids, amino acids acquiring the beginnings of "life" and eventually evolving into organisms, and so forth, some of these organisms forming voluntary organizations known to us as communities with governments and an array of associations.

The first three parts of this book surveyed this concept of self-organization in practice among humans. We looked at what the emergence of syntactical thinking did for human society. We saw community underlying Japan's repeated successes at managed change, as well as the collapse of community in Hawaii. Orange County displayed how complex community can become in its vast web of mutual dependencies and need for communal meaning and identity. The 1990s have seen biologists and economists pooling their respective expertise (such as at the Santa Fe Institute) to tackle the challenges of complexity, with other fields of science now joining in.

Though seldom mentioned by scientists grappling with turbulence, another conceptual spin-off seems unavoidable. I refer to what chaos/complexity means for that traditional criterion in evaluating scientific explanations, that of Occam's Razor.

Occam's Razor provided a workable approach: go with a simple explanation rather than an equally good complicated one. Unfortunately, a simple explanation for some phenomena might appear valid because the observer has not adequately recognized the complexity (the full interactive aspects) of its context. Seeing human behavior as entailed within complexity renders it impossible to judge whether an explanation is simple but inaccurate for lack of depth as against an explanation that is more complicated because it more fully encompasses the web of mutually dependent variables.

What becomes apparent at this juncture is a need to better understand the nature of systems, especially what might be seen as "living" systems focused on in this book. Science, thusly, comes out of the closet: it is an art form—albeit a rigorously disciplined art form—dependent largely on the perceptive sensitivity of its practitioners (the scientists) whether on the so-called hard or soft side of academic divisions.

LIVING SYSTEMS

Genetics deals with the interaction of genes in a process which not only creates a new organism through birth but continues to guide that organism's growth, maturity, reproductive drive, and eventual aging. Social science deals with interactions as they function in culture-based societies through political, sociological, and economic processes. Humans who function in communities have both genetic and cultural dimensions. Conceivably those dimensions interact with each other.

One need not hold a PhD in a science to make many accurate predictions about how the human body works and what humans will most likely do under ordinary circumstances. That such predictability suggests the presence of a system or systems does not mean that any unpredictability encountered negates a systemic reality. It may simply mean that our comprehension of biological and social systems is inadequate. It may also raise the possibility that the complexity far exceeds our ability at this stage to fathom all of the systemic properties of life on Earth.

In any case, using a systems model at least provides a convenient "basket" for collecting, identifying, and examining not only chance deviations from the expected but also patterns of change, especially fundamental change. And since change seems inherent to our planet and the life thereon, comprehending systemic change may well open windows in heretofore blank walls. Focusing on how systems change opens a most productive avenue for discovering how biological and social life functions.

While both fields of science study living systems (whether fully recognized as such or not), we should ask what their respective systemic worlds have as common characteristics. Indeed, what attributes distinguish a living system from any other form of system? At least three characteristics occur in common and so might start to answer both questions.

- The whole is greater than, and distinctive from, the sum of its parts due to interaction of those parts.

- All parts of a living system are interdependent; an impact on any one part affects all other parts.

- A living system perpetuates itself *both* by reproducing *and* by self-adapting to a changing environment.

Just these three can allow us to separate out a vast range of "nonliving" systems.

We saw in Orange County that the community system actually goes beyond these three basic criteria. Community entailed an adaptive, multi-scaled, self-reinforcing, synergistic process with backup redundancies to meet challenges, to cope with members' needs, and to interact successfully with other systems It is, in essence apparently, a highly complex evolutionary process, not a homeostatic mechanism. It is a continual intricate, interactive process of self-organization. This distinction could prove crucial—and largely distances it from previous systems theories in the social sciences. For, it necessitates nonlinear thinking.

Immediately we ask whether any other systems meet not only the three basic criteria but also this last description evidenced by community as a system? Various observers have offered different perspectives and sets (see Appendix A). I find only two other systems—the organismic and ecological, beside community—which fulfill all parameters. These parameters might then serve as a common frame of analysis, whether in biology or in social science, to bridge the chasm of specialization.

Limiting the concept of living system to just the foregoing criteria raises questions about other forms of interaction with systemic characteristics that do not meet the full set of stipulations. For instance: people participate in economic systems and political systems. Why shouldn't they be thought as "living" since living people conduct them?

In having structures and processes, they are systemic—just as are the respiratory, circulatory, immune, endocrinal, and neurological subsystems operating within us as an organism. But they cannot operate on their own. They can function only within, and in support of, a true living system, though their failure can damn the rest of the system.

Take a group of people for example, even a group as rigorously organized and self-operating as members of a warship. While in operation, this group constitutes a systemic network that functions as an ersatz community. But once in port and on shore, members of this group revert to their real communities, and the "networkness" of the ship's contingent becomes quite evident. It is not a living system, only part of a larger one.

What we have then is not a clean line between living and nonliving. Gradations span across the spectrum, just as spectra occur in other aspects, too. For instance, we cannot draw exact borders to delineate specific human communities any more than we can demarcate particular ecosystems in their web of webs. Interactive complexity exceeds our knowledge and even our imagination for drawing precise lines.

No magical solutions lie in employing this view of reality. It simply offers a framework for handling the horrendous complexity we operate in when we deal with either human community as a system manifested at the full range of scales from family to clan or village to city to nation, or with biological systems spanning the range from individual organisms to the interplay of vast combinations of species/individuals within the ecosystem. At least we can take conscious note that subsystems operate within living systems and that all living systems are interdependent.

∨ISTAS AND ∨ICISSITUDES

Once this common perspective takes root, we can more readily explore a common means for viewing the seemingly uncommon phenomena which the biological and social sciences focus on. Their differences in theory and methodological techniques diminish as obstacles for coordinated investigation. We may now examine living systems in whatever form they take without fear of trespassing on some other's professional turf.

We can cease seeing *H. sapiens'* culture and hence human behavior as totally unique. Instead, we see a continuum of behavioral programming from overwhelmingly (if not totally) genetic to nearly overwhelming in its sensitivity to cultural programming. *H. sapiens* may stand at one end of this continuum; but we are not alone in coming under the influence of culture.[2]

We may reach this position because we can now define culture as behavior learned from conspecifics, either among peers or from generation to generation. To varying degrees, numerous species—obviously apes and cetaceans, probably elephants, and quite possibly song birds (at least for their songs), among others—have what amounts to cultures. Lionesses must *teach* their cubs how to hunt, for example.

Even combined though, genetic and cultural programming cannot account for the full diversity of behavior within a species, much less between species. Each individual differs not only in minute degrees of genetic material but in one's environmental experiences. Interaction with the world—we call it individual learning—affects behavior by neurological (psychological) programming. Virtually all species within the animal kingdom are capable of individual learning.

If they can learn, they have a "mind"—regardless of degrees of consciousness discussed in Appendix B. Behavior then expresses programming from genetics (for temperament and physical capabilities), from society's cultural influences (for expectations), and from an individual's neurological responses to prior experience. Complexity prevails even at the level of individual organisms; how much more so in the on-going adjustments to change by ecological systems and in the evolution of species' phenotypes. (We return to this in the last chapter.)

In essence a phenotype involves an evolutionary system of systems. Although the general characteristic factors/forces differ for each species and in slight particulars for each deme and individual within a species (their genes and experiences differ), the interactive framework of analysis applies to all.

This analytic framework facilitates a more concerted research strategy when focusing on any of its parts: We must relate all findings—be they in the realm of biology/genetics or in social science—to a larger systemic universe engulfing interactions between both kinds of phenomena. (Please note that we can thusly bring biological and social sciences together without getting bogged down in controversies raised by sociobiology; see Appendix C.)

In a view which sees reality as a systemic web of interlinked dependent variables (with virtually no independent ones) there occur no causes, only contributing factors. All relationships then become in effect circular—except time and even it may seem curved in that human anticipation of the future can influence the present.

Being willing to approach reality in its utter complexity highlights a particular danger. Nuclear physics has Heisenberg's uncertainty principle where establishing one fact sacrifices certainty about a linked variable. If observing a variable in physics can change it, it most assuredly happens in social and biological sciences. (For instance, a person interviewed competently and thoroughly has had to think and hence is not the same person after the interview, thereby invalidating the survey results to that extent.)

Biological and social sciences have their own uncertainty principle: that the phenomenon under investigation affects the eye of the observer. As sensitive social animals, social scientists in particular have great difficulty acting in an ideally clinical manner.[3] For a while in the 1970s many gave up any pretense of objectivity and became open activists for social/cultural change. Biologists, too, can let a desire to accomplish a goal color what they see, even to affecting how they go about investigating phenomena.

We encounter in science the difficulty of cultural bias and political (yes, let's admit it, economic) pressures. Ideology comes into play also, as when some social scientists refuse even to explore a role for genetics in programming human behavior lest "science" be twisted once more to support discrimination and eugenics as happened earlier in this century.

To those who doubt that genes might play some role in how we humans behave, we might ask: How do genes make owls build owl nests and sparrows build sparrow nests and not any other kind? Or make cardinals sing melodiously and not caw like crows? The answer is: we don't know how, just that they do, whether directly or via what Ernst Mayr calls somatic programs.

We do know that only some five percent of the genetic material in our DNA suffices to produce the human organism. What purposes the other ninety-some percent serve remains far from fully uncovered. Political correctness not withstanding, there does appear to exist plenty of DNA available to handle whatever behavioral (or somatic) programming might occur in our own species.

But not knowing everything about the genetic system does not prove that genes cannot influence behavior in humans as they surely do in other species, though not as extensively since our capabilities for culture (increasingly so over the last fifty-thousand years) modify the expression of those genetic instructions so much.

The crucial aspect to bear always in mind is the infinitely complex interactive web of living and nonliving systems we participate in. To borrow a Biblical phrase, we can only see as through a glass darkly. Yet what we think we see and then act on can have horrendous implications and impacts, as we shall review in the next chapter.

CHAPTER FOURTEEN

IMPACTIVE IMPLICATIONS

Having spent so much of this book on the processes of change over time-spans running into millennia, having laid so much emphasis on the interwoven complexity of life on this planet, having framed that complexity in systemic terms so as to emphasize the connectedness of community, please do not expect me to offer panaceas and quick-fix strategies so beloved by bureaucrats, politicians, reformers, news media, and general public alike.

It should have become abundantly clear by now that this book does not portend to promote "solutions" to modern-day problems. A remedy is only feasible if the problem is definitively established. I cannot offer pat solutions because I argue that we cannot isolate simplistic "causes." If everything affects everything else, then we must deal with entire systems, not individual items myopically. This demands imaginative, holistic thinking, exceedingly difficult though that may be.

Rest assured, this message does not infer a retreat into nihilism or fatalism. It simply acknowledges nonlinear reality. The question instead becomes one of how to live within that reality without either giving up or blissfully, blusteringly, bombastically ignoring it.

By taking a systemic perspective, this book views human behavior as one ingredient in a vast whirl of interactive forces. Hope here lies in the belief that greater familiarity with the inherent complexity of living systems—with all of their inherent turbulence—may better prepare us to make more benevolent (or at least less detrimental) choices as citizens, consumers, parents, and community members.

After all, quick-fix solutions for momentary ills (whether for crime or drugs, violence or disease, pollution or unemployment) tend to bounce us from one crisis to the next, the next one often created by the previous "solution." Far better, through a firmer appreciation of the systemic context, to avoid problems in the first place. Proactive, instead of merely reactive, strategies spring far more often from a better informed position than from one of ignorance.

CASES IN POINT

Without a constant awareness of community as a pervasive system, we can readily lose sight of the requisite balance between individual rights and mutual responsibilities. We can equate societal values with market measures of value, in large part because market values lend themselves to exact calibration within a discount rate scaled to individual lifetimes and uncomplicated by the rather amorphous measurements of communal and ecological values in their far longer temporal spans.

If we deny the centrality of connected community, we are left with merely individuals and social-economic-political institutions devoid of a systemic arena/process to give comprehensive meaning to the interactions of human life. Seeing interactions as discrete items rather than as integral aspects of complex systems has us seeing modern society composed of segmented rather than integrated functions.

Eliminating the centrality of community fosters a segmentation of our lives between such niches as school, work, play, religion, romance, and death. We get our food, water, entertainment, protection, employment, health care, education, etc. from disjointed suppliers. The round of daily interactions divides into distinct blocks of people and events as social, political, economic, recreational, religious, racial or whatever. Generations become segmented, destroying any sense of continuity and heritage and hence any real sense of responsibility to past and future generations. Instant gratification can prevail.

A segmented worldview lets employers forget that employment carries far greater meaning than mere compliance from hirelings and pay cheques for the hired. Work equates with either self-respect or self-denigration, with a sense of participation and achievement or anxiety, ill-health, and declining productivity. Stress on the job means stress in the home and in the community—and those stresses bring violence and alienation which not even consumerism to the max can alleviate.

A segmented view of the world allows educators to focus on individual pupils to the neglect of those pupils' full learning environments. Educational systems therefore deal with segmented subject matter in segmented days without regard for the important roles played by peers, families, neighborhoods, outside role models, etc. In pursuing the safety of a monastic model, schools simply shut out all of these crucial influences rather than take the educational process into the streets and homes and bring families and peers into the classroom.

The question here concerns the extent to which today's chopped-up life style affects people's mental health as well as their sense of belonging—their personal and societal sense of being. For lack of a sufficiently sophisticated model of community, we may suffer severe handicaps in even trying to assess how people emotionally treat the totality of their human experience. Do they try to transform it into an integrated whole or simply resign themselves to a world of disconnectedness?

It takes little imagination to hypothesize that a world characterized by disconnectedness might facilitate—possibly even encourage—senseless violence, drugs, crime and other so-called anti-social behavior. But it is not that simple.

Some of the most communally integrated of people can engage in the most hideous acts of violence. We see repeated instances nowadays of this among fanatic fundamentalists and ethnic/racial bigots around the world. Their extreme form of integration, however, extends only to one narrow segment of humanity, not to the larger connected community.

If we contentedly relegate "community" to local place or some buccolic entity, then of course it has little relevance to a modern, urbanized world. But what does exist to provide people a sense of order, of direction, of protection? Laws, litigation, and government tend to provide a poor, even counterproductive substitute because these devices can disengage (instead of integrate) providers from consumers of public functions thereby undercutting potentially positive symbols and processes.

Some seek their human needs in racial awareness, or in tight-knit religious congregations, or in ideological cells and crusades. But try as they may, they can never escape the reality that much of their existence still remains functionally (and hence emotionally) linked to providers of services and influences by people with different beliefs, different lifestyles and from different ethnic/racial backgrounds. They are, in effect, begrudgingly beholden to people outside the borders of their circled wagons.

Indeed, why do so many of us feel we must circle the wagons against the world outside? To what extent are we genetically programmed to distrust sociological "others" and "stick to your own kind?" Or does our genetic system program within us a sensitivity to cultural dictates which in turn, irrespective of genetic instructions, programs us with a herd propensity—to go with the crowd, to defer to the group's collective judgment (despite any personal qualms) in the pursuit of survival? Or perchance, does a widely differing combination of these and other possibilities exist in each of us, thereby producing a diversity of attitudes and actions—and rendering scientific investigation, theory formulation, and applied strategies both more difficult and more hazardous?

It boils down to this: How really great is our need to sense community— to fully sense connected community? And how long can we neglect this question?

Leaders of the October 1995 "Million Man March" on Washington, DC seem to have intuitively sensed the working essence of community. They apparently felt the necessity for societal functions and group symbols to reinforce each other. Consequently they emphasized taking the initiative to resolve local problems, to develop Black-run businesses and industries, and to pull themselves up by those proverbial bootstraps through education and production—rather than waiting for government to act. For, a viable community involves members feeding themselves and policing themselves, as much as by rallying around positive symbolic images.

As long as the sustenance of life must come via merchants from other ethnic groups and as long as basic services and economic support comes most notably from distant welfare workers, any self-identifying symbol sets will inevitably lack substance and hence meaning. Only from a stronger sense of community can come a stronger commitment to family, both being dimensions of Black lives too long abused by others for their exploitation. But herein lies a crucial irony, an irony not readily acknowledged by all sides.

In seeking to redress the onerous Jim Crow discrimination and indignities imposed on individuals, the civil rights drive of the 1950-60s inadvertently also freed individual Blacks from the confines of their once rather self-contained and effective communities led by Black society, Black churches and schools, and Black-run businesses. Not unlike Jews freed from Euro-pean ghettos a century ago and upwardly mobile post-WWII American whites whom we observed in Orange County, they bought personal escape at the sacrifice of a coherent sense of community. They gained greater op-portunities for individual expression, professional advancement, and artistic creativity. But in so doing, many more lost the moral direction and cultural support of a strong localized community. And like the students at my alma mater UC Berkeley who sparked the 1960s' so-called Free Speech Move-ment, three decades later many of them (or their children) have begun—by repeating the mantra of "family values" —to search for what they had pre-viously lost.

COMPLICATIONS

We noted earlier that our human behavior stems from some combination of genetic programming, cultural influences, and personal interactions with other people and with one's environment. We can readily discern what form of communal interaction each culture promotes. We have, however, a long way to go before we can determine within a reasonable degree of assurance whether the genes which make us human also orient us toward communal life in general, much less toward any particular orientation.

Has evolutionary selectivity over millions of years (or at least over the last fifty thousand years) favored interpersonal cohesion for survival within small groups where social direction, identification, and mutual support operate for both functional and symbolic advantage? If a genetic factor does bear on the centrality of community in human life, what happens when the scale of community favored by a culture drastically departs from the scale of community in operation during those thousands of generations of genetic evolution and selectivity? Where is the pain and strain felt when the two underlying programming forces in our lives (the genetic and cultural) go in diverse directions? Does it hit us individually in our psychological state or does it primarily affect the community system—or both?

In a small scale community such as a band of hunter-gatherers or early pioneer villages in New England and the western frontier, the network of personal interactions remained quite limited and on a face-to-face basis. The more people congregate and the more work specializes, the growing complexity no longer allows communal decisions on a consensus basis. Structured organization and politicians generally tend to arise and take over the management of communal affairs.

To illustrate: 1013 potential linkages can occur between ten people whereas the number of potential linkages jumps to 1,048,555 for twenty people, a thousand-fold increase by adding ten more people. Each added participant roughly doubles the potential links for interaction. Even a group of two-hundred people, much less two-hundred thousand or two million, quickly reaches complexity beyond comprehension. Not all of these potential linkages come to fruition; obviously. Still, we must ask whether the fundamental forces which program human behavior—the cultural as well as any genetic programming—evolved with sufficient safeguards to deal in modern-day levels of complexity. Have we overwhelmed those programming processes?

As long as networks of interaction spread rather evenly across the full body of community participants, we saw that chances seem to improve for successfully meeting challenges. But where networks become sliced into marked cleavages (such as between classes, ethnic/racial groups, religions, castes, sexes), the community system tends to grow brittle and hence less flexible in coping with other systems, other cultures, and other groups. Today's exponential rate of complexity's growth readily allows leaders, members, and even social scientists to lose sight of community under a fog of absolute reverence for individualism unbalanced.

Consider one implication here. We have seen how important rituals of mutual identification are in facilitating the effective functioning of support services. In contemporary society, sporting events constitute one of the most, if not *the* most effective form of communal ritual. This happens with football and baseball in America; as much or more so for soccer in many other countries. Sports provide a function beyond mere entertainment; beyond even cathartic exuberance. They give focus and identity not unlike religious observances once did or still do for some societies.

If an athletic team means so much for community vitality, might not that community have a vested interest *and* responsibility in maintaining a team in that community? We might rightly ask: Haven't sports become so vital to the health of large-scale community until their franchises take on more the complexion of a public utility than that of strictly a money-making enterprise for a few wealthy individuals to profit from or indulge their vanity in?

A similar question has arisen in towns devastated by a loss of jobs from a plant closing when the productive activity moved elsewhere for the benefit of the corporation without regard to impacts on the community and people who had previously served that industry's needs. Doesn't the local community have some vested interests in such horrendously important decisions?

Let me assure you immediately that this line of argument does not have to lead to any form of socialism. Having earned my living over four decades working for public agencies (whether for local and state government, for public universities, as a consultant to them, or in the military), I am intimately aware of the real limitations and dangers of big government. Indeed, I close this chapter by citing a few personally observed situations where governmental intrusion did more harm than good in dealing with community concerns.

The objective in this section seeks to encourage alternative ways of viewing and hence of approaching contemporary problems, especially those with a community component to them.[4] In this it becomes absolutely essential to avoid the trap of equating community with government. This temptation increases as we consider ever larger scales of community. That is why I have focused on *connected community*, a systemic world.

Government amounts to no more than one among many instruments for conducting community interests—just as do agencies for education, health care, employment, commerce, production, religion, news media, and all the rest that comprise a modern community system. But as complexity has grown, government has expanded (especially since the Great Depression and WWII) until it has come to supplant community instead of serving it. Perhaps a reawakened interest in more fully understanding community can lead to new ways of viewing government—other than those periodic ground-swells of acrimony and cynicism that seek to "throw out" all incumbent "public servants," whether in a local Orange County or at national scale.

When the founding fathers of this country drafted our Constitution, they intentionally built in inefficiency so as to protect both individual and communal interests. Yet despite those built-in inefficiencies (or because of them), our system of governance has muddled through all manner of crises rather well, compared with seemingly more efficient governance structures elsewhere. Perhaps a similar kind of "inefficiency"—instead of the current injected inefficiencies from excessive regulation—just might serve the economic component of community well too.

Difficulties here stem, in part, from a confusion between "efficiency" and "effectiveness." A political or economic system may appear efficient, such as in how decisions get made. But when we calculate in the customarily disregarded indirect costs, we move into consideration of true effectiveness, and it often differs markedly from what an economist or manager would herald as optimal efficiency. We obviously need to know far more about complex community systems before charging off on any simplistic crusade, be it regulation or deregulation, or communitarianistic reforms.

Further Probing

So we need to know far more about human involvement in community systems and what programs this orientation into us. What kinds of studies might contribute to enhanced knowledge and awareness? Two in particular might pay off.

After completing its initial mission of cataloging all of the 100,000 genes in human DNA and tracing how they interact to produce a biologically functioning individual, the Human Genome Project could continue to probe how genetic interaction deals with behavioral programming. I suspect, though, that scientists in this project might have to shift to work on less socially complex species which more fully depend on genetic rather than cultural programming. Otherwise the huge cultural component in the human phenotype will cloud any observations about the genetic component.

Meanwhile, social scientists might take a fresh look at small, less complex societies. To some extent, clan, sect, caste, town, metropolis, and even nation can fulfill the criteria of a systemic community. Yet no forms of human collectivity better evoke the combination of ritualism, common ancestry, cultural practices and customs, common language and symbolism of identification, plus productivity, than do family and tribe. And since in most cases family tends to involve too limited a slice of human interactions to provide a solid basis for understanding the system of community, tribalism probably more than any other form of societal organization best typifies or demonstrates community as a systemic process.

Unfortunately "tribalism" has, from anthropological practice, acquired an undeserved limitation to nonliterate (or at least nonindustrial) societies. This is unfortunate in that it dysfunctionally blinds us to what we might learn from looking at the tribalism in "modern" societies/cultures and their core community system.

Tribe carries with it quite emphatically the practice of controlling who may mate with—who may share genes with—the group's daughters. This aspect, perhaps more than any feature, gets at the heart of tribalism. It most typifies the central concern worldwide for preserving the symbolic "purity" and tight cohesion of patriarchal groups. What term then better than tribalism fits the social scene in Bosnia, Northern Ireland, Israel, the Indian sub-continent, Quebec, the former Soviet Union as well as Somalia, Sudan, and Rwanda? In this light, what better term than tribalism conveys the essence of America's suburbia vs. inner-city bifurcations and other flashpoint delineations?

Herein lies a disconcerting anomaly. The more cohesive an immediate community (such as in a tribe), the less the incentive and opportunity for positive interaction with members of other comparable units. But the wider one's opportunities to interact with different people, the less cohesive and hence the less protective one's sense of community. The former condition sacrifices individual caprice for collective security which benefits individuals. The latter sacrifices general security in preference for individual caprice which can disturb individuals by neglecting communal concerns. This, perhaps, explains some of the perseverance of tribalism in whatever its guise. A sense of community never ran higher in America than during WWII when the nation pulled together as a single tribe to defeat the enemy tribes of Germany and Japan.

We saw earlier how a system of community involves a vast range of scales and formats. It is not limited to the antiquated traditional image of a small town in isolation. Orange County's experience revealed quite dramatically how complex (and amorphous) the connected community has become. Actually it always was complex; we simply did not recognize adequately such complexity because we sought simplicity. Now the complexity is no longer deniable.

Personal Observations

Recent decades have heard an increased clamor for a sense of community, indicating rather stridently that the realization of community must have correspondingly decreased for Americans. Even President Clinton in his State of the Union addresses expressed a yearning for a reemergence of community and its central characteristic of mutual responsibility.

We can readily attribute the demise of community (especially its spiritual dimension) to burgeoning complexity, technology with its phenomenal advances in aspatial networking, and to consumerism. I fear, though, that we in the social sciences have made a regrettably large contribution toward this dilemma. We have done so by failing to perceive in depth this phenomenon of community as a living system. Consequently we failed to provide community leaders and decision-makers with a realistic appreciation for the implications of their choices and for the counterproductive remedial programs which we helped them impose on society.

The decades involved in this odyssey provided me abundant opportunities for firsthand, participant-observer probing of "real world" conditions. Although I grew up in what we would now call an industrial slum of immigrant families during the Depression, I was quite unprepared for my first encounter with the tragic insensitivity of American officialdom for pluralistic communities, especially where they involved "undesirable" neighborhoods.

Armed with university degrees and great enthusiasm in the 1950s, I found my first city manager refusing to provide fire protection to one locale. He wanted to expand the city's airport and its surrounding industrial area. This particular neighborhood of hardworking minority families stood in his way. But without fire protection, it was slowly burning down, one house at a time, often taking people's lives in the progress.

Shocking though his callousness was, it paled in comparison to what I would see in well-intentioned social welfare programs. Tragic as that first situation was for folks there, they at least retained a strong sense of community, led by a spirited school teacher and a few Black ministers.

The welfare programs I observed later dealt with individuals one by one, thereby eroding people's sense of mutual interest and mutual responsibility, the essence of community. Administers of those programs unwittingly created an atmosphere of suspicion and hostility between givers and receivers of aid. They forced people to prove that they were dependent which in turn they became even when initially they still had some self-respect and resilience. Those programs destroyed good people by tearing down their sense of family and community, just as federal programs had already driven Amerindian and Eskimo communities to alcoholic violence.

Model Cities legislation in the late 1960s supposedly sought to undo that damage by allowing local neighborhoods to manage their own recoveries. But once residents in those areas proved (to the trauma of university-educated bureaucrats and politicians) that they could manage their own affairs better than patronizing officials could do, mayors all across America went into high gear to alter the central thrust of the Model Cities program. They wanted to keep ghetto and public-housing dwellers segmented and hence dependent so that they the mayors could control all incoming federal dollars. Mental health and community viability among these segmented residents held far less concern for them than using federal money for what the politically dominant interests wanted. And so Model Cities died aborning in its own naiveté.

Power brokers at both local and federal levels had really learned nothing from the earlier Watts Rebellion where Martin Luther King had warned Mayor Yorty what would come, only to be denounced as an agitator. They had learned nothing even from the white-student uprising at Berkeley over being treated like IBM punch cards ("do not fold or spindle") where administrators used to joke that they could run a good university if they did not have to bother with students.

When local people warned Honolulu's big-time mainland consultant for Model Cities (the person who had drafted that legislation for Congress), he threatened to sabotage our funding if we did not focus on getting federal money instead of working on the real needs of community vitality. By blackmailing local residents this way, he did push through his agenda. But the results were what we had predicted.

Conditions grew worse, not better, as alienation deepened with the inevitable disillusionment. In this, Honolulu differed none from (though perhaps not as explosive as) dozens of other municipalities with MC pilot projects. It is probably not an exaggeration to conclude that metropolitan centers have continued to slide more toward chaos in the two decades since then, seemingly in direct proportion to government's replacing community in people's lives.

Here and there an occasional police department has acknowledged the benefit from working with, for, and through local people and their networks rather than keeping so aloof. Here and there individual schools have made a difference by becoming havens of human warmth and intellec-tual/artistic/creative stimulation. But for the most part, alienation between the controllers of public services and their intended recipients has grown. And that alienation—aided by hypocrisy and greed among national leaders in finance, industry, and government—has gnawed at the sense of mutual respect and responsibility.

Open Questions

Might the current crisis in American cities get so bad until it crashes and thereby gives birth to a new and possibly more vibrant community system— a system balancing mutual responsibility with individual rights? Might a polity emerge out of the experience typified by Orange County in the 1950s-60s with a restructuring of large metropolitan sprawls into federations of local entities handling local problems locally at a scale people can compre-hend and relate to, while appropriate combinations of units tackle problems at other scales? Or have interest blocs, government officials, government employee unions, attorneys, and social scientists become too entrenched in their respective ruts to look at the systemic complexity in new ways? Can they plot more appropriately flexible courses of strategic action than the simplistic concepts and measures from the past? Or will public myopia and vested interests stymie this need?

When will we social scientists and writers cease using the term "man" in referring to people or humanity? When will we stand tall enough to recog-nize honestly the central importance of females in the evolution of our spe-cies and thereby cease subliminally (and not so subliminally) making males the center of our world. As the trend runs increasingly once again toward matricentered families albeit this time in a male oriented culture, aren't we needlessly heightening tension within the connected community—between social/economic reality at family/neighborhood level and political/ economic reality at a larger scale? Aren't we stacking the cards in favor of violence?

Might recent moves toward cumulative voting for political representation in some states indicate a growing awareness for some people that networks hold more meaning for community ties than do place delineations? Might we not face a growing challenge to rethink democratic participation as modern community systems continually evolve more complex linkage webs? Or must political process continue to drift away from sociocultural reality, thereby acquiescing power to economic and ideological blocs?

We have seen that for survival the connected community needs to function symbiotically among its participants for their biological survival and symbolically for their emotional health. These require roots in both place and networks. Segmented however, aren't these crucial ingredients likely to work at cross purposes and so spur anxiety, frustration, alienation, "me-ism," and eventually violence?

Boiled down to its essence, doesn't our community system need a sense of stability so as to undergo change effectively *and* a sense of change so as to retain vitality while identifying with stability? Is it not likely that enhanced awareness of this systemicity of the connected community could go far in helping society find an optimal mix and process?

Isn't it time we recognize—and hence adjust our public strategies to the recognition—that individuals cannot stand alone? Individuals may be only as healthy, productive, and communally responsible as their connected community is healthy, meaningfully responsive, and systemically sensitive. The systemic depth of community in human life would appear far more significant than current political/legal ideas acknowledge in America and in most of the economically developed world. In taking community for granted, might we really be undercutting its vital role for humanity, a role neither government, nor commerce, nor religion/ideology have adequately filled?

Might it not be time, too, to bridge the chasm between the social and biological sciences so that we can fathom community as a living system? If this means social scientists must know as much as do geneticists about how the genotype and environment interact to produce the phenotype, wouldn't we find ourselves in a far better position to address those troubling questions about ethics inherent in our increased tampering with DNA? And might such an advance prove especially beneficial as we face a new wave of eugenics—a potentially more dangerous wave of eugenics shimmering in the reflected light of enhanced science—already welling up like a wave about to break over a naïve and ill-informed but panacea-craving world?

CHAPTER FIFTEEN

BEGETTING BEHAVIOR

I have drawn on violence to introduce considerations of behavior. I have also brought genetics into this discussion. Since an emotionally hot debate now rages over linking the genetics of race to the genetics of behavior, what I have covered lies vulnerable to distortion and erroneous interpretation by those who seek to distort and misinterpret in the misguided promotion of some agenda, whichever agenda that may be. It thus becomes necessary for me to address this area pointedly.[5]

Consistent with the argument throughout this book, I find it beneficial, first, to lay on the table the kinds of factors which go into affecting behavior whether violent or benign, and then to note their extensive interaction. In short: to note that we cannot throw blame at any one "cause" or even at a few but must reckon the systemic web of interactive factors.

BIOLOGY AND BEHAVIOR

An individual's phenotype (like a species') is the product of genetics and environment. Environmental factors come in an awesome range of forms. Such as (and I name only a few): 1. cultural attitudes (e.g. the individualism, manliness, and readiness to fight for one's interests so typical in America); 2. social expectations, both of oneself and of others; 3. myths and self-fulfilling prophecies about "race", ethnicity, religions, and socio-economic strata; 4. quality of public and private sector services; 5. ambiance of noise,

clutter, crowding, and fear; 6. positive or negative opportunities and rewards for self-respecting, productive involvement within the community
system.

Each of these (and many more) are shaped and magnified by linkage
networks, whether through social groups, religious connections, and contacts of daily life, or through the media and education. Availability or
nonavailability of jobs, of police protection, of garbage collection services
affect the self-images and images of others we wittingly or unwittingly base
our actions on. And these constitute the stuff of either a functioning or a
stressed and brittle community system.

The field of factors on the biological side of the equation is no less complex. Genes alone definitely do not comprise a person's entire biology. Biological factors go well beyond what genes influence. But let's start with the
genetic.

The vast range of temperaments, personalities, and hence behavior evident among individuals identified as members of any ethnic group or race
should dispel all myths that try to link one kind of behavior with any particular group. All large groups have a diversity of people: some considerate,
some nasty. This does not mean that genes cannot affect behavior, only that
they do so on an individual basis. Each person is unique in both genes inherited and life experienced, hence in outlook and behavior.

Everyone of us inherits a combination of genes which start us off in life
with a generalized temperament that gets shaped (or misshaped) into per-
sonality by our family, neighborhood, disease, nutrition, accidents, and an
infinite variety of other factors experienced. What is more, any one of us
might incur noninherited genetic mix-ups (mutations) with all manner of
potential impacts on us as human beings.

Quite likely nongenetic aspects of our biological systems exert more influence on behavior. Take these few examples: whether your pregnant
mother ingested drugs, be they prescription or illicit, caffeine, nicotine, or
alcohol; whether she had suitable nutrition and prenatal care for you;
whether you received healthful nutrition and received love, care, and intellectual stimulation during your infancy and childhood. All of these could
and would have affected your neurological system and hence your mental

capacity and attitudinal outlooks. These would have channeled your behavior into socially acceptable or unacceptable paths. Even more so: whether you suffered debilitating diseases and did or did not receive adequate care; whether you were abused or encouraged as you grew up; and what role-models were available to follow.

Given even these few factors, we may safely conclude that socio-economic status, neighborhood/peer groups, and the behavior of others quite likely had much to say about how you or I or any of us behaves. And those factors lie at the heart of any community system, whether for good or ill. From evidence now available, race (whatever it is) has in and of itself virtually no relation to behavior—except in so far as it provides mythical markers for setting self-fulfilling prophecies by segregating people and then adjusting accordingly the quality of community functions they experience.

While race, a biological phenomenon, makes no determinable contribution to behavior, ethnicity does because ethnicity is a cultural force in shaping and guiding lives. The more networks span the full breadth of society, the healthier its community system can be. The more ethnicity—whether in actual practices or in commonly-held images (some of which may employ racial markers)—splits a community system and dehydrates it thereby rendering it brittle, the less satisfactory a community's ability to function. In these, race gets a bad rap for a failed community.

As we saw, the less well a community functions, the more it is susceptible to social/economic/political turbulence; and the more such internal turbulence occurs, the less well it functions. A downward spiral of community erosion accelerates with the undercutting of mutual respect and mutual responsibility among members as identification with the self-organized community comes apart. As community thusly unravels, so do constraints on individual behavior—not just in anti-social acts by marginal members but by core members of the establishment ripping people off via stock manipulations and exaggerated advertising, through environmental pollution and legal/political games, by spouse and police violence. These not only dramatically symptomize the communal malaise; they can traumatize it and suck communal vitality.

Although race is in essence fictional, ethnicity (in all of its forms, be they life style, religious, or national origin) is real. It can serve as a positive force for orienting people's lives into productive, self-respecting, community participation. Or it can divide and thereby generate communal turbulence. Its tribalism can strain community; or its diverse cultural richness can enhance to communal vitality. The crucial factor in what happens is not race, ethnicity, or government's floundering intrusions. Case studies in this book suggest that the central factor is how the community system as such functions with its overwhelming multitude of webbed factors and forces.

We are left, then, with the question: What sets this pattern of human behavior in motion that both configures and expresses the connected community? Let's see.

"Programmed" Behavior

The term "programming" has appeared in this book modified by "cultural" and "genetic," seemingly to imply that culture and genes deal with us the way we deal with a computer: punching in instructions which must be followed slavishly. Intuitively we doubt, if not abhor, this connotation.

But by what process, then, did humans acquire the vast set of behaviors we routinely, often unconsciously, act out? I refer to gestures, habits of hygiene, mannerisms, body language, and modes of social exchange, all peculiar to each society. (Indeed, what makes children intuitively from infancy want to imitate others?) I refer also to how and why people in every society orient themselves to each other and interact in ways that allow their society to carry on its business of survival and reproduction. (What actually makes us a social species?) *Going further, I refer most of all to how a society creates its culture and how a culture creates its society.*

If human behavior stemmed from a process so straight forward as the term "programmed" implies, we should by now have a firm handle on what the program is and how it got that way. But we obviously do not. Several explanations arise: Possibly we lack the mental capacity for such profound discovery because it is too complex. Or possibly we have yet to look in the correct area. Maybe it's a combination of both, and more. Or is it?

Perhaps in thinking of cultural and genetic *programming* we have mentally boxed ourselves in to expect determinism of some sort. But what if *Homo sapiens*—and hence human behavior within its full social-cultural context—evolved through a nonprogrammed, nonlinear process? What if the closest analogy to this process of change resembles the seemingly random way a multitude of neurological cells in parallel and in web handle incoming signals? Though still at a "what if" stage (not yet even a hypothesis), this possibility might run something like the following.

From work in artificial intelligence, some scientists now suspect that a key factor in neurological systems is the self-organizing iterative interaction between nerve cells. Instead of one line of linked cells handling the learning and subsequent recognition of a specific bit of information, many parallel cells in webbed nets all deal with the processing of this unit of information and its subsequent recall.

Neurological cells' ability to learn, recognize, and recall information rests on their interactive "communication" while processing that information. Redundant circuits may not only provide backup; their iterative interactivity may reinforce significant signals, thereby fixing them more securely for subsequent use when needed. And since these same cells web with others processing other information, they might more readily link and draw up related information as needed. Could some similar sort of process occur in the evolution of culture among humans? Consider the following scenario.

A group of individuals encounters a novel challenge. Each person acts on this matter spontaneously albeit tentatively. As social beings, they routinely compare their responses to see which worked best. Thereby they prepare themselves, not only for dealing with the challenge when subsequently encountered, but for dealing with each other's diverse reactions, thus strengthening their interdependence. In facing different challenges, each such group would evolve a unique set of procedures. Hence there could emerge over time a vast diversity of cultural systems for a diversity of groups to self-identify by—with languages improvised accordingly.

Depending on how mutually dependent these individuals become, they will unobtrusively seek a consensus strategy and evolve a collective approach. This generally agreed-to approach then becomes another facet of their on-going, working culture—without consciously thinking about it. And as a solution to a challenge, this collective strategy reinforces the cement of society. While thusly gaining a body of operating procedures for countless aspects of its culture, each society also creates a working modus operandi noted here as a connected community. The greater a society's capacity for effective interaction, the greater its prospects for evolving an effective community system and hence a more viable culture which can more effectively identify that society. Voila: self-organization in practice; order out of chaos.

It is this connotation title of this book speaks of connected community operating as a force in a systemic web. The web is not merely a two-dimensional one like today's computer internets; nor even three-dimensional as in a static Gordian Knot. It is four-dimensional as a process ever in evolution. We (especially scientists) readily admit how little we know about the forces of self-organization that evolved galaxies and solar systems out of primordial dust and living organisms out of chemical bondings. Why then should we suppose we know all there is to the existence of social bonding and cultural formulation? Take turbulence ("chaos") for instance: it may well be the factor which, in shaking and rearranging the raw ingredients, prompts new structurings and processes of order and thereby in a ay encourages the evolution of new systems, whether genetic/biological or cultural/societal.

Be that as it may, for humans this process of cultural formation becomes a medium of "collective memory" with built-in feedback loops: namely in how people adjust their behavior in relation to each other. Neither for the human trinity of society-culture-community, nor for other species' evolution do we find optimization here, only a "muddling through" or "make-do" resolution of problems—just enough to survive and meet the next challenge. Where optimization does inadvertently happen, a species or society can become too well adjusted to a particular set of conditions and so render itself unable to adjust when conditions drastically alter. We saw this happen in Hawaii and see it among countless species currently going extinct.

For humans, this suggested muddling-through process meant societal learning and increased organizational potential. But these rested on how interactive learning facilitates further learning at neurological, individual, and societal levels. Here then would exist a process of self-organization without need for any overall "programming" much less any need for an omniscient/omnipotent orthogensis. Somewhat parallel processes of adjustment might, conceivably, underlie ecological and organismic living systems as well, albeit without of course any cultural development accompanying the genetic changes. For, their equivalent central force would differ in substance from the connected community so relevant to the human experience.

As biological changes abetted individual and group survival, change could build on itself at an accelerating rate: Not just via Darwinian natural selection but through "learning" by both the genetic and cultural systems as they evolved—somewhat like dancers. As each one adjusts to the other's adaptations to change, the more the other can change in concert. Might they not, in this manner, learn how to enhance their adaptative capacities? If life on Earth could evolve the eye some 40 times, why deny nature a full range of potentials for self-organization?

Eventually the cultural form of change would emerge as the more obvious influence on human evolution and human behavior. But culture could not have done so without certain biological (genetic) changes. Yet biological change could succeed so fast only as it remained in tune with the societal capacity for adaptive survival. (Lamarckian heresy need no longer frighten us.) Culture and society, then, could evolve as two sides of the same coin— *with the community system serving as the coin.*

Why the hominid line (more so than the pongid or most other lines) experienced its particular record of so much change in so limited a span of time remains far from resolved. It remains unresolved largely because we have so much more to discover about the genetic system and so much more to comprehend about the elaborate phenotypic dance performed by the partnership of *H. sapiens'* genetics and culture.

While other species have evolved varying degrees of simple cultures, their biological systems have neither facilitated nor prompted the evolution of complex culture and society akin to that evident among all humans with our capacity for elaborate communication. Nor have they undergone the interactive exchange between culture creating its society and society creating its culture so characteristic of our species. They have not, apparently, fully experienced the synergistic, multi-scaled, adaptive process of change explored here as a *connected community* and its great expansion due to our recent capacity for syntactically symbolic interaction.[6]

Community, in turn it would appear, not only serves humans as our arena and process of interaction for society to realize its culture and for culture to identify its society. Community has emerged as a major catalyst and nexus for human adaptation. Communal vitality becomes a crucial (albeit subtle) force for change as well as for stability. Myopia in the social and biological sciences as well as in the civic professions risks peril by neglecting community as an intricate, highly complex system.

This peril can come, by analogy, like a runaway cancer as human society/culture eats on itself by letting individual greed run rampant—and, in the process, threatens to destroy the other living systems of organisms and ecology which share our planet. All the rhetorical ballyhoo in the world about family values can do little if families lack a viable community system to function in, a prospect given more words than tangible commitment. Look back at the case studies (Japan, Hawaii, Orange County) from which these observations derive and test heir validity; then try them elsewhere.

In Part One we saw the emergence of complex community—well beyond the clustering propensity among other primate species and hominids previously—for funtional/biological survival and procreation. We observed that only recently mutated capacity for self-conscious syntactical thought almost suddenly allowed humans to organize increasingly complex community systems with and for societal and cultural expansion. Not only could they now fabricate far more sophisticated tools and operate far more intricate political and economic subsystems; every tool and operation carried symbolic meaning and every symbolic meaning had impact on functional survival. Part Two compared one case where community system broke down, first in its symbols of life and then functionally. Using the case of rapidly growing Orange County, Part Three demonstrated how complicated community can become in its self-organizing process.

Currently we encounter a bombardment of political rhetoric about "family values" and crime, followed by a menagerie of simplistic solutions. From this analysis, it would appear that an atmosphere of violent crime and

lost family values may far more represent symptoms than causes. Consequently, focusing on the symptoms of malaise rather on the malaise itself
can produce more futility and hence frustration than resolution. Like weeds
taking over a weak lawn or a healthy lawn squeezing out weeds, crime can
readily fester where community is weakest because the prime acculturation
force, that of the family, has sparse context of significance to relate to and
even less societal and cultural vitality to support it.

Beating society's collective breast about violence gained and family values lost misses the point. Family values, crime, violence, justice, rights and
responsibility are facets of an intricate complex of iterative interactions.
Focusing on a few of them at a time merely impedes our envisioning the
systemic whole. Alas, the whole is far too complex for politicians, dema-
gogues, journalists, ideologues, and pundits to deal with in the usual 30-
second sound bites which the public will tolerate. Yet it is the interactive
nature of human though (symbols) and action (functions) that constitute the
essence of human life and behavior. And this interactivity, as it evolves, is a
turbulent system. No amount of over-simplifying will make this reality go
away.

EPILOGUE

Several linked propositions emerge with regard to the self-organizing process of this human trinity of society, culture, and community. First: enough
cultural specificity must occur for a society to achieve self-identification and
hence cohesion. Yet second: too much complexity—whether from sheer size
or divisive diversity—can overload the system and cause it to break into
more readily self-identifying, self-integrating blocs. Thusly third: time and
mass—namely the rate of change needed, the number of participants involved, their organizational capacity, and the scope of factors (technology,
structure, mores, values) under pressure for change—will shape the systemic results. And fourth: those results will always differ because the number and the interactive mixes of the variable factors/forces involved approach infinity.

The vast complexity and the inherent turbulence involved in this process of cultural/societal self-organization readily obstruct our vision in probing it. We may only take consolation in the difficulties we faced earlier in fathoming the "miracle" of self-organization made possible by covalence (periodic table) in chemical interaction and complicated by the horrendous complexity (quantum mechanics) of subatomic particles and waves.[7] Even how gravity functions over intergalactic space remains less than fully comprehended; so too for Einstein's elusive quest, a unified field theory.

Where virtually all variables affect all others, we should not expect to successfully project our puny depictions of "order" onto reality. We have barely begun to envision the potential complexity that constitutes the living systems we partake of and participate in. Caution and humility, therefore, seem most essential when trying to impose any public policy that would channel society toward some simplistic image of order, whether that image be prescribed by ethnocentric myths, by ideology/religion, by political expediency, or by sophisticated science.

I hope you have gained from this book a bit of the challenge we all (scientists, officials, and public alike) face, a challenge that has obviously fascinated me, increasingly so over these many years of professional participant observation and academic analysis.

Please permit me to end on an editorial note about what this study has meant to my own outlook after decades of wrestling with the issues and unknowns involved. The chaos and complexity that surrounds—yes, engulfs and permeates—community can seem intimidating to scholars and threatening to us all as members. Yet these need not mean a lack of order.

It's just that the order achieves a magnitude, a diversity, a potential strength beyond what we look for when we cripple community with myopic vision. Diversity can mean vitality rather than disorder and threat. Strength can stem from flexibility rather than from rigidity. It depends on our individual and on our interactively consensual outlooks—on outlooks willing to accept nonlinear complexity instead of only simplicity. One major obstacle to overcome: recognition that the interactive complexity of our systemic world vastly exceeds the naively simplistic universe which sociologists/economists/anthropologists, biologists, Darwinian sociobiologists, and religionists have heretofore segmentally theorized and too often dogmatically portray it to be.

Our problem here may lie in the fact that our outlooks stem largely from our community experiences. We are caught in systemic spirals that can go up positively or down negatively. The challenges come in turning a disintegrative down-spiral around and in making a positive up-spiral realistic enough to grow in strength. Toward this end I believe, more concrete knowledge (rather than more impassioned rhetoric) can help. Hence the writing of this book with the possible vistas its questions open.

End Notes

1. Using the words "myth" and "science" in this book makes no judgment about how well any viewpoint or methodology expresses reality. Both myth and science have their successes and failures in this regard. Both myth and science have their forms of "proof" which their adherents swear by. My distinction between them concerns their process of formulation and acceptance.

   We either accept myths on faith or reject them, period. Ideally, science should ask for no faith. The basic modus operandi of science is the opposite of faith: we must remain consistently skeptical and constantly question. While we may close our eyes and simply enjoy myths, science ideally demands eyes that never close. Admittedly, scientists as humans can at times accept supposedly scientific propositions with stubborn faith thereby rendering them myths. Such human failures do not provide a basis for rejecting a scientific method of subjecting every explanation to critical review.

2. A few quick examples of culturally learned (nongenetic) behavior among animals: Orangutans on Borneo tend to live rather solitary lives whereas on Sumatra a male will far more often remain with the female who has borne and is rearing his offspring. The adaptive factor is the existence of dangerous tigers and siamangs on Sumatra but not on Borneo. Anubis baboons living in African forests move through an area and react to the presence of baboons from other troops in markedly different patterns of behavior than do those living in open savanna even though both kinds of baboons have the same genotype. Some killer whales remain within tight matriarchal family pods in one area of ocean where they hunt cooperatively for fish and use a markedly different "language" from other ocra who migrate independently and live on a diet of sea mammals.

3. Social scientists face a fundamental dilemma. In being totally, clinically objective (if that were humanly possible), an observer would miss the emotional nuances of considerable significance in human affairs and in community viability. But the more empa-

thetic an observer, the less one can minimize the dangers of emotional distortion to phenomena observed. Achieving a workable balance is an art, and artistry inescapably plays a central role in all sciences.

4. A systemic conceptualization of community led a handful of us in Hawaii to champion fiberoptic-linked satellite work centers in the early 1970s. We saw it as a far less costly and far less intrusive alternative to ever more freeways and rail transit relative to potential results achievable. Alas, officials, professional planners, and urban leaders could not envision any alternative except pouring more concrete—to increase com-muting—as a way to cope with increased commuting.

    Ironically, state officials at that time had a campaign on to attract electronic indus-tries to relocate in Hawaii which of course did not happen but could have if officials had demonstrated even a little comprehension about the potentials of an electronic world.

5. See *Discover's* November 1994 special issue on "The Science of Race" for easily read and quite enlightening articles by James Shreeve, Stephen Jay Gould, Jo Ann Gutin, Christopher Wills, Jared Diamond, and Juan Williams. They penetrate far deeper into this issue than I could do given the primary focus of this book.

6. But to what extent do some other species experience community as conceptualized here? In playing political games, bonobos and chimps certainly read body language and interrelationships as fully as we read our symbol systems. Porpoise pods huddle close by a bereaved mother who carries her dead infant for days—as much of a funeral ritual as any attributed to Neanderthal: indeed, our funeral rituals focus far more on the immediacy of bereavement than on some abstract concept of eternal life. Social species with advanced intelligence may well have a sense and process of community. They simly lack our digital dexterity for making tools, our larynx for complx speech, and our recently evolved capacity for fully sysntactical comprehension and speculation.

7. See H.C. von Baeyer's "The Philospher's Atom," *Discover*, Nov. 1995.

INTRODUCTORY BIBLIOGRAPHY TO "CHAOS" AND "COMPLEXITY":

Gleick, James. *Chaos: Making a New Science.* 1987.
Horgan, John. "From Complexity to Perplexity." *Scientific American*, June 1995.
Lewin, Roger. *Complexity at the Edge of Chaos.* 1991.
Stewart, Ian. "Does Chaos Rule the Cosmos?" *Discover*. Nov. 1992.
Waldrop, M. Mitchell. *Complexity.* 1992.

A Few Diverse Additional Approaches.

Drucker, Peter. *The Ecological Vision.* 1993.
Foldvary, Fred. *Public Goods and Private Communities.* 1994.
Gusfield, Joseph R. *Community: A Critical Response.* 1975.
Kemmis, Daniel. *Community and the Politics of Place.* 1990.
Selznick, Philip. *The Moral Commonwealth.* 1992.
Sturm, Douglas. *Community and Alienation.* 1988.

Structure and Delineation

Scientists hope to formulate models of reality with which to test hypotheses about variables. We may have heretofore lacked adequate models of intricate living systems due to inadequacies in depicting them, even when we could imagine them. This situation may have begun to change during the past decade with the emergence of "chaos" and "complexity" theories. As a new generation of scientist takes its place in social and biological research and willingly interacts (as at the Santa Fe Institute), we may at last achieve the requisite capability for the exceedingly sophisticated analysis entailed.

But even with this requisite mathematics, there remains considerable rethinking for us so as to put this advance in model-making simulation to optimal advantage. While the math can help our exploration of reality, it can as readily obfuscate if core systemic concepts used remain fuzzy, ethereal, and segmented between disciplinary fields, or just plain jargon-ridden. These new breakthroughs in analytical capability may serve well if they broaden (instead of narrow) our grasp of reality's horrendous complexities.

The more phenomena display commonality, the easier to come up with models. However, there ever exists a temptation to carry commonalities between diverse sets of phenomena too far—to force phenomena to fit an elegant analytical "structure." For instance, James Grier Millers' work into living systems theory some two decades ago, a forerunner of today's research and modeling of complexity. While sincerely impressed with his pioneering perceptivity, I retain my skepticism on the grounds that it tends to push metaphor into dangerous waters.

Miller's hierarchical set of eight levels and twenty "critical subsystems" sought to serve analytical purposes. Yet it inadvertently planted in disciples' minds a fixedness of structure that does not exist in reality—the way we easily slip into thinking of taxonomic nomenclature (kingdom, phylum, class order, family, genus) as reality when at most only species truly exist. The rest is invention for our own convenience.

Chaos and complexity theory, still experimenting and feeling its way, has yet to reach this point. But it might, simply by the esoteric nature of its math, a math that could put it out of reach of the vast majority of decision makers who would benefit from its potential in perceiving reality afresh.

As viewed in Miller's living systems and in more recent complexity theory, some sort of as yet barely glimpsed process of self-organization did occur whereby certain chemical compounds collected into amino acids and proteins to produce RNA and eventually DNA. These proceeded to self-organize into cells which evolved into self-perpetuating organisms which organized into groups, some of whom eventually would consciously form voluntary organizations.

A magnificent challenge here calls enticingly for scientists to discern the process or structure (or both) common to all of the wide ranging types of self-organizations identified thus far. Discovering this ultimate fractal would rank for biologists with physicists' resolving a unified field theory.

We may surmise that some self-organizing processes have occurred since these phenomena do exist and structures with subsystems have evolved. While fractal-like processes and structures may exist, present facts do not of themselves necessitate commonality. Until we have far more information, we might do well to resist the temptation to force the issue.

That's what complexity theory would like to use simulation testing to probe. Meanwhile we can, even without the esoteric math, begin to think in terms of horrendously complex networks of interaction, as explored in Orange County.

Another difficulty arises, that of delineating living from nonliving. By definition, all systems involve interaction, hence all require energy to underwrite their activity. Weather systems, for example, involve tremendous amounts of energy but certainly do not fulfill any other qualification for "living-ness." Interaction and the use of energy, therefore, cannot provide criteria for distinguishing a living system.

Many systems, but not all, process "information." Again, this aspect does not provide a useful criterion since some of them involve mechanically or electronically predetermined processes of interaction. They neither self-adapt to change nor can they opt to reproduce themselves within a context of multi-scaled, multi-directional, systemic interaction.

The three living systems identified here—organisms, ecosystems, and community—remain distinct despite their interaction, interrelatedness, and common criteria. They are similar in having long life-spans measured in hundreds or thousands of years for community, millions of years for ecosystems, and up to hundreds of millions of years (via genes) for organismic systems. Otherwise they mostly differ.

A species (simply a collection of units capable of specific reproduction) would not qualify because impacts on one part do not necessarily affect all other parts. For the same reason, a society (as a collection of units identified by their adherence to a culture) would not qualify either. Furthermore, neither species nor society becomes both the arena and process of interaction for its component parts the way organisms, ecosystems, and community systems do.

The fact that a species shares a generally common phenotype among its member organisms (just as a society shares a set of cultural practices and attitudes among its members) does not make them analogous to an organism, ecosystem, and community even though the latter three are composed respectively of interactive subsystems, species, and groups.

Nor should we see these living systems fitting a single metaphoric structure. An organism has recognizable boundaries to its system, namely its body; ecosystems and communities, as open systems, allow participating species and groups respectively to join or depart. For the latter two, self-organizing self-adjustment becomes a more obviously continual, tangible process.

Ecosystem and community as systems can occur at an almost limitless range of scales—from that in a petri dish or family to the entire globe. Both can enlarge or contract rather extensively by changing adaptively without destroying their system. Whereas the more complex an organism, the more likely death will follow dismemberment; the more complex either an ecosystem or community is, the more versatile its dynamic capabilities. What is more, ecosystems function only symbiotically; community has an emotional dimension expressed in symbols and rituals.

If analysts feel they must have a structure of some sort, a V-shaped one might serve better than Miller's unitarily hierarchical one. At the V's apex come organisms composed of subsystems which cannot function on their own—such as the genetic, immune, neural, endocrinal, respiratory, digestive, and circulatory. The V's two legs—the ecological and community systems—may resemble each other in being populated by organisms yet differ in their form of interaction. Ecology operates on an interspecies level; the interchange constituting a system of community occurs at an intraspecies level. Besides, community systems fall within the overall ecological system. Ironically, the Millers only recently added community to their analytic framework and have yet to designate ecosystem by name.

Not only are organisms, ecosystems, and communities multi-scaled (having living subsystems) and adaptively interactive with other systems; their characteristics rest heavily on the workings of phenotypes. All of the others cited by the Millers can be subsumed (explained) as subsidiary to these three basic forms of highly interrelated living systems. For, these three, in essence, alone are not only evolutionary processes but also constitute both the arena *and* process for member interaction.

Having stated the caveats, I must leave open possibilities for all manner of as yet undiscovered or at least inconclusively explored fractals, commonalities, and rhythms in these living systems. Here are two to illustrate the many areas whose complexity we have barely begun to fathom:

1. What governs the reliable periodicity of mtDNA mutations? How does any particular mtDNA "know" when it is the "correct" time to mutate?

2. How do the gametes of mating individual humans "know" to produce a male or female embryo so that just enough surplus boys are born to offset their higher childhood death rates so that males and females are numerically even at the onset of their reproductive years? Chance alone would seem to dictate an even distribution at birth, not sixteen years later.

We are a long way from knowing how ignorant we are about the complexity of living systems and the essence of their orderliness within the seeming randomness of their turbulent contexts. While statistical information may define the parameters, it throws no light on the interactive processes involved.

See James Grier Miller's *Living Systems* (1978); J.G.Miller and Jessie L. Miller, "The Nature of Living Systems," *Behavior Science* (July 1990) and "A Living System Analysis of Organizational Methodology" (October 1991); J.L.Miller, "The Timer," *Behavior Science* (July 1990); Miller and Miller, "Reproducers" and "Boundaries," *Behavior Science* (January 1992). *Organization and Change in Complex Systems*, edited by Marcelo Alonso (1990), employs the Miller conceptualization of living systems.

CONSCIOUSNESS /
SELF - CONSCIOUSNESS

"Mind" and "thinking" do not require "consciousness," only the neurological capacity to recognize and hence react to stimuli in an optimal manner based on past experience. A major portion (if not the vast majority) of human actions occur like this without our having to consciously in words command our body parts to act in a desirable way to each situation, much less each stimulus, encountered. (How else can we drive a car, talk, and chew gum at the same time?) Our human neurological processes apparently proceed as they do among all animals with the mental capability to make choices. Other species simply do not talk about their choices the way we do.

Indeed, even when we communicate in words, our mind has had to think out our thought subconsciously before we can translate and express the thought with communicative symbols. To the extent a person's mind has not subconsciously worked out a thought before translating it into symbols, to that extent the words will lack syntax, spilling out in a muddle. As the old joke has it: "How do I know what I'm thinking until I hear myself say it?" Which may be why we talk to ourselves so much.

Part of the debate about the supposed uniqueness of Homo sapiens rests on the relative degrees of consciousness among species. Difficulties in addressing this issue stem initially, as so often the case, from what we might mean by the concepts involved.

The look of horror in a rabbit's eyes as it flees for its life from a fierce predator bounding down on it, the frightened cries of small birds when a hawk menacingly circles above, the guilty body language by a pet dog when it has misbehaved, the plaintive bawling of a calf when first separated from its mother in the weaning process —these kinds of behavior certainly indicate that other species can acutely sense what happens in their world. Obviously they can experience many of the same emotions we humans feel, for they can express them quite unmistakably. Isn't this consciousness at work? Since most if not all mammals dream, they must have neurological systems capable of feelings and imagination not unlike our own, at least in their keenest senses such as, say, hearing and smelling—though not demonstrated verbally

When protohumans several million years ago moved through the African savanna, they must have felt aware of their environment quite keenly. Otherwise how would they have survived to locate sources of food and evade much larger predators? Must we conclude that they lacked consciousness simply because their small brains and non-human larynxes would have too severely restricted their repertoire of verbal symbols to allow some minimum level of communication about their lives and feelings?

If consciousness equates with sensitivity to stimuli, then which species are the most conscious? Dogs, among many other species, certainly attain a far higher level of sensitivity to smells and sounds than do we humans. Eagles have sensitive powers of vision that put us to shame. It is not just a matter of processing such stimuli; they utilize their sensitivities for the ultimate purpose, that of survival. Some species acutely sense variations in Earth's magnetism, air pressure, and some as yet unidentified indicators of approaching earthquakes. Some may even orient themselves by the stars. Can we do these? Are we more "conscious" than these species?

The question really concerns self-consciousness rather than consciousness. In the former, an organism might not only recognize him/herself in a mirror; it must deliberately undertake play-acting roles as on a stage (by perceiving others' thoughts and emotions via understanding its own thoughts and emotions and strategies) and must make deliberate decisions at self-expression, even choices about alternative options. Going that far still does not exclude other species from some degree of self-consciousness. Chimps and bonabos not only recognize their reflections as themselves; they deliberately act out political games. Some chimps and elephants have even become quite enamored with self-expression through artwork and do surprisingly well at it.

Actually this debate tends to revolve around diverse sets of definitions and undocumentable conclusions—not unlike Medieval debates about angels standing the head of a pin. After admitting that it will likely remain never fully resolved, we might at least break "consciousness" into its multiplicity of elements so as to note their continuum from slightest through greatest neurological receptivity to both external and internal stimuli, at some point or other arriving at self-consciousness.

At one end of the spectrum comes that basic neural programming that keeps body functions performing whether conscious of them or not—such as heart beating, lungs breathing, alimentary canal under control. Next comes that shot of adrenaline for "fight or flight" in the conscious face of a real or imagined threat. Third, the response to sexual signals for procreation and parenting. Fourth, deliberate control of motor functions as in walking for mammals, swimming or flying for other species. Fifth, sleep dreaming, a set of internal stimuli whose purpose is less than fully clear but whose need seems essential among most mammals to cope with life's challenges; our brains/minds continue to work even while our conscious self sleeps.

As species' neurological systems become more complex, they can solve more complicated problems through insights and innovations, at times almost as if they had reasoned out a situation. Soon we reach neurological systems capable of sensing others' thoughts and thereby purposefully manipulating conspecifics through attention and the use of symbols, including dress and grooming. This applies largely to our species, though apes can and do display some of this condition. At this point comes the sense of awe associated with an aesthetic experience and of reverence linked to ancestors and things noble.

Although seemingly a characteristic only of humanity, this sort of behavior has been observed among elephants when they come upon the skeletons of other elephants. Chimps sometimes intently watch a brilliant sunset. Some observers of cetaceous behavior even suspect that their sonorous communications may have a poetic, hence an aesthetic, quality to them. That their songs change like fashions from year to year may indicate more than a genetic component behind them.

We now reach the point of syntactical consciousness capable of complex analytical, creative, abstract conceptualizations and their precise expression—to a point where we have apparently eliminated all other species except *H. sapiens sapiens*. Ironically, beyond this point of neurological sophistication comes a level of self-consciousness capable of controlling all neurological programming, even the otherwise automatic pulsing of the heart, the regulation of body temperature, hormonal flow, brain waves, and the breath of life itself. At this point a person enters into an altered state (sometimes irreversibly) beyond anything experienced by more than a few unusually self-disciplined individuals in monasteries.

Given this spectrum of neurological activity, self-consciousness becomes whatever slice of it we chose to designate. We can make that slice either so narrow as to flatter our own species or broad enough to include many other species. In fact, self-consciousness may no more mark us off as distinctly different and hence superior to all other species than does the presence of culture. Acknowledging this possibility might facilitate an exploration of the potential role of genetics in behavior—in humans as well as in other species. What then of "artificial intelligence," that programmed by humans into a robot? Done well enough, it could achieve sufficient sensitivity o its environment to reach a state of consciousness equal to some living species. But if the analysis in the last chapter has validity, a computerized robot programmed by an outside intelligence (us) will not have experienced a genetically self-organized capacity to evolve nonlineally the integrated unity of culture, society, and community requisite for full self-consciousness. Any seeming self-consciousness would merely express what we had implanted.

THE ENIGMA OF INCEST AND ALTRUISM

It would appear that no discussion of possible genetic influence on human culture can long avoid the controversies raised by sociobiology. At its heart lie the issues (enigmas) of incest and altruism. If the genetic system seeks to maximize itself, then what better way to accomplish that goal than via incestuous reproduction? Yet all cultures bar it, with exceptions made only for royalty (as in ancient Egypt, Peru, Hawaii, and Europe). If the genetic system seeks to maximize itself, then what worse way than by allowing altruism? Yet altruistic sacrifice occurs in virtually all thriving societies.

* * * *

The argument centers on whether the universality of incest taboos is instinctive or culturally imposed? By now this long argued enigma should have reached the conclusion that it is neither one nor the other; it goes far beyond either alone. Yet that has not diminished the passion it can generate among those who debate it.

Consistent with the analysis throughout this book, I find it counterproductive to look at an issue such as incest taboo in cause/effect terms. Since both biology and culture operate within highly intricate systems, then an issue with possible links to both deserves analysis in a systemic context, too.

And a systemic context inherently involves intricate webs of complexity, not one-to-one linear formulas.

In earlier decades, social scientist/philosophers could structure their arguments for a cultural explanation on such unbiased assumptions as utter promiscuity among the great apes, the nearest species to our own. They could do so because none of them had spent years in the wild meticulously observing ape behavior. We no longer have that excuse; Jane Goodall, Diane Fossey, and others have taken the time and exerted the scientific care to provide us with accurate accounts of primate behavior.

Their findings? For the most part, other species do avoid incest. A basis for hypothesizing a built-in genetic factor for humans then does exist. And that possible factor appears imposing enough to disallow our sloughing it off. We must account for it or prove it does not affect humans.

If humans still feel a genetically programmed avoidance of incest, the question usually raised next concerns why societies throughout the world need to include rules against it within their cultures. Why not ask the same question about the avoidance of murder within one's family and group? Primates tend to act differently (more protective, accommodating) toward family and group members than to outsiders. So why do all human societies feel it necessary to establish and generally to enforce rules against murder and violence, at least within the group? In-group violence and murder are no less repugnant to human cultures worldwide than incest, yet receive less scrutiny when scholars explore sociobiological theory.

I do not raise this latter question frivolously. Incest and family violence may have more in common and hence may more legitimately call for concerted consideration than customarily conducted in this debate by either cultural or genetic determinists. After all, people do engage in sexual intercourse (especially within the family) for more reasons than procreation; even more than for recreation. Sex often involves either violence to establish dominance or seduction to establish control—among primates as well as among humans.

Ethologists have observed various uses of sex beyond insemination. Sexual activity can bear on strategies for success in pair-bonding and offspring-rearing among other species as well as among our great human cultural diversity. A few examples: Females may practice promiscuity to gain the protection of all unrelated males who might otherwise abuse, even murder, their children. Sister and/or daughter swapping for marriage (actually mutual hostage taking) may gain the protection of other families by sealing alliances.

We noted that private property, inheritance, and male willingness to observe institutionalized marriage may partake of the same process of change. Then as a society and hence its culture grow larger and more complex, the above strategies—and many others—require societal recognition and hence more elaborately defined cultural rules.

Observance of cultural rules serves purposes beyond their immediate objective. Indeed, the secondary impetus for such rules can become so important in and for themselves that their original objective may lose immediacy, even to the point of being forgot. For, observance of rules provides a very obvious way to distinguish in-group members from all others and to determine commitment among those members. It provides as obvious a set of markers for whom to trust and whom to avoid as do the symbols of racial features, dress, and prescribed rituals.

If this hypothesis stands on firm ground, then why should it not apply to incest as well as to all other facets of human life governed by culture within our community system? While incest avoidance may stem initially from some ancient genetic device for protecting the species—just as mating is essential for species propagation—how humans act it out within any particular culture will take on the shades and rituals which evolved largely by happenstance over the centuries and millennia for that community system. And people may do so for societal concerns unrelated, or at most tangential, to biological incest.

Just as the institutions of family and religion occur in all cultures but take a myriad of forms, incest avoidance too comes in many formats. Yet despite this diversity, several general principals do emerge and they correspond with cultural proscriptions against in-house violence: One, elites and ruling families may not have to conform, at least not as narrowly as the rest of society. Sibling (or at least first cousin) marriages and brother rivalry to the point of murder among a ruling class may serve the interests of that

class so often as to become institutionalized. Two, incest and in-house violence occur so consistently among people on the margin of societies that
conformity to societal prohibitions takes on the symbolic function of marking community membership for the bulk of society.

Even among this main body of conforming community members—even
in the best of conforming middle-class families—incest and in-house violence still happen. They may occur far more often, especially in times of
communal strain, than people admit. American courts, for instance, have
tried valiantly over the decades to avoid opening this proverbial can of
worms. Quite possibly it strikes too close to the heart of our culture (namely
the family) and at the values we as a society pay lip service to. Only our
current epidemic of HIV, drugs, juvenile violence, and welfare problems has
begun to unlock closet doors on these skeletons of abuse.

Acknowledging the existence of incest and in-house abuse does not deny
the possibility of a genetic effort to avoid actions detrimental to the species.
Acknowledging the above situation simply acknowledges how far human
culture has come to override genetic programming and characterize human
behavior over these last forty millennia.

Another facet of incest similarly draws less than full attention. I refer to
sexual interaction between spouses and tie it to an apparently natural
(noninstitutionalized) avoidance of mating with persons one grew up with,
as observed for one example in Israeli kibbutzim. If the kibbutz experience
has validity elsewhere (and no evidence has emerged to the contrary), then
whatever the genetic factor is, it might operate on us in terms of proximity
to the opposite sex rather than being blood-relationship specific. Translated
into daily life: if we get turned off by some one of the opposite sex in a family context so as to avoid incest, then couldn't this same factor eventually
turn us off sexually with the spouse we share so much of our life—
especially as wife becomes more like sister and even mother to her husband
with the passage of years?

In this perspective the old excuse of "the grass is always greener on the
other side of the fence" no longer satisfies in fully explaining actual (or
yearnings for) infidelity. The question remains: why is the other grass
thought greener? We are not horses who must crane our necks to reach the

distant grass when surrounded by a field full of grass. Might not this incest avoidance "mechanism" (whatever it is) have served as useful a purpose in curtailing late pregnancies as in protecting the species from biological degradation through incestual unions?

I do not know the answer. Nor do I propose this possibility to obfuscate the original issue of incest avoidance as a biological or cultural phenomenon. I cannot help but note, though, that societies throughout the world have invented all manner of cultural rules to accommodate male desires for sexual diversity while curbing any real or imagined parallel desires by females. Moreover, family violence to assert "honor" (really dominance) quite possibly erupts more over this troubling and often buried matter than perhaps any other.

All we might safely surmise is this: Incest, like culture generally, does not lend itself to a simplistic explanation. Until geneticists have learned enough to fathom how a genetic system can program behavior in other species, we have no way to discern how it might happen to humans. Human behavior has become so overlaid with cultural programming until it seems utterly foolish to keep speculating about what we have so little evidence to base any argument on.

Saying this, however, does not suggest that we should necessarily credit cultural programming alone for such universalities as religion, family, violence, incest avoidance or whatever. We simply do not have a firm enough basis now for making this or any other conclusion. But the underlying complexity of incest avoidance leans toward the hypothesis that we would do better viewing it as one of countless interwebbed systemic factors in the human organism and human community.

* * * *

Similarly for that other sociobiological enigma, altruism. Human genes might retain a proclivity for "inclusive fitness" (maximizing the perpetuation of our genetic material) even if in certain circumstances it means sacrificing oneself so that others bearing some of our genes can live and reproduce surviving offspring. But the heavy overlay of cultural programming still leads some of us to sacrifice ourselves for others —even for strangers—with no apparent reproductive advantage. What was genetically programmed over millions of years for hominids in small bands of relatives may have remained in force even though the community of our involvement has expanded to encompass thousands and millions of unrelated individuals.

The fact that altruists act without thinking suggests an innate drive, not something one calculates strategy over. Yet it is not all genetic. Altruism and cooperation decrease where community erodes, whereas a strong sense of mutual respect, mutual trust, and mutual responsibility encourages altruism. In contrast, selfishness is counterproductive by undercutting community. Indeed, nepotistic family has prevailed throughout human evolution—until slavery and later the Industrial Revolution mandated individualized workers devoid of community as a way to ensure their compliance and rigorous exploitation.

We might hypothesize then that genetic evolution, like cultural evolution, may have mostly favored cooperation, especially where the two reinforce each other. Darwinian competition falls short of fully explaining evolution in many species including that of *Homo sapiens*. An *over*emphasis on the individual (individual rights over individual responsibilities) may run as contrary to biological evolution as to cultural evolution.

Suggesting this, however, in no way gives credence to eugenics, communism, fascism, or any other ideology that would rationalize inequality or individual suppression. They utterly lack any basis in evolutionary biology.

POLITICS IN MATING

A popular song of a generation ago reasoned that, since love and marriage are so inextricably linked ("like a horse and carriage"), a person could not or should not have one without the other. Now, obviously there occur all kinds of love not associated with marriage--love between relatives, love shared with friends, love of a pet, love of country. For those singing this song, however, no confusion arose. "Love" in this instance clearly meant: no marriage, no sex.

A major debate in Congress today focuses on what to do about unwed teenage pregnancies, especially since so many of them add to the nation's welfare burden. Oft overlooked is the fact that, in most cultures today and throughout the entire course of human life, childbearing began in the teens. This has been true in America as well--until the technological revolution of the twentieth century has increasingly forced young people to remain "children" even into their twenties by having to attend even more schooling in order to gain desirable (often even minimal) employment.

Has nature (or God) always been wrong and only we modern-day people correct to deny mating to teenagers? Or is it just a case of today's complex (convoluted) economics imposing demands on fundamental human drives well beyond what our biological systems can genetically adjust to so suddenly? And with fuller diets, the age of puberty keeps dropping thereby compounding the problem. Note though that not only did mating begin in the mid to late teens; so did parental responsibility and productive work; conditions not typically accorded teenagers in modern society.

I do not of course pretend to offer solutions or even resolutions to this debate. More than enough proposals have already spilled forth from our elected representatives and the many nonelected contenders for public opinion. What does prompt our attention here is the web of social, cultural, biological, psychological, genetic, and hence political factors and forces, processes and outcomes surrounding a central fact of life: that virtually all humans at virtually all ages (especially those in their teens and twenties) feel a tremendous, sometimes overpowering drive to mate--with or without mutual affection; indeed, with or without mutual agreement, much less legal license.

Darwinian sociobiologists in particular can readily and rather convincingly explain this drive in terms of perpetuating one's genetic material: as a way of achieving immortality. Geneticists can see what a significant role this mating drive plays in the perpetuation of our species and that of most species. Sociologists/anthropologists look more at the outcomes: at how societies organize themselves within their culture to institutionalize some sort of bonding between mates and/or between adults and children to take responsibility for the latter's necessary care and acculturation. Such arrangements assume myriad forms, from concubinage and marriage to adoption, and occur across a range from nuclear to extended families or communal agencies.

The literature from each of these academic perspectives has already reached avalanche proportions. Political scientists, in contrast, seem strangely reticent to apply their analytical expertise to the general arena of mating even though story-tellers and dramatists have mined its inherent political machinations for centuries and millennia. What else has provided a more pungent force or at least a more fateful force throughout the recorded history of human affairs than the politics of sex, be it ensuring "legitimate" offspring or arranging for intended inheritance of property, be it fulfilling societal rituals or the management of prestige/status, or be it simply the manipulation of other people via sex for one's own purposes, for one's ego, or for one's amusement?

Given the vast panoply of human interactions over the millennia and throughout the horrendous diversity of cultures extant on this planet, evidence for a pervasive reliance on purely romantic love is optimally determine mating actually appears rather elusive--at most a test of a male's sincerity. And given the high rates of failure of romance-determined matings, we might question how solid a basis romantic love provides. Whether idealized "love" enters into the equation or not, virtually all cultures dictate that mating should go beyond the two immediate individuals to involve others as well, especially the pair's families.

Immediately, an onslaught of interests converge, especially when the mating involves pregnancy, child-rearing, support costs, inheritance, religion, habits of life style, expectations of fidelity, all the while achieving or sacrificing each person's selfish desires. The more money and emotional commitment (as in religion, ethnicity, cultural orientation) exert pressure and the more public and personal power come into play, the more mating departs from a strictly biological act.

Further complicating the intricacies of mating are differences in sensitivity and perception between how women and men read and internalize their interactions. Whether these differences stem from some inherent genetic/biological predisposition or from what expectations and interpersonal strategies their society instills in them, the differences are real. (For the most part for instance, little girls become heterosexually conscious well before little boys sense something strangely intriguing about girls.) Basic differences should not surprise us, given the differential burdens imposed by nature on the two sexes in bearing offspring and given most societies' heavily weighting of females with childcare responsibilities. These cannot do other than further affect how females view sex as compared with how men approach the act of mating.

Not surprising then, the interplay of outlooks, interests, and strategies between the two individuals--often complicated or at least altered by family ties, religious institutions, and community--can grow quite complicated. This interplay quickly takes on the characteristics of a political game with all of its subtle (or open) exercise of power, influence, manipulation, even at times physical and/or psychological violence.

Let's consider a sample of scenarios. Go back some thirty-thousand
years to an age when humans had few material possessions, when their
technology was still crude and life depended upon everyone's pitching in to
gather food. In that setting, women could as easily have provided whatever
they and their children ate and wore. Women might also have provided sexual gratification in exchange for goods and services. But a woman need not
do so unless she wanted to; no man had claim to her time, talents, and
charms. She could have elected to mate with a strange on the sly (behind the
local bully's back) or temporarily joined a different band of hunter-
gatherers, thereby intuitively ensuring a healthier diversity of genes instead
of just inbreeding.

By six thousand years ago in many parts of the world, population density
had risen markedly. Agricultural production, resource extraction, manufacturing, and labor specialization had attained sizeable significance. Commerce, even international trade, had grown extensive. For the most part,
males had come to dominate this production and economic activity, along
with a hold on emerging organized religion, government, and war-making
capabilities. Men (powerful men at least) now had far more leverage with
which to secure sexual gratification. Their economic resources and military
prowess could usually translate into increased chances for their children to
survive by virtue of having better food, better care, and better protection.

These father-bestowed benefits could also lead to better preparation
(education, favoritism) for an offspring's continued survival into adulthood
and hence for continuing that genetic line. Under those conditions, competition between women for access to the richest, most powerful men appears
only logical--to gain protection, status, and their survival benefits for themselves and their children. If a woman brought herself to have an emotional
attachment to (that is, to stand not only in awe of but believe herself in love
with) such a man, so much the easier to play out the politics of mating. Otherwise, safety lay with acting as if she were in awe of the mate chosen for
her. Survival depended on reading others' thoughts and body language perceptively enough to pursue the most effective ploys--not unlike slaves, ambitious bureaucrats, and disadvantaged minorities everywhere have also had
to do.

But as happens so frequently in human affairs, reality seldom remains a simplistic one-to-one relationship, even between sexual partners. Her family (and his) would have much at stake too. They would seek to ensure the most prudent (most secure and profitable) set of family alliances possible, regardless of the girl's (and boy's) momentary emotional preferences. Strategic political and economic considerations would likely claim a high priority. Having a sense of communal history would have helped, too. Given that context, she would find her best strategy in going along with the game and making the most of it--leveraging the most from her own family for her sacrifices as well as from her mate's family by how she played the game.

This might involve feigning feminine submissiveness, proving one's devotion to family propriety, performing well in bed, bearing healthy heirs of whichever gender were preferred in that culture, and outliving other contenders for influence until she achieved matriarchal status or at least became the "power behind the throne." If she happened to have an abundance of talent and her mate were weak, she might shortcut to dominance by sheer dint of personality--provided she had no equally talented and ambitious rivals within his harem or family. Unfortunately this involved far more potentially disastrous risks. Histories of China, India, Greece, Rome, to name a scant few, provide many a dramatic example down through the centuries.

Move closer to our own time and culture: The ideal of romantic love might go so far as to produce a life-long commitment to a chosen mate whom fate removed; Longfellow's Evangeline for example. But an Evangeline never has a chance to fulfill her inner drive for reproduction, the impetus for that irrepressible romantic attachment. In real life Evangeline would more likely have kept her options open to eventually seek some other likely partner for mating and child-rearing with. While it might make for less heroic literature, it would come closer to how people the world over tend to function.

The trouble with idealized romantic love emerges soon enough--when diapers need changing, bills need paying, the house needs cleaning, when in-laws intrude to make demands, when the real world squeeze for jobs and housing closes in , when the man expects expert kitchen and bedroom service, when he goes out to drink "with the boys" (or another woman) and forbids his wife to leave the house lest she be tempted to act as unfaithful as her spouse. Tensions can rise further if she wants a career of her own, especially if she eventually earns a higher income or expects him to share responsibility for some "women's work" household and child-rearing tasks.

Where considerable wealth, power and prestige ride on a marriage, the politics involved can rise proportionally. But elites do not have a monopoly on political games between the sexes. Men and women less endowed still have their lives, their pride, their parental drive, and their security at stake when they begin to mate, whether casually or (they hope) permanently. Each gender tries to advantage itself by seeking out and manipulating the other's relative weaknesses (whether those lie in the areas of economics, physical strength, self-esteem, or social status) as much as both sides seek to profit from the other's endowments.

Women can readily (intuitively or calculatingly?) manipulate men's exaggerated and vulnerable desire for sex; men more often succeed by "selling" themselves to a potential mate on the basis of their prowess, financial if not physical. Women may say they look for strength, reliability, and congeniality/empathy even though these desired male attributes frequently prove mutually, often dangerously incompatible. (Yet look at how many women seek copulation with famous rock stars, athletes, and powerful politicians--as if their fame somehow translates into phallic virility.) Men tend first to notice women's physical features--the features largely associated with childbearing and nurturing potentials, features often accentuated by feminine dress and make-up but which tend to lose their allure after a pregnancy or two and then turn a mate off.

Troubles in inter-gender communications begin with males generally less able to read other people's faces, thoughts, and body language than females do, thus missing messages which women think they have made abundantly clear. From there, men and women interpret interactional games of mating differently. Soon both begin to read the worst into the other's motives; especially in times of stress. Where women might more likely express themselves verbally, men tend more to give vent to their feelings in physical form. One attacks with sharp words, the other with hard fists and sharp knives. The reaction of each mate allows the other to reinforce his/her now increasingly negative appraisal of the other's character and of their relationship. Earlier misinterpretations of appearances, actions, and of the heady process of courtship arise to add acid to ;worsening strains, bitter disillusionment, and fears of having been embarrassingly manipulated or devastatingly put down.

Where a couple lives distant from other family members or old friends who might buffer and siphon off tempers, or where no trusted communal leader (a minister or shaman for instance) has acquired an effective role of mediator, there the political game of mating can get completely out of hand. It can turn into open warfare when economic pressures, poor living conditions, or unrealistic expectations (even among the well-off) exacerbate tensions beyond the individuals' capabilities to cope. Note here the potential importance of keeping inter-gender relationships out in the open as game playing so that referees can intervene. Again reality is, alas, not so simplistic. Those other parties have their own games to play, and these may go as far in heating up as in cooling down any particular couple's troubles.

A strong sense of community membership and hence a sense of mutual responsibility might contribute to keeping the politics of mating within workable bounds by providing clear rules and processes for easing tensions. Heavy-handed community rules can, however, just as readily ameliorate marital strains by unequally imposing painful burdens upon only one of the parties, namely the party with the least political and economic leverage, most often the young wife.

Note that simply having a rigidly structure hierarchy does not equal a strong community system. Neither does Western culture's granting complete license to young people to mate as they chose ensure that individuals (most often the female) won't suffer as much as where traditional rigidity of, say, an India or China prevails. The few remaining matrilineal societies, in contrast, appear to go farther than other cultural systems in leveling the playing field between the sexes.

One intriguing aspect of the politics of mating emerges in how the games played end up dominating and even replacing the reproductive drive which started all of these inter-gender activities in the first place. The examples which sociobiology uses to demonstrate the underlying drive for reproductive fitness among humans (as well as among other species) readily become human ends in and of themselves to the detriment of the reproductive drive they supposedly intend to serve. For instance: devoting one's entire being to reach the top of the corporate or career ladder, accumulating vast amounts of money, or exercising world-shaking power goes far beyond what one needs for successfully maintaining a marriage and raising children. Indeed, the very driven sacrifices necessary to achieve those material goals quite often force participants to neglect their families at a vital personal level of caring. How really important are chic clothes, vast trendy houses, luxurious cars, and a deluge of recreational play-things (such as for golf, boating, "home entertainment") for the future of our species?

Studies have found that women dress more to impress other women than for man. Whether men do the same to impress other men seems less certain; they surely do acquire flashy cars, big bosomed women, and the accoutrements of power to outdistance other men and reassure their own masculinity--not unlike women gaining status by the "fish" they attract. To what extent such staging really does seek to gain advantages over members of one's own gender (or just assuage real anxieties) in today's pressure-packed competitive games of survival is a tantalizing question for sociobiologists and psychologists alike. Does one really play the mating game to better one's sexual selectivity or to enhance one's ego?

The political maneuvering and one-upmanship involved certainly offer some fascinating interactions for analysis, especially as they become stylized and institutionalized by what was once called "polite society" and among what we now call the jet-set. (Segments of today's media make considerable profit from portending to "reveal all.") Some would argue that accumulating wealth and public power can open access to the opposite sex and thereby allow successful men to spread their genes to more women, serially or concurrently. Maybe. (In some cultures, men reserve affection for other men and conduct much the same mating games homosexually.)

We might just as easily demonstrate that wealth, power, and access to women actually become mere poker chips to provide a handy measure of a man's apparent success. (Do young teenage boys--or grown men for that matter--really want sex with a female or just bragging rights to demonstrate their hoped-for masculinity among male peers?) Before long, these cultural indicators of power replace the real purpose of life, that of perpetuating the species, the sine qua non of our existence. So what actions are genetically prompted and what culturally orchestrated? Can we say for sure?

Ironically, being dominant does not ensure a procreational advantage. Observations by competent scientists have found (with DNA testing) that supposedly dominant males can spend so much time and energy on the politics of dominance that they have less to devote to insemination. Other studies have revealed the prevalence of infidelity amount supposedly monogamously mated species as well as extensive infanticide in other species by newly established dominant males wanting to eliminate the offspring of their predecessors and to proliferate their own. The animal kingdom offers examples of just about any kind of mating politics we can imagine. Yet all seek to perpetuate their species and their DNA. The extent humans can and do adjust behavior to cultural pressures simply complicates this drive for us. Men tend to respond to those female "come-on" body-language signals (real or imagined) about as predictably as males of other species respond to female pheromones.

Just raising these few enigmatic aspects of the universal mating drive should readily suggest the naivete of touting quick-fix solutions to current issues about teen pregnancies, welfare, and the not unrelated delinquent behavior among young men. For, the politics of human mating occurs at two levels: culturally shaped self-conscious behavior and genetically engineered unconscious decisions. But touted solutions tend inevitably to tackle aspects of issues at a verbalized (cultural) level of consciousness whereas much if not most of the "mechanisms" underlying sex occur at the nonverbalized level of what, for lack of ;a better term at this state in our knowledge, appears to be genetically (somatically) prescribed "instinct."

As in all other sexually reproductive species, games of inter-gender politics may be so deeply inherent until about all we humans can do is rationalize our strategies and actions after the fact. Even then the "spin" (to use a Washington DC term) we put on such spoken rationalizations likely become a political ploy in and of themselves--at the cultural level. Yet much of the energy involved may well lie so far beyond conscious scheming that we may be quite incapable of explaining why we really act as we do--or why our culture leans in the direction it does--in so fundamental an area of species survival as mating.

And because the mating drive is so fundamental to behavior within our own species as in every other species for survival, it may underlie a larger share of what prompts people of different ethnic and religious groups to seek to perpetuate their group and protect their genetic investment, even to confronting, threatening, and warring on each other. The politics of mating extends well beyond interaction between the sexes; it may well power--quite subliminally if not overtly--much of what we call "race relations," international conflict, and politics in general. Quite likely we bias both our academic research and our efforts at pragmatic problem-solving to the extent we overlook the fundamental role of the sex drive and its related politics within virtually all other sociocultural phenomena.

SOCIETAL STRUCTURE BY CLASS

A ny discussion of society, culture, and community as lengthy as this one can hardly avoid the question of how society structures itself--largely meaning how it stratifies its classes. At least those of us from a EuroAmerican academic background seem to think we must address this area of sociological theorizing. I have sidestepped the issue here simply because I harbor doubts about class as a useful tool of analysis and hence about any beneficence from its implications for current social programs.

At least three basic flaws in prevalent conceptualizations about class call for fundamental revision in our desire to depict a structured society. These stand out most graphically in America today, but increasingly run true for other modern, economically complex societies. First: thinking in terms of class structure can fog our vision to the horrendous dynamism of modern life. Structuring a society by class tends inherently to impose a degree of status that appears steadily drifting away from reality.

Second: we must ask what criterion (or concerted set of criteria) can effectively and realistically portray how a society is structured if it is indeed structured at all. Third: if structuring by class imposes more rigidity than exists in reality and if usable criteria for delineating classes have progressively grown less clear, then a continued reference to classes when describing society risks the danger of imposing unwarranted invidious distinctions. Hence, it risks doing more harm than good, both by disrupting cross-community networking and in framing social policy for the political arena.

The terms upper-class, middle-class (or white collar), working-class (blue collar), and intellectual did have real meaning and utility in nineteenth century Europe. (Peter N. Stearns, for one example, could appropriately refer to such blocs when examining events in his *1848: The Revolutionary Tide in Europe*.) Admittedly vestiges of class distinction still linger in Europe. But they express a particular cultural/economic/political heritage not necessarily applicable to other industrialized societies--certainly not to Japan, Australia and America.

What criteria can provide (for those social scientists who insist on class structure) a workable approach to that task in America? If one cares to do it, we can readily delineate "classes" by wealth, or by income, or by fame, or by life-style, or by power, or by willingness to delay gratification. Ethnicity has long provided convenient markers for assigning class. but ethnicity too readily changes, like the other candidate criteria, to last more than one or two generations; fame, barely one. Only race has remained in some people's minds (though not, of course, among social scientists) as a firm determinant because its markers do not adjust as quickly as the economic and life-style aspects of ethnicity. But how can even what we call "race" serve when people, lumped together by just one fuzzy category, partake of the full range of all other criteria such as income, wealth, education, power, fame, and life style evident in society today?

As late as the 1930's, sociologists could point to observable classes in America. Certain families did tend to monopolize land and capital ownership, better educations, cultural/artistic leadership, and hence political power while other families could only hope to earn their livelihoods by heavy labor, to dream of home ownership and having some of their children survive long enough to carry on their parents' way of life. World War II, more dramatically perhaps than any other milestone, brought a demise of old class thinking here--especially with so many veterans getting previously impossible college educations, professional careers, and opportunities for home ownership and upward aspirations for their children. We saw this happen markedly in Orange County.

Now the overwhelming majority of Americans (similarly for Japanese) consider themselves "middle class," whatever that is. They watch the same television programs, cheer for the same football or baseball teams, send their children to public schools and colleges, eat the same hamburgers when in a hurry, and buy their clothes off the rack. Few if any publicly admit to being upper class or lower class. Even the once proudly held badge of "intellectual" has in particular become a word of derision. Teachers and university professors, artists and composers have virtually all joined the ranks of employed workers. And today's computer revolution has transformed an even larger portion of work into an exercise in manipulating information once reserved for intellectuals. So what "class" do you or I or anyone belong to ? And who cares?

Repudiation of class enjoys a long tradition back to the earliest American colonists. Many an aristocrat, unprepared to work, ended up a poverty-striken mountaineer while impoverished immigrants willing to work eventually prospered. Their descendants understandably rejected Old World notions of class-by-birth. The current rejection of class in America allows those managing to make it to cast the blame on those in poverty for failing to take suitable advantage of opportunities.

If structuring by class no longer provides a realistic depiction of society because it is too static and lacks a convincing set of meaningful markers, then perhaps we would do better to scrap it. Better perhaps to see myriad delineations that categorize to the point of lacking any structure; at least not a static one. Better instead to look for the linkages between this maze of categories and for how those linkages--both functional and symbolic--allow a community system to thrive or strangle. Better, then, to focus on interactions, communications flow, and adaptations to change..

THE ROUTE TAKEN

A mixed bag of career experiences sparked the questions that ultimately drove me to write this book.

My concerted focus on community began in the mid-1960s with Dr. Daniel G. Aldrich Jr, Chancellor at the University of California's Irvine campus. Previously as statewide dean of agriculture, he knew better than anyone what a positive impact the University had in making California the nation's most agriculturally productive state. He intended to have UCI interact as positively with the urban sector, starting with the burgeoning urban scene of Orange County surrounding the new campus. But he needed more information.

As his campus-community planner on the initial team that created UCI, I presented a logical target (before faculty arrived) for the chancellor's incisive questions about community systems undergoing rapid change and evolution there. When to my chagrin I could not find answers that would satisfy me much less him, we agreed on a two-year project. I would gather all the data I could, whether or not I could immediately convert them into useful theory and pragmatic proposals.

At the end of those two years he had a 700-page report, the basis for this book's Part Three. About the time I felt I would drown in the mass of information collected, colleagues at UC Berkeley pioneered a view of community as a communicative process. Using their breakthrough, my work on Orange County began to make sense. But I needed to test it elsewhere.

Soon I had my chance, first as a consultant to Stanford Research Institute (now SRI International) for a study on land reform out in the villages of Vietnam at the height of the war there. Then with that completed, I returned via Hawaii where old colleagues brought me on board the just-launched Model Cities program. Subsequently as a consultant to local community groups on the windward side of Oahu, I could continue my participant-observer work of exploring the essence of community.

My first attempt to publish some of this work (other than for particularized journal articles) came in the 1984 book, *Strategic Management: Public Planning at the Local Level* (J A I Press). By that time I had become engaged in conducting evaluations of public programs for the State of Hawaii. One such project concerned drug rehabilitation; several focused on crime/punishment and juvenile justice, among others. By now I automatically posed the kinds of questions Chancellor Aldrich had shot my way and I found existing social science theories no more satisfactory in these areas than I had found them for interrupting community earlier.

Consequently I began looking into biology and genetics for contributing factors. This move soon brought me to examine sociobiology for its possibilities and weaknesses (there was no way to avoid it at that point despite the controversy swirling around it). A year providing staff for the Hawaii Commission on Comparable Worth (equal pay for women) further expanded my realm of research, in particular reading some eye-opening books by anthropologists Sarah Hrdy, Nancy Tanner, among others.

Meanwhile my second book came out. Entitled *Global Positioning for the Twenty-first Century: Rethinking Strategic Planning* (Michigan State University Press, 1990), its exploration of American foreign policy (and hence unavoidably of war) made me pursue the unknowns about violent human behavior. Again more questions arose than answers.

Actually my habit of challenging existing explanations for human behavior began even earlier. As a young military officer arriving in Japan soon after WWII, I looked out that first day over miles of utter destruction. A question rose in my mind and would not go away; indeed, it would change my life. That question: What drove this small country to accomplish the horrendous industrialization and military prowess that encouraged it to take on the world?

After six years of military service, I did not return to college to study architecture as intended. Instead I enrolled at the University of California Berkeley to major in Asian Studies and did my graduate work with Dr. Eberhard in sociology to grapple with my ever nagging question about Japan.[1] Continued interest produced the portion of Part Two on that culture.

Membership on state commissions in Hawaii concerned with population, environmental protection, and innovative education, and on advisory bodies for urban renewal and transportation (as well as some involvement in local politics there) caused me to look closely at cultural and ecological changes in the islands, especially as they related to ethnic Hawaiians. Consequently I had a chance to view political processes from the inside, the basis for that portion of Part 2.

Taking early retirement so that I could do what I had long wanted to do but could not afford, namely teach at university level, I began to pull these various areas of research together for use with my students. Again I was not satisfied until I became acquainted with developments in chaos and complexity theory. Here was what I had been struggling with for years but had lacked an adequate set of analytical tools for. At last it all began to gel.

Some order *is* possible even in apparent chaos, just as turbulence occurs in seeming order. A conceptualization of the reality of "order," however, may have been captured as well within Vedic and Taoist cosmologies, even by Papuan or Amazonian animism, as in the Cartesian rationality that we ethnocentrically place our modern Western faith in. The expansion of recognition about the vast complexity of particle physics, of time/space, and of biology just within my 6 years on Earth makes me quake at how ignorant we still are about the systemic intricacies of human life.

This is how this book came into existence and why it took so many decades to complete.

---

1. Other great teachers at UC Berkeley under whom I had the distinct fortune of studying during the 1950s included: Professors Bendix, Blumer, Bock, Kornhauser, Selznik, and Shibutani in sociology; Bisson, Lepawski, Park, and Scalapino in political science; Glacken and Parsons in geography; Heiser and Mandelbaum in anthropology; Li and Wendt in economics; Bauer, Foley, and Kent in city/regional planning. Those stimulating years provided much of the initial thrust for this continuing odyssey.

Subject Index